WHO WILL DEFEND EUROPE?

'Keir Giles has been warning us for many years of Russia's determination to re-arm, remilitarise and rebuild an empire. Now he offers a stark warning for Europe and the world: the only alternative to planning for a war is planning to lose it.'
— Anne Applebaum, author of
Autocracy, Inc.: The Dictators Who Want to Run the World

'A powerful and urgent analysis of Europe's looming security challenges—this book is a wake-up call for anyone who cares about the future of the continent.'
— Eliot Higgins, founder of Bellingcat

'Keir Giles has been right about Russia for 20 years. In Central and Eastern Europe we read his work, comforted that at least some Western scholars understood what Russia was doing. Western leaders, though, refused to listen. For all our sakes I hope they listen now.'
— Toomas Hendrik Ilves, former president of Estonia

'Keir Giles presents the reader with a disturbing catalogue of Europe's weaknesses, and how Russia is planning to exploit them. As regards Europe and the West in general, Russia is a hostile actor, has always been, and will always be, and collectively, Europe should expect that Russia will exploit to the fullest, not just the vulnerabilities it can create, but the vulnerabilities Europe has created for itself.'
— Gen John R. Allen, US Marine Corps (Ret),
former commander NATO International Security
Assistance Force (ISAF)

KEIR GILES

WHO WILL DEFEND EUROPE?

An Awakened Russia and a Sleeping Continent

HURST & COMPANY, LONDON

First published in the United Kingdom in 2024 by
C. Hurst & Co. (Publishers) Ltd.,
New Wing, Somerset House, Strand, London, WC2R 1LA

Distributed in the United States, Canada and Latin America by
Oxford University Press, 198 Madison Avenue, New York, NY 10016,
United States of America.

A Cataloguing-in-Publication data record for this book
is available from the British Library.

ISBN: 9781911723486

Printed and bound in Great Britain by Bell & Bain Ltd, Glasgow

www.hurstpublishers.com

This book is dedicated to the people of Ukraine,
who at immense cost have formed the front line
of the defence of Europe for over a decade.

CONTENTS

ACKNOWLEDGEMENTS

This book would not have appeared without Michael Dwyer at Hurst, and his skills of persuasion, specifically at transforming determination not to write another book into a firm plan to produce one as swiftly as possible. Thanks also go to the entire team at Hurst for their cooperation and support.

Once I had agreed to write the book, Antoni Dziwura and Laura Halminen contributed underpinning research for the passages on Poland and Finland respectively, and James Hanson and Susan de Nîmes provided essential project support. Thanks are due to *The Guardian*, CNN and *Maanpuolustus* for permission to adapt for this book short passages that previously appeared in pieces written for them.

Invaluable help, advice, technical guidance, or permission to repeat specific comments or incidents came from Samantha de Bendern, Stefan Forss, James Nixey, Melania Parzonka, Jim Townsend, Jack Watling and Stefan Wurwal.

I must also thank the serving military officers and government officials from the US, UK, Ukraine, and other countries ranging from Canada to Poland, who gave generously of their time and insights, but had to speak anonymously in order to speak frankly.

Regardless of all the help and support listed above, any errors of fact or interpretation are of course entirely my own.

INTRODUCTION

This book is about Russia's plans for war beyond Ukraine, and whether it's possible to deter the Kremlin from putting them into action. It looks at what the return of war to Europe means for people across the continent if either or both of two things happen: Russia's war on Ukraine comes to an end, with victory, defeat or a ceasefire; and a new presidency in the United States scales back the American commitment to the defence of Europe. It compares how the countries of Europe are – or are not – preparing their armed forces and their civilian populations for the likelihood of conflict on their own territory. And it concludes that for all the heroic efforts of Ukraine holding back Russia's onslaught and blunting its military power on land, the rest of Europe is in a race against time where the stakes of winning and losing cannot possibly be higher.

In a way, this is a natural continuation of two previous books that I've written over the last four years. In 2019, *Moscow Rules* described the beliefs and assumptions that drive Russian state behaviour – and how they meant Russia was on a path to conflict with the West, and in particular the countries around Russia's Western periphery. That book warned that if the fundamental disagreements with Russia were not addressed by Western countries, open warfare was inevitable. And then in 2022, after that open warfare had begun, *Russia's War on Everybody* explained the many ways that Russia was already also covertly attacking the rest of the world far beyond Ukraine. The book you are holding now looks at the growing risk that those ongoing and increasing covert attacks could turn into an open assault on Europe – and what European countries are and aren't doing to reduce that risk.

It is a fair question for readers to ask: is Russia really a threat? For some people it is hard to imagine that in the twenty-first century, Europe is once again threatened by a megalomaniac dictator seeking to expand his territory by force. After all, figures like Hitler and Napoleon are supposed to be the stuff of history rather than the present day. And when we read news reporting of the war in Ukraine highlighting the evisceration of Russia's land forces there since 2022, it's tempting to assume that now they have been rendered harmless – or that their lack of progress in Ukraine in the last two years means they don't have the ability to mount a meaningful attack anywhere else. But as we will see in Chapter 1, Russia has been working hard to reconstitute its armed forces, and Putin's intention to take what he (and many Russians) see as rightfully theirs has never been clearer. Even when Russia's war on Ukraine ends, there will be no simple return to the notional state of peace that much of Europe liked to think it enjoyed before 2022. The war, and the broader confrontation between Russia and the West, are symptoms of the fact that we are once again living in an era where brute military force will determine the lives and futures of millions of people across the continent.

This is hardly breaking news. In early 2022, anybody that was willing to think hard enough about the implications of Russia's preparations for a full-scale invasion of Ukraine had no doubt that President Putin's ambition did not stop at the Ukrainian border, and it was time for Europe's second line of defence – the front line states of NATO – to begin urgently preparing for hostilities.[1] Ukraine itself stands as a stark reminder of the consequences of underestimating Russian ambitions. For now, the conflict there continues to absorb Russia's hostile energies. But if it is resolved or stabilised – for instance by a ceasefire – there is little doubt Russia will look to its next target or objective in Europe.

How different groups of countries have responded to the challenge – and whether that response will be sufficient – forms a major part of this book. You will see that I repeatedly refer to countries "west of Warsaw". That is a shorthand for the divide in Europe between the front-line states bordering Russia (plus, to some extent, the Nordic states and the United Kingdom) that are in no doubt as to the seriousness and immediacy of the threat from Russia, and the rest of the continent that has in the past felt protected by distance and geography and so preferred not to think about the problem too hard. That divide shows starkly when, for example, the Polish Prime Minister Donald Tusk warns of the threat of looming war but adds that his Spanish counterpart has asked other EU leaders not to use the word "war" in order that people do not feel threatened.[2] And it has direct results in terms of which European countries are, and are not, taking seriously their duty to protect themselves and their citizens, as we will see in Chapter 5.

You'll also find that far too many people in this book have had to be anonymised. That includes many of the officials and military officers whose direct quotes I've used to introduce each chapter. Many of them were speaking under the "Chatham House Rule", a convention whereby you are allowed to use the information they give but you're not allowed to indicate the source.[3] That's a useful tool for the essential conversations that government officials sometimes have to have without putting their name to them. But it's also frustrating, when it demonstrates how widely a problem is recognised, and yet how little can be publicly said or done about it. Over more than a decade I've listened to government officials and others in close to a dozen countries raising the problems described in this book over and over again behind closed doors, with use of the Chatham House Rule highlighting the gap between the real situation and what can officially be admitted to. In Brussels in late 2022, I sat in on a joint meeting of top-level EU and NATO officials, gathered to discuss their response to "hybrid threats". "Russia is at war with us. We can admit that in this room, but we can't say it outside," one of them observed, to a series of grim nods around the table. However valid the reasons might or might not be for that conspiracy of silence outside the room, it amounts to an official state of denial and results in a public that is wilfully under-informed about the threat facing it. And NATO itself is now dealing with the consequences of decades when its members had the luxury of pretending that the problem of defence had gone away altogether. The return of war brings with it a need to overcome deeply embedded assumptions and political behaviours among not only a generation of politicians and decision-makers, but also of the voters that will approve or obstruct the investment that is required for withstanding military threats.

Russia's full-scale invasion of Ukraine ought to have proven beyond any doubt that Europe is under threat. And President Putin's continuing declarations of his undiminished ambition to recapture territory that he feels should be governed from Moscow show clearly how more countries than Ukraine are in his sights. Russia isn't the only threat, of course. But it's the one with the nearest and most immediate ability to bring catastrophic consequences directly to us at home. And yet, for years it seemed recognising and responding to the threat demanded a leap of imagination that was beyond the capabilities of most western politicians. Nobody that seriously studies Russia is in any doubt that European voters need to be persuaded of the need to invest in defence and deterrence – because as Ukraine shows, the alternative is vastly more costly. But there is little evidence that this realisation has permeated the top layer of politics in countries beyond the front line states. Elsewhere, some national leaders continue to pretend to their electorates that the situation is not desperate, or that it is somebody else's problem, instead of presenting a looming threat to their own country which if not confronted will blight the futures of their children and grand-children.

Europe's situation today has been repeatedly compared with that of the late 1930s and the slide towards the Second World War. Even Germany's defence minister has compared Russia's war on Ukraine today to Adolf Hitler's annexation of Czechoslovak territory in 1938, to explain that if Russia is not defeated there, a much larger war may follow.[4] Like all such historical analogies, the comparison isn't perfect – but there are enough points in common to confirm that anybody who isn't alarmed just hasn't been paying attention.

Then, as now, the threat came from an alignment of authoritarian powers that sought to challenge the world order. Instead of an axis developing between Germany, Italy and Japan, today it is Russia that has embraced fascist and nationalist ideology backed by a (for now) loose coalition of Iran, North Korea and China.[5] Then, Europe suffered a combined assault by two aggressors, Germany and the USSR, and once Japan entered the war, faced a strategic choice of which adversary to defeat first. Now, as we will see in Chapter 3, US decision-makers are facing the same quandary between Russia and China.

In 1939, it was Poland and Finland who resisted the aggressor powers, while Czechoslovakia had already been abandoned as a victim of British unreadiness and French unwillingness to confront Nazi Germany. Today, it is Ukraine that is the victim, buying time for Europe to rearm through its own sacrifices.

And now, as then, the threat is existential and yet far too many European citizens consider Russia's war on Ukraine to be a quarrel in a faraway country, between people of whom they know nothing. Meanwhile people across Europe who might have grown up not understanding how in the previous century the world could have slid inexorably towards war but seemingly with nobody able to stop it, now find themselves powerlessly caught up in a grim repeat of that process. There are the same excuses for inaction from politicians, and a similar cast of cheerleaders for the aggressors, with public figures willing to excuse or applaud Putin now as there were Hitler and Stalin then.[6]

In 1940, France collapsed in part because its huge and powerful armed forces had not evolved and adapted to the new form of warfare pioneered and implemented by Germany. Today, some armed forces are closely studying the development of military technologies in Ukraine and how they are being applied to transform warfighting techniques, and thinking carefully about how much of that will carry across into the kind of combat they themselves will face with Russia. Regrettably, it seems, not all of them are.

While there are similarities between today and the 1930s, it's useful also to consider the differences – even though it's a disturbing exercise because those differences are not in our favour and in several respects the situation of countries like the UK is even more dire now than it was then. In the second half of the 1930s, understanding of the looming threat drove Britain to a crash rearmament programme to prepare for conflict. That included urgent expansion of the Royal Air Force and investment in technologies like radar, and innovations such as the world's first fully co-ordinated air defence system, without all of which the country would have been in much greater danger of total defeat in 1940. But in the 2020s, as we will see in Chapters 4 and 5, attempts to ramp up arms production across Europe have instead been slow and faltering. That is despite the fact that boosting defence production will if anything be more challenging now than then. In the 1930s, the UK for instance had a solid manufacturing industrial base that could be repurposed, and military technology could be produced by dispersed cottage industries and craftsmen. That is something we still see today in Ukraine's widely distributed military drone industry, but it's hard to imagine how that pattern could be replicated for high-end Western military equipment. Parts for Spitfires could be fabricated in bicycle factories. The same cannot be said of an F-35.

Rearmament has also been held back because the need for it comes at a financially inconvenient moment. Many European governments are already coping with high levels of public debt following the emergency spending during the coronavirus pandemic. And their economies, like their societies, have transformed rapidly, leaving far less scope for government-mandated reinvestment in defence than in previous decades. But that obscures the fact that countries like the United Kingdom have previously rearmed at times when their financial position was much worse – not only when emerging from the economic trauma of the early 1930s, but also in the early 1950s when the country was still crippled with debt from the Second World War. In both cases, recognition of the gravity of the threat, from Nazi Germany and the Soviet Union respectively, led to a prioritisation of national survival over waiting for a better economic outlook. That's a policy choice – the same one that faces the British and other governments today.

There is another vital difference that will make a unified response to the challenge that much harder. 1939 was almost a century ago, and in that time the societies of western European states have undergone enormous change. Demographic transformation driven by decades of unconstrained immigration and societal attitudes that have evolved over generations combine with lack of common understanding of the danger to mean that military or civil mobilisation to meet an existential threat can no longer assume widespread cooperation from the populace – despite efforts in several countries to prepare public opinion for that possibility.[7] And social cohesion is likely to be far more brittle when faced with civilian casualties, disruption and destruction at home.

One key advantage compared with the 1930s is that the United States is for now not an isolationist state but a partner in global security, tied into the future of Europe, in particular through its NATO alliance commitments and a clear understanding of where its economic interests lie. But as we will see in Chapter 3, the strength of that commitment is now, for the first time in decades, in doubt – and that makes Europe's challenge vastly greater. Whether Europe will cope with that challenge, with or without the United States, is the theme of this book.

Who Will Defend Europe? describes some things that are permanent, like Russia's ambition to subdue its neighbours, by force if other means do not suffice; and others that are changing rapidly, like Moscow's capacity to do so and the ability of European countries to resist. That means that as this book went to press in summer 2024, some of the decisions and processes it describes were still in motion. It may be that by the time you read this there has been some good news to offset the generally pessimistic picture. Equally, some of the dangers it describes may have become even more clear. Things are moving fast. But the question is, are they moving fast enough? And in particular, have western European countries grasped that tinkering around the edges of the military and making small increments to their defence budgets is just not enough? Only a radical transformation of their defences will render them capable of actually surviving a full-scale war.

INTRODUCTION

All of this means the book you are reading describes events up to, approximately, mid July 2024. Even while it was being written there have been significant steps forward – in the approach taken by France, for example, where, as we will see in Chapter 5, President Macron has pivoted decisively (for now) from wishing to partner with Russia to seeing the need to defend the continent against it. But in France, as elsewhere, the new-found resolve may be undercut by shifts in political power following parliamentary elections in mid-2024. And there are still alarming indications that the message has still not sunk in with other major European partners, like in particular the UK, discussed in Chapter 4. Furthermore it is political change in the United States, most of all the outcome of the November 2024 presidential election, that will overshadow all of the questions that will be decided in Europe.

Whether US support is available to Europe or not, the challenge from Russia will remain. But the withdrawal of America's military backing for NATO is the surest possible way of turning the possibility of Russia attacking beyond Ukraine into a probability. In January 2024, not long after agreeing to write this book, I gave a presentation on the Russian threat to a group of naval helicopter pilots from a Western nation. Their colleagues were busy in the Red Sea, dealing with attacks on global shipping and doing their best to keep navigation safe and secure – but those in the lecture theatre were intently focused on the prospect of being drawn into a direct conflict with Russia, whether in Ukraine or elsewhere. They hoped, above all, that leaders in the West would recognise the scale and nature of the threat, and respond accordingly in terms of defence funding and revitalising the ability of their country and others to withstand the threat from Moscow. But also, they were looking with foreboding at the cycle of elections throughout Europe and the United States in 2024. One female officer asked me directly: "Do you think Russia is going to win the next US election?" Their intent focus was because they recognised that they might have to fight Russia without US support, and with a political leadership at home that was unwilling to face up to the challenge before it was too late. Unfortunately, as we'll see in Chapter 3, it wasn't necessary to wait till November 2024 to assess the impact of Donald Trump, who was already working hard to undermine NATO and the security of the US and its allies even before winning the Republican nomination, let alone being actually elected to office.[8] And his distorting impact on US politics even when out of office means that Europe has an America problem whoever is in the White House in 2025.

In Europe itself, that same process of rapid change might make you wonder whether the suggestion in the title that it is a "sleeping continent" is fair. After hitting the snooze button for over a decade, some parts of Europe have definitely woken up. The problem is, as this book shows, it's not nearly enough. And that is clear to see whenever European leaders get together to try to agree on what to do. The Munich Security Conference is an annual gathering of bigwigs discussing the state of the world. Observing it is good for taking their collective temperature and gauging the mood and outlook for global security. Much of the speechifying may be performative rather than substantial – so much so that it has been dubbed the "Munich Security Carnival" by veteran US and NATO hand Jim Townsend. But it also serves as a regular venue for big news. It was during the 2024 conference that news of Alexei Navalny's death broke, while his wife was among the attendees. And it was at the same conference in 2007 that Vladimir Putin startled those that had not been listening, in other words much of Western Europe, by pointing out that Russia was not entirely happy with the way things were going. In 2024, participants and commentators noted a change of mood from the previous year. But their overall impression was of a sense of gloom accompanied by resignation, rather than scrambling to do something about it.[9] German think-tanker Jan Techau reported that there was "a sense of urgency, without a sense of action". "It's a very strange state of affairs," he went on.[10] In short, although the danger of the current situation is now widely accepted, the resolve to take action about it is far too unevenly distributed across Europe.[11] And that's a theme that will come through strongly as we compare how different countries are responding to the Russian threat.

Today, there can be little excuse for not recognising the gravity of the danger. A succession of international crises and acts of aggression over several years served as warnings of what was to come in 2022, and Russia's growing confidence and aggression – as well as Vladimir Putin's own statements of his intentions – have by now removed any lingering doubt as to Moscow's further plans. But across much of Europe, that hasn't led to widespread recognition that the lives of ordinary people will inevitably change, and for the worse. The reason for that change, as we will see in the first chapter, lies in Moscow.

1

RUSSIA'S NEXT WAR

"Russia shows no signs of stopping. Nor does Russia intend to stop with Ukraine."

General Christopher Cavoli,
Washington, 10 April 2024

"We cannot deter Russia through threats of casualties. The only number of Russians to kill that is enough to deter them is all of them."

Commander of the Defence Forces of a front-line state,
Tallinn, May 2023

Whether or not Europe really faces the threat of new Russian military attacks beyond Ukraine depends on two factors: first, whether Russia has the means to carry out such attacks; and second, what would drive Moscow to do so. In other words, the threat is as ever a product of capability and intent. This chapter looks at each of those in turn, and concludes that there is no doubt as to the intent, and there is a strong risk that Russia might persuade itself it has the capability too.

Western views on Russia's military tend to swing between overestimating and underestimating its power. Both are dangerous. In the lead-up to the February 2022 invasion, it was widely assumed that Russian military strength meant its outcome was a foregone conclusion, and it was only a rare dissenting voice that expressed doubt, arguing that Ukrainian resistance could drag Russia into a quagmire.[1] That led to a misguided expectation of Ukrainian collapse which fuelled arguments that Kyiv should receive no foreign aid at all.[2] Later in the conflict, once it became clear that Russia had been fundamentally unprepared for Ukraine to fight back effectively and was suffering huge losses in men and equipment, the argument ran the other way: that Russia's forces were broken and could be on the verge of total collapse.[3]

Yet over the course of the conflict Russia has been transitioning to a new type of army ("yet another" new type of army, to those of us who have watched Russia's efforts at military reform over previous decades). It is building a bigger force than it had before, more than replacing the staggering number of killed and wounded it has suffered since February 2022. Towards the end of that year, then Russian Defence Minister Sergei Shoigu announced plans to expand the armed forces by approximately 30 per cent to 1.5 million people by 2026, with a clear focus on preparing for conflict with NATO.[4] There is scepticism as to whether that target will be hit (one thing for which the Russian military is entirely reliable is the unreliability of its publicly released manpower statistics), but by April 2024, NATO's military chief General Christopher G. Cavoli reported to the US Congress that despite suffering huge losses, the Russian army was now 15% larger than it was at the start of the full-scale invasion, and was continuing to recruit about 30,000 new soldiers each month.[5]

That expansion happened with unexpected speed, in part because of the way it is being carried out. In December 2023, the UK's Defence Intelligence assessed that it "will likely [sic] take Russia five to ten years to rebuild a cohort of highly trained and experienced military units".[6] But highly trained units are not Russia's immediate aim; it has shown itself willing to throw untrained and inexperienced soldiers forward to soak up Ukrainian bullets with "meat wave" tactics. When just three months later a senior US official assessed that Russia had "almost completely" reconstituted its military capabilities after its heavy losses in Ukraine, that didn't mean with like-for-like replacements.[7] The new force has more people, but less well trained and with fewer items of modern equipment.[8] Russia was able to transition into a long war of attrition by dredging manpower from across the country as well as recruiting or press-ganging foreign citizens, mercenaries and prisoners, reversing a decade and a half of faltering Russian attempts to build a more proficient and professional military that at least attempted to treat its members with a degree of humanity.[9] Russia is also digging deep into its Soviet-era weapons stockpiles and vehicle parks at the same time as ramping up domestic arms production.[10] Armoured vehicles more than half a century old have been pulled out of storage, refurbished and sent to the front. In the previous decade, when discussing why Russia still retained thousands of apparently useless obsolete vehicles in reserve, I suggested it reflected a lingering view that in the final analysis, if Russia had more armoured vehicles of whatever quality than its adversary had anti-armour weapons, then in spite of heavy losses it would overwhelm the defenders and win. That suggestion prompted laughter at the time; today, we see Russia apparently acting on precisely that principle.

In short, Russia's military doesn't always have to be competent or high-tech to deliver destructive effect. But nor does that mean the Russians don't adopt new technology. A distinctive feature of the force's evolution is how it is merging antiquated and hyper-modern weapons systems, vehicles, techniques and capabilities in what experienced Turkish defence researcher Can Kasapoğlu calls "Mad Max warfighting tech" and Jahara Matisek of the US Naval War College described as a "cyberpunk form of warfare" that "is blending old fighting styles with new technology."[11] The "Mad Max" impression was reinforced in 2024 by Russia's adoption of motorcycles and dune buggies to charge across open ground in motley flotillas, inevitably suffering heavy casualties as a result.[12]

In defence, the blending of new and old ways of war includes building extensive fortifications. These halted Ukraine's mid-2023 counter-offensive and are in greater depth than even the US Army's current equipment could breach under equivalent circumstances. And in intelligence and situational awareness, Russia is adapting to a form of warfare where unmanned surveillance platforms are ubiquitous across the battlefield. But Western militaries are also realising that they are unable to move undetected even when far from the fighting. The new information environment means that practically every Western military vehicle can be tracked from the moment it starts moving from its home base, or is unloaded from the ship delivering it to the European mainland. And when they get to the front, they will find Russia has been drawing upon its experience in Ukraine to rapidly learn and improve ways of making Western weapons systems obsolete – for instance by jamming the guidance systems of American precision weapons like HIMARS rocket artillery.[13] That means that Western militaries need to feel the same sense of urgency that is driving Russia and Ukraine if they are not to be technologically outflanked and bring weapons systems to a war where they have already been rendered ineffective.

It is important to note that only Russia's ground forces have been substantially damaged by the war and need to be rebuilt.[14] Other Russian military capabilities, such as its air force, have in relative terms remained unscathed, while Russia's enormous nuclear arsenal has of course not come into play at all. Russia has lost only 80 out of approximately 1,000 front-line aircraft in or near Ukraine, and Ukrainian success in sinking warships of the Russian Black Sea Fleet and effectively regaining maritime control there shouldn't distract from the fact that elsewhere, the Russian navy remains untouched and consequently is no less dangerous to NATO than it was before 2022.[15] And that danger lies not just at sea. The ability to fire missiles against land targets from warships that may be hundreds of kilometres away was demonstrated in Syria and then formed a major part of Russia's campaigns against Ukrainian cities and infrastructure. Russia's own experience of losing ships to missile strikes while they are in port or drydock around the Black Sea will have confirmed its conclusions about the utility of these strikes, meaning that in the event of conflict with NATO, European naval dockyards and civil ports receiving shipping with reinforcements are likely to be prime targets for long-range Russian attacks. That is also a role in which Russia's Long Range Aviation (LRA) force has proven its worth in attacks on Ukraine, with heavy bomber fleets keeping up a sustained campaign of stand-off strategic missile bombardment. As we'll see in later chapters, that should be a serious concern for European air forces that have closed many of their airbases and concentrated their aircraft and maintenance organisations in a small number of locations, making cost savings but also greatly simplifying the work of Russian targeting planners.

The net effect is that Russia is successfully building a neo-Soviet-style mass army. While it may be technologically inferior to NATO forces in some – but not all – areas, it will benefit from numbers, combat experience and deep reserves.[16] And the less damage Ukraine can do to Russia's forces, the faster and better Russia can rebuild, develop and train them.

Doubts have been raised over how Moscow will pay for it all. Russia has almost tripled its spending on defence since 2022.[17]

Not all of this is accounted for in buying arms: salaries and bonuses for military personnel and defence industry employees alike have grown rapidly. There will also be hidden costs to the state budget, like death benefits and long-term health and disability care – such as it is – spiking as a result of Russia's enormous casualty figures. Sanctions too increase costs in sourcing vital equipment for defence manufacturing. All of these pressures have led to speculation that the Russian economy may be unable to sustain the war. But for as long as oil prices remain acceptably high and foreign buyers like China and India continue to buy Russian hydrocarbons, it seems that Moscow can survive indefinitely on its pre-war financial reserves and ongoing energy income.[18] The long-term damage to the economy caused by turning it into a war machine will be immense, of course; but that reflects Russian priorities. In June 2024, a senior official in Russia's Presidential Administration listed the government's most important goals. The economy came after the military – because, he explained, "there can be no successful economy without a successful army".[19] That is the opposite approach to that ordinarily taken by Western governments; but it drives the threat that those Western governments will need to face.

The military-industrial build-up has seen Russia converting shopping centres, bakeries and other civilian facilities into drone workshops and weapons factories, and Russians have been asked to work six-day weeks and volunteer in manufacturing plants as part of the intensified war effort.[20] That too is a stark contrast with those parts of Europe still operating at peacetime scales and schedules. Corruption and inefficiency will inevitably take their toll on Russia's rearmament efforts: production statistics will be inflated, huge sums of money will be embezzled, and sub-standard weapons and munitions will arrive at the front line and cause the deaths of Russian soldiers. But these challenges are likely to hamper, rather than prevent, the transition to a war economy and the widespread repurposing of industry in order to continue to fight in Ukraine and beyond.[21] If successful, that may mean that Russia over time becomes less dependent on munitions supplies from North Korea and Iran. The industrial drive has already led to significant increases in production output, with Russia now apparently delivering new and refurbished armour to its forces at a rate of about 1,500 tanks and 3,000 other armoured fighting vehicles per year.[22]

And for now, there has not been a concerted effort by the West to fully block Russia's oil revenues that help pay for it all.[23] The political will to undercut Moscow's war effort by doing so has been lacking, in part due to US fears of a resulting rise in energy prices.[24] Consequently, money even from EU states is still pouring into Russia in energy payments,[25] and Western trade with Russia overall continues to boost the Russian state budget and pay for its war.[26] Despite sanctions, Russian oil is still even being delivered to countries including the United Kingdom after refining.[27] The Russian war machine is still being helped by British companies in other ways too, including a roll call of enablers for Moscow like those I identified in *Russia's War on Everybody*.[28] And failure to enforce sanctions effectively means that Russia is not only sustaining its economy through oil exports, but also succeeding in importing vital components for its defence industry through third countries like Kyrgyzstan and the UAE, including microprocessors and materials for manufacturing explosives and propellants.[29]

Neither is there any likelihood of support for the war fading among ordinary Russians.[30] Polls in March 2023 suggested Russia was capable of sustaining ongoing heavy casualties without loss of popular support.[31] That suggestion has been borne out by the subsequent year and more of fighting, while the Russian authorities have continued to work hard at fostering popular anger and resentment against the increasingly remote

West.[32] In fact there are consistent indications that those around Putin – and Russian society more broadly – are not dissuading him but looking forward with keen anticipation to a more open and honest confrontation with NATO.[33] In the middle of the nineteenth century, a French visitor concluded that the perpetual grimness of most subjects' lives in Russia was "like war, but with less enthusiasm".[34] Now, an actual war has given many Russians not only a sense of unity and purpose, but the enthusiasm that was missing too.[35]

That has contributed to Russia abandoning all pretence to be anything other than a rogue state. Early in the war, Russia's propagandists worked hard at offering excuses for strikes on civilian targets like schools, hospitals and shopping centres, trying to tell the world that they were being used as headquarters by Ukrainian or even NATO forces. By 2024, they no longer bothered pretending. The commission of atrocities against Ukrainians was carried out unconcealed, in the same way that Russia's security services saw no reason not to disseminate images and video of its torture of suspects in detention after the Crocus City Hall terrorist attack in Moscow in March 2024. Russia's opposition, meanwhile, never a significant force in politics, has been suppressed or emigrated; as has happened repeatedly through history, Russians with initiative are using it to leave the country rather than staying behind in the hope of improving it.[36] The remaining individuals who set themselves up as challengers to the existing regime, like Igor Girkin (also known as Strelkov), who was sentenced to a four-year prison term for extremism in 2024, tend not to have any real policy disagreement with the current leadership. They want to achieve the same objectives for Russia through even more aggressive behaviour, and abandon the relative restraint of the Putin administration (relative, that is, to the former rulers of Russia whom they idealise like Ivan the Terrible and Stalin). With Putin himself fully committed to confrontation with the West, and no constraints on his authority or genuine dissent from anyone in a position of power to do anything about it, there are simply no circumstances – including any conceivable change of leadership – under which Russia would no longer be a threat to Europe.[37]

Intent

As a result, after long-running and entrenched disagreements across Europe over the nature of the Russian threat and even whether there was a threat at all, early 2024 saw unprecedented unanimity among intelligence and defence chiefs that Russia was preparing to attack a NATO state in the near future. US,[38] Danish,[39] German[40] and other leaders confidently stated the likelihood or certainty that Putin would not stop at Ukraine, amid widespread expectation that one of the three Baltic states could be the next target.[41] The result, according to former NATO Secretary General George Robertson, is that "Ultimately we're going to be in the firing line".[42] That's a consensus that was strikingly absent before the invasion of February 2022, suggesting not only that European intelligence services have learned from that experience, but also that the evidence available to them is even stronger now than it was then.

Where there is disagreement, it is not over whether Russia will attack, but when. An authoritative US study released in September 2023 attempted to look forward two to four years – and noted that the window of opportunity for European defences to be strengthened would only be open for as long as Russia was tied down in Ukraine, and China continued to hesitate about paying the economic and diplomatic costs of throwing its weight fully behind Moscow.[43] But the setbacks suffered by Russia's ground forces in 2022–3 led to early estimations that it could take as long as a decade to rebuild them, and even in early 2024,

NATO officials were talking in terms of being ready for full-scale conflict in the next twenty years.[44] During 2024, however, the unexpected speed with which Russia reconstituted its forces led to a rapid re-appraisal of how soon they might be ready to move against NATO, and a spate of warnings to prepare for conflict more urgently. Inspector General of the Bundeswehr Carsten Breuer said in early 2024 that his country should be ready for war in five years.[45] British Defence Minister Grant Shapps pointed to the same period, but with the potential for conflict in multiple theatres with Russia, China, Iran and North Korea.[46] Polish,[47] Norwegian[48] and joint Baltic[49] assessments meanwhile indicate three years as the time NATO has left. Denmark's Defence Minister Troels Lund Poulsen split the difference and quoted three to five years before Russia could attack NATO.[50] Naturally, this depends on the progress of the war in Ukraine. The outgoing commander of the Estonian Defence Forces says the threat will become critical if and when Russian military power is freed up from the campaign there. Thereafter, "one year is enough for them to do something horrible in our direction".[51]

But the one thing all these estimates have in common is that NATO and its European member states will not be ready if they continue to prepare at their current pace. We'll look at European efforts to rearm, rebuild their defence industries, expand their militaries and bolster (or construct from scratch) civil defence in later chapters. But for now, a simple comparison should be enough to demonstrate the problem: while Russia may be ready in three to five years, French Defence Minister Sébastien Lecornu said in 2023 that France "will need a ten-year period of time to upgrade all infrastructures and equipment of our military".[52]

It's worth pausing for a moment and thinking where we were a decade ago. In 2014–15 the world was still adjusting to the new security situation in Europe that resulted from Russia's seizure of Crimea. The question then, as now, was where Russia's next move would be. The three Baltic states were intensely vulnerable – since NATO had not just failed, but actually refused to put together defensive plans for protecting them against Russia. As a result, analysts considered a wide range of ways Russia might employ an attack on one or more of the Baltic states to achieve one of its long-standing goals. One of the most commonly cited scenarios involved Russia seizing a small piece of NATO territory, seeking to replicate in miniature the success of its 2014 seizure of Crimea, then calling a halt to its operations and challenging NATO to respond – bolstered by a bout of nuclear sabre-rattling to concentrate minds. As we will see in Chapter 5, the calculation in this scenario was that NATO would prove incapable of responding meaningfully, and thus the entire rationale for the alliance – that it protects all of its members – would collapse and consequently so would NATO.

At the end of the last decade, however, these scenarios disappeared from discussion altogether because NATO did the right thing. The so-called Enhanced Forward Presence (eFP) contingents were its direct answer to the challenge of ensuring that NATO member states would be involved in the defence of their forward allies, and so avoid any equivocal situation where they might be inclined to back out of their commitments. These multinational battalions in each of the three Baltic states and Poland were made up of contingents from many different NATO allies – so the decision on whether to send troops from those countries would not need to be taken in a crisis, as they were already there. The results in assessments of the options open to Russia were immediate and dramatic. The "fait accompli" scenario disappeared altogether from the spectrum of possible action, and the Baltic states briefly enjoyed the greatest period of security that they had in hundreds of years.

But since 2023, those scenarios are back, and increasingly becoming one of the most likely avenues for Russia to seek to regain influence. The simple reason is the lack of demonstrated will by Western allies to act with sufficient urgency to improve their defences coupled with the potential for the United States, the keystone of Allied security, to refuse to get involved or even to withdraw its support altogether.

Russia may have failed in its successive efforts at undermining foreign support for Ukraine, such as grain blockades or restricting gas supplies. But its options are far from exhausted, and Moscow will be constantly looking for new ways to turn Western public opinion such that citizens put pressure on their governments to abandon Kyiv. As we will see in Chapter 6, that has led to a campaign of sabotage attacks across Europe. That campaign is intensifying, and chemical or biological attacks, or resuming Moscow's long-term practice of sponsoring terrorist attacks to wreak havoc in the West, are all still options for a Kremlin leadership that long ago abandoned all restraint along with any aspiration to salvage its relationship with Europe.

The reason why Russia invaded Ukraine is the same reason it will attack other countries too if it feels it can do so at a cost that it finds acceptable. And that is the simple fact that Vladimir Putin, and many other Russians, feel that the borders that bound Russia today are incorrect, unjust, and need to be put right, by force if other means fail.

In my work as a professional explainer of Russia, I routinely have to describe how Moscow sees itself and the world around it to military and government personnel at establishments like the NATO Defense College or the UK's own Joint Services Command and Staff College. For almost a decade I've been using in those lectures a slide showing a children's wall map of Russia, found on sale in Moscow. The map is called *Karta nashey Rodiny* – "Map of Our Motherland". And the striking thing about it – and the reason why it is such a useful teaching point – is that it is completely unrecognisable from the political map of Russia that we have taken for granted for the thirty years since the end of the USSR. Instead of showing the borders of Russia as we know it today, it shows the "Motherland" extending to the boundaries of the former Russian Empire, and including not only the other countries of the so-called Slavic heartland – Ukraine and Belarus – but also Moscow's former dominions in Central Asia, the Baltic states, Finland and Poland.

That a map like that is on sale at all (and remains so, indicating that at least somebody is buying it) speaks of a mental geography in Russia that is completely different from what is taken for granted outside the country. For many Russians, including the youngest generation who have been brought up on propaganda devices like this map, the current official borders of Russia are an anomaly. Instead, it is Russia's normal and rightful role to exert power over a far wider domain.

This assumption was an explicit part of the justification for the full-scale invasion of Ukraine in February 2022. In explaining the reasons for the invasion, President Putin referred specifically to decisions by the Bolsheviks in the earliest days of the USSR a hundred years before. The establishment of the constituent republics of the Soviet Union, broadly along ethnic lines, was, Putin explained, a mistake – and one that led to the entirely unnatural creation of the sovereign states that now surround Russia, some of them now full-fledged members of the EU and NATO.[53] The war on Ukraine is an attempt to correct that historical error, and bring at least one of those wayward nations and peoples back under Moscow's rule.

Of course, historical "corrections" like that are only a one-way process. Many in Russia would laugh scornfully if it were suggested that the same principle could be applied to revise the status of Karelia or Kaliningrad, seized by Moscow at the end of the Second World War, or – further back in history – the territories of the Russian Far East. Nevertheless the same Putin speech justifying the dismemberment of Ukraine also contained chilling warnings for the rest of Europe. His warped description of the way countries achieved their independence from Russian rule was aimed at Ukraine, but there was little in it that did not also apply to Poland, Finland and the Baltic states. This wasn't, of course, the first time Putin has said these things.[54] But with his move on Ukraine, he removed all doubt that he is intent on acting on them.

A different explanation that was strikingly absent from Putin's justification for the invasion was NATO "approaching Russia's borders". The role of NATO enlargement in driving Russian aggression is a subject that's been discussed many times before at enormous length, and there's no need to repeat it all here; but anybody that is still in doubt about the real reason for Russian aggression need only look at what Moscow is saying today. Putin has stepped away from the pretence that NATO accepting new member states is dangerous and provocative, and instead is quite frank about the assault on Ukraine being a colonialist war to recover lost imperial territory, that the Russian Orthodox Church is happy to bless as a "Holy War".[55] In fact the only people who still repeat the line that NATO enlargement "provoked" Russia are those who have been so seduced by Russian propaganda narratives in the past that they haven't realised that Russia has discarded them in the present. Putin didn't invade Ukraine in 2022 because he feared NATO; he invaded because he believed that Russia should take Ukraine back, and that Ukraine's friends and partners in the West were too spineless to prevent him from doing so.

It is not just about Putin, however. The assumption of Russian privilege over its neighbours is prevalent even among educated, internationalised Russians. There is a maxim among students of Russian society and politics that a Russian liberal's views are only liberal as far as the borders of Ukraine. Even

Russians who might be opposed to Putin, and inclined towards democratic ideals, do not as a result necessarily sympathise with the idea that Ukraine can possibly be a sovereign independent nation that can determine its own future, or has borders that should be respected.

Borders are an enduring security preoccupation for Moscow, and a component of a self-perpetuating cycle driving Russia to attack its neighbours. The old Russian joke goes that the only secure border is one with a Russian soldier standing on both sides of it. And that principle has found practical application throughout Russia's history of expansion, dealing with the hostility that Russia's aggression causes by expanding still further, in order to control as much territory as possible and neutralise threats by pushing them further away. But ironically, today the "security concerns" Russia claims over disputes with its neighbours would be resolved by Russia itself remaining within its internationally recognised 1991 borders. Neighbours have always respected these borders; it is only Russia that has not.

Nevertheless Russia still believes that the small states around its periphery should by rights be governed from Moscow. Since Western states believe instead that they are countries in their own right, and entitled to determine their own foreign and security policy and their own future, this represents a fundamental clash of world views that leads unavoidably to confrontation between Russia and the West. Ukraine is the tragic victim of this confrontation finally coming to a head.

The unfortunate conclusion from long-term observation of Russia is that this attitude towards Russia's borders will persist for as long as its assumption of entitlement to Empire does. And that, it has long been clear, will persist unless and until Russia suffers some kind of strategic reverse – a clear, unambiguous and undeniable defeat that sets the limits of Russian power. A defeat of this kind has been an essential ingredient in the historical path of all former empires – including the British, the French, the Portuguese, the Dutch and more. In each case, it was only strategic shock that led to a national re-appraisal of the country's status and role in the world.

This provides yet another reason to support Ukraine to the maximum extent possible to eject its Russian invaders, as well as investing in deterring Russia from further attacks. The choices made by the West in how to respond to Russia determine not only the futures of allies and partners in Europe, but shape Russia itself. Setting a firm limit to what Russia can achieve through force will not only preserve Ukraine, but also start the long, difficult process of change within Russia itself, from a frustrated former empire into, eventually, a normal country that can coexist with others. That change will be painfully slow. Even in democracies, it takes generations to change entrenched attitudes. Yet it is the only way of laying the foundations for an eventual future Europe that is secure, because its one and only hard security threat has been finally resolved.

For now, though, Russia shows no signs of changing and thus will remain a threat for the foreseeable future. In part that's because of its leadership's indifference to the scale of the slaughter that results from pursuing its goals.

Russia has never been in the habit of counting its human or economic losses when assessing whether it has achieved its aims. Its resilience in extended, attritional wars has often lain in greater willingness than the adversary to subject its own population to misery and destitution in pursuit of victory – and that population's willingness to accept this, up to a breaking point which is never entirely predictable but lies far in the future for today's Russia. Success in Ukraine would be presented by the leadership, and largely accepted by the population, as a triumph and a sign of the return of Russia to greatness – and the greater the Russian losses incurred, the greater the victory.[56] That's one reminder that it doesn't matter whether Russia is ready and able to fight as measured by NATO standards. Its willingness to send its own soldiers to their deaths in the tens of thousands for marginal gains tells us that this is an adversary with entirely different metrics for effectiveness and success. Moreover Vladimir Putin's evident sense of personal grievance and emotional investment in the restitution of Russian power will work against objective assessment of national interest, with the likely result that Russia may accept still higher costs in pursuit of its aims.

Russia's war effort has been significantly underwritten by its partner rogue states, with Iran supplying attack drones and North Korea sending artillery shells in the millions.[57] China too has played a key role in keeping Russia's defence industry revitalisation on track, through not only facilitating sanctions evasion but also massively stepping up supplies of its own war-related components and materials to Russia. There's no reason to think that support won't continue and expand. China's interest is clear: it has every reason to keep Russia in the game for as long as it is a co-challenger to the US, diverting American attention and resources. And just as I was completing writing this book, there came the first reports of North Korea supplying military units to support combat engineering on Russia's front line.[58] If the trend continues, it's reasonable to think that North Korea and others would eventually support Russia with armoured vehicles and artillery pieces when Moscow's own stocks finally begin to be exhausted, which according to some estimates could be in late 2025.[59]

What happens on Ukraine's battlefields has a direct impact on the future security of countries further West that are still notionally at peace. The more damage Ukraine can do to Russia's armed forces, the longer it will take to rebuild them for the next war, and the more reason Russia's leadership will have to hesitate before launching it. In the best case scenario, Ukraine could reduce Russia's military power until it poses only a manageable threat to its neighbours. But that would depend on willingness by the United States and others to offer Ukraine more support, with fewer restrictions attached, than they have to date.

Still, Russia's ambition for its next war – and hence the future of Europe as a whole – depends on the outcome of its current war. You can arrange Russia's possible futures by reference to that outcome. If Russia achieves anything from the war, and retains a land war capability that it believes is usable whether or not it is by anybody else's standards, Vladimir Putin will have been vindicated and the next step in achieving his vision will follow shortly. At the other end of the scale lies a different threat for Europe, in the form of a catastrophic Russian defeat bringing social change, instability and a return to the unpredictability of the 1990s with the ever-present threat that it could spill over into a direct danger to Russia's neighbours. The most likely outcome is somewhere between the two: a peace deal is imposed on Ukraine forcing it to accept Russian territorial gains; or Russia is eventually ejected from some or all of Ukraine's territory but survives to lick its wounds and once again prepare for the next attempt after a number of years.

There's one thing that's common to all of these possible outcomes. None of them removes Russia as a threat; it is only the type of threat and its imminence that varies. That means NATO and Europe's most important task after the war remains the same: to reduce to a minimum Russia's ability to harm its neighbours directly across state borders, or its adversaries further afield indirectly. As we'll see in Chapter 6, that requires not only credible armed forces, but also a defence and resilience mindset that encompasses society as a whole – which for many countries west of Warsaw is a remote aspiration. Nevertheless Russia is in no doubt that Ukraine is merely the front line of a much broader, and longer-term, contest with the West.[60] That means that the West in turn needs a long-term strategy that recognises Russia as a determined adversary for the foreseeable future, rather than a temporary challenge.[61] NATO Secretary General Jens Stoltenberg may have explained that Western populations should prepare for a confrontation that could last decades;[62] but far too few national politicians have echoed him and explained that the attacks across Europe discussed in Chapter 6 are merely a foretaste of what Russia has in store.

It is the Kremlin that will decide when to act, but it is not the Kremlin that will determine what options it has for action. That instead is a function of Western will and interest in constraining Russia. It depends on ongoing support to Ukraine to destroy Russian military capability faster than it can be rebuilt; on sanctions, and their enforcement, to put grit in the gears of Russia's war machine; on undercutting where possible the support Russia receives from third powers like North Korea and Iran; but most of all it depends on the rest of the West maintaining its resolve and focus during the United States's ongoing political nervous breakdown. But the contest is uneven. Russia doesn't need to rebuild a force that will match NATO's strength; it only needs to persuade NATO that the costs of confronting Moscow are unaffordable. Much of the groundwork has already been laid: Western governments have a consistent history of misguidedly believing that responding firmly to Russia will make the situation worse not better. In Georgia, Syria and Ukraine they have repeatedly fallen into the trap of negotiating with Russia to end a conflict while Russia is focused instead on winning it; while fearing that attempting to deter Russia will only "provoke" it and lead to escalating conflict.[63]

It's a mental paralysis rooted in an assumption that Russia is too big, too strong, too irrational or has too many nuclear weapons to be influenced – and the result is that Russia can attack with impunity, while any response to the attack is ruled out as a dangerous "escalation". Russia's network of propagandists, mouthpieces and influencers continues to insistently push the idea that confronting Moscow risks almost inevitable escalation to nuclear war. That obscures the fact that a clash with the US and its allies is the worst-case scenario for Russia, and the prospect is one of the few genuine deterrents for Putin. As a result, Russian state behaviour seems to be treated as a natural phenomenon that must be observed helplessly, rather than the result of decisions by a leadership that can be influenced.

But history, and the current conflict, demonstrate conclusively that it is weakness, not strength, that encourages Russia to aggression.[64] In September 2021 I wrote a detailed survey of what deters Russia, looking back over the history of Western attempts to dissuade Moscow from doing something stupid, and tracking the pattern of when they succeeded and when they failed.[65] That study revealed a simple and straightforward pattern: that Russia does not stop unless it is opposed by a strong and credible military force and the demonstrated will to use it, since that is the only obstacle that the Kremlin takes seriously and that causes it to think twice and step back from aggression. The multiple examples of success in setting boundaries for Russian action that the report considered included Turkey shooting down a Russian aircraft in 2015 – a far more direct challenge to Russian power than those currently causing such hesitation among NATO allies in the context of Ukraine, but one which demonstrably failed to bring about a broader conflict let alone open warfare between Russia and NATO. Sadly none of the points made in that report were acted on by Western powers while Russia made its preparations to invade Ukraine over the following five months, and as a result, Russia was not deterred.

In late 2021 and early 2022 I visited a series of British military units that were expecting to be sent to the Russian front, that one after another called me in to talk to them about what they might expect to find there. This was when options under consideration included a troop presence from NATO member states in Ukraine to deter Russia from invading – swiftly ruled out as implausible without US support, which was not forthcoming. I had no access to the classified information that made the British and US governments so sure the invasion was imminent. But in briefings to governments on both sides of the Atlantic, I was describing what we could see from the outside – the fact that Russia had changed strategic gear. The Kremlin, it was clear, had abandoned any aspiration to have a constructive relationship with the West, and instead was pursuing its own goals in its own time.

Two key factors shaped Putin's decision that the time was right to mount a full-scale invasion of Ukraine. One was confidence that Ukraine would collapse swiftly, which proved wildly wrong. The other was confidence that the West would not intervene, and in this Putin was entirely right. Russia had observed the previous three decades of defence drawdowns across Europe, and repeated demonstrations that Europeans were unwilling to fund their own defence. That left the United States as the main guarantor of European security – but with assurances in place from then President Joe Biden that there would be no military response to Russia's moves, Putin knew that this too could be discounted.

The vital task for the West now and in the future is to try to ensure that that confidence does not arise again, and that Putin and his advisers don't conclude, either rightly or wrongly, that the time is right for further attacks beyond Ukraine. Ukraine's experience shows that Russia doesn't have to be successful, or correct in its assessment of when to go to war, to inflict horrific damage on its victims. Russia will have its own estimate for when it is ready. It may well not be right, just as in February 2022. But the fine distinction of whether Moscow's next assault is perfectly timed or wildly misguided won't help those in the path of Russia's troops or subsequently rounded up for detention, deportation, rape or murder in the occupied territories.

Whatever the outcome in Ukraine, the end of the current fighting will not bring "peace" without effective means of deterring Russia from starting another war. Russia will remain a threat to Europe until its imperial ambition is broken. This is why the outcome of the conflict in Ukraine is of such vital importance not only to Ukrainians, but to the West and arguably to the whole world. We'll look at just how important that outcome is to all of us in the next chapter.

2

THE FUTURE OF UKRAINE AND THE FUTURE OF EUROPE

"It's amazing how unprepared we are for the big war. It will take years – but fortunately the Ukrainians are buying us time."

Chief of Defence of a central European state,
Tallinn, May 2023

Not enough Europeans west of Warsaw realise just how much their lives will change if Russia defeats Ukraine – or even if the war there ends without a sufficiently convincing defeat for Russia itself. That's not only because of Russia's direct promise to attack elsewhere in Europe, but also because of the social and economic upheaval that will be required to deter it from doing so – and especially how those essential changes will be paid for. Whatever kind of peace prevails in Ukraine will define the fundamental principles of Europe's future, including whether borders and sovereignty are negotiable, and aggression is accepted or punished.

But Russia doesn't even need to match NATO or Europe in conventional military power to challenge it. If Russia can turn confrontation into a poker game where the loser is the first to fold when daunted by the stakes – while Moscow whips up the ever-present nuclear threat – there is still the risk that Russia can make Western military power irrelevant by winning before it is brought to bear.

That is why the campaign of strikes against Ukraine's vital civilian infrastructure should be considered carefully by other European states. For Russia, a "Strategic Operation for the Destruction of Critically Important Targets" is a means of coercing an enemy state into submission by demonstrating the ability to inflict more and more damage on the basic infrastructure that keeps its civilians alive. In Ukraine, that campaign failed in the winter of 2022–23, in part due to the extraordinary resilience of the Ukrainian people, only to be resumed in earnest during 2024. But conducted against a western European state, a similar onslaught could have a very different impact on the continuing will to fight. So too would the savagery and barbarity with which Russia wages war. Western militaries in Afghanistan became accustomed to fighting within the strict bounds of international humanitarian law while their adversaries faced no such constraint; but in a war in Europe, as tragically demonstrated in Ukraine, it is civilians too that feel the direct impact of Russia's methods of terrorising populations into submission through unimaginable brutality. This too sadly should have come as no surprise. In briefings to NATO militaries long before 2022, I was explaining how in the event of war in Europe, nobody should expect the Russian armed forces to operate with any less murderous inhumanity and gratuitous viciousness than they had done in Chechnya, Syria, or any other conflict further back in history. Russian actions in places like Bucha and Irpin, and throughout the occupied territories of Ukraine, together with the systematic torture and starvation of both captive civilians and prisoners of war, proved this prediction sickeningly correct.

And yet, fear of Russia in a way made the invasion of February 2022 inevitable. As the crisis unfolded, the US and UK almost immediately ruled out direct military support on the ground to Kyiv. Moscow will have been delighted, as once again the West helpfully took Russia's greatest fears off the table. But even after the US and UK had ruled out direct defensive support to Ukraine, it would have been possible to put in place no-fly zones or maritime exclusion zones, presenting Russia with the risk of direct clashes with NATO nations if it supported an attack by use of air or sea. This didn't happen either. The extent of support to Ukraine was supposedly limited by the fact that it is not a member of NATO, but there's no shortage of examples where Western powers have offered protection from aggression beyond the borders of the alliance – and as we'll see in Chapter 3, there have been more such cases since 2022. Even two years into the full-scale war, the US practice of supplying weapons but prohibiting Ukraine to use them to hit targets within Russia – even those directly involved in mounting attacks into Ukraine – has been another telling symptom of Washington's extreme reluctance to confront Moscow. In sum, Russia's confidence to act against Ukraine stemmed from a failure of deterrence by the West overall. What stops Russia, and has done so reliably over the centuries, is credible military force being present and ready in advance. The West was not willing to put that force in place, so Russia saw no reason to stop.[1]

Instead of direct involvement, the global coalition backing Ukraine has kept it in the fight primarily through massive supplies of aid. Kyiv's dependence on foreign support was highlighted in 2023–24 when domestic political hostage-taking in the US Congress stepped on the hose delivering support, leading to a months-long interruption in aid. That had direct results in choking Ukraine's ability to resist, since shortages of munitions and supplies have direct impacts on the battlefield. To take a simple example, this happens when Ukraine loses ground because it observes Russian troops preparing to attack, but is helpless to break up that attack because there are no artillery shells available to do so. But that immediate effect in turn contributes to a long-term building of advantage for Russia, through increased Ukrainian losses of both defensive positions and personnel that cannot be recovered.[2] Politicians sacrificing Ukraine's ability to prevail for their own narrow motivations in Washington or Brussels – or simply being timid and indecisive and not taking the necessary decisions – have a direct and potentially disastrous impact on what happens at the front line of Europe's defence against Russia. It's a matter of grim accounting which of Russia's tools will kill more Ukrainians in the long run – Iranian drones, North Korean shells, or US Republican Party politicians in Congress.

As a result, early 2024 saw increasingly strident warnings from Ukrainian, US and European officials that the interruption of support from the US was translating directly into critical vulnerabilities for Ukraine.[3] A joint appeal by five European leaders in January 2024 to increase supplies to Ukraine and invest in expanding industrial capacity at home contained brave words about renewing resolve and redoubling efforts, but also highlighted that they had been powerless to bring this about so far despite being heads of state in their respective countries.[4] And like so many other EU decisions, aid from the EU depends on a consensus between member states, which means that there too individual politicians can take the process hostage for their own, much narrower aims. During 2023 both Hungarian Prime Minister Viktor Orbán and Slovak Prime Minister Robert Fico temporarily did so.[5] With Hungary scheduled to hold the EU Council presidency in the second half of 2024, there was concern this might be used to extract further concessions from the EU in exchange for allowing the free flow of aid – concern which only grew when one of Orbán's first actions after the start of the presidency was to visit Vladimir Putin in Moscow, a mission immediately disavowed by the EU.[6]

The US block on aid to Ukraine emphasised Ukrainian reliance on military assistance to continue effective resistance. But economic aid to ensure that the Ukrainian economy and state can continue to function is equally vital. Just as supplies of shells help Ukraine hold back Russian forces on the battlefield, financial support is vital for staving off an economic crisis that would severely compromise the country's ability to continue resisting.[7] The two are inter-related, of course. In the clearest link between military aid and economic gains, cruise missiles provided by Britain and France have targeted Russian warships in conjunction with Ukrainian attacks using exploding sea drones. The attacks have forced Russia to base its Black Sea Fleet farther from Ukraine's coast, which has allowed regular commercial shipping to return to Ukrainian ports that handle grain and steel, key export commodities, and contributed to keeping the Ukrainian economy afloat.

What if Ukraine Loses?

Russia and Putin have been open about, and even proud of, their genocidal intent to destroy Ukraine as an independent state and Ukrainians as a distinct people. That aim is pursued at the highest state level, and against individuals on a daily basis. It includes determined attempts to eradicate the Ukrainian language – even speaking Ukrainian in the Russian-occupied territories risks detention and torture.[8] That means that there is no middle ground or partial solution to the conflict, because there's no scope for compromise with an aggressor that is bent on extermination of its victim. The disappearance of Ukraine from the world's maps in the same way that countries swallowed up by the USSR were erased in the last century isn't just a theoretical possibility, but a clear goal that Russia is striving for.

A just and fair outcome to Russia's war on Ukraine would be Ukrainian success in liberating the occupied territories, justice being done for war crimes and atrocities, Russia paying reparations and reconstruction costs, and a change of heart in the Kremlin leading Moscow to realise that aggression does not pay. Sadly, justice and fairness remain in the realm of fantasy. Short of that ideal outcome, as things stand in mid-2024 there's a wide spectrum of possible futures for the war, ranging from substantial Ukrainian advances, through a ceasefire and freezing of the conflict, to Russia breaking through the front line and part or all of Ukraine being overrun.[9] But the key point that's common to all of those possibilities is that they all absolutely require not only maximum possible support to Ukraine by the countries of Europe, but also massive reinvestment in those countries' own defences.

That's because even the remote prospect of a complete Ukrainian "victory" would not remove the underlying problem. A simplistic view of victory is that it consists of a successful military campaign to evict the Russian invader from Ukraine. But that's only one of the essential changes needed to ensure the safety of Ukraine and Europe over the long term. That's partly because simple retreat to its own borders will not cause Russia to stop the war, or to stop missile and drone strikes and attacks by conventional and unconventional means from behind its new front line. Liberating Ukraine's overrun territories and the people there suffering under savage Russian occupation would on its own be a huge achievement and is essential – but strictly in terms of ending the fighting, it is no better than a ceasefire or peace agreement at the current front line if Russia remains undeterred and has no incentive to change its objectives. In fact when President Zelenskyy put forward a plan for peace in October 2022, only two of its ten points were related to removing Russia and recovering Ukrainian territory.[10] The remainder were about ensuring Ukraine's longer-term future by protecting energy, environment, food, nuclear security and more – all of which are threatened by Russia – plus security guarantees to prevent a future repeat invasion.

In other words, victory implies peace. But peace can only come when Russia is no longer both determined to attack and able to do so. Of those two factors, it's easier to erode Russian capability than to change Russian intent. Most objective analyses of Russia's own possible futures agree that the only thing that will deflect the Kremlin, and Russian society as a whole, from imperial ambition and aggression is traumatic defeat followed by coming to terms with being one country among many rather than a frustrated and resentful former empire. That process would have to run far deeper than the tumultuous changes that followed the collapse of the USSR in 1991, since those demonstrably did not bring about a transformation in Russia's assumption of rights over its neighbours and determination to assert them through invasion.

That transformation remains a distant prospect, just like any hope of justice or reparations. What's left is opportunities closer to hand – primarily reducing as far as possible Russia's ability to threaten Ukraine in the short term, while building up the capacity to deter it from future attacks against Ukraine and Europe in the longer term. In that respect, Ukraine's sacrifices bought time for European states to urgently build that capacity, through rearmament and bolstering their civil defences. Sadly, after two years of war much of Europe is only now embarking on this process, and even aid to Ukraine to continue the fight is consistently under threat. As a result, in mid-2024, defeat of Ukraine is still a clear possibility – and with it, a series of cascading second- and third-order effects that threaten disaster for the rest of Europe and, in turn, severe disruption globally.

Defeat for Ukraine would lead to a stronger, emboldened Russia still more convinced that overt aggression is the best route to achieving what it wants – and that puts the whole of Europe at risk. Former Estonian Prime Minister Kaja Kallas has laid out the challenge with her customary skill in reducing a problem to its essence. "Russia will not continue if they lose in Ukraine," she says, "they will continue if they win in Ukraine."[11] Russia's new front line with NATO from the Black Sea to central Poland would pose a new and direct threat to Romania, Hungary and Slovakia, not only fixing NATO forces there and diverting them from defence of the Nordic and Baltic regions, but offering Moscow the potential for further encroachment if sufficiently Russia-friendly governments arrive in power in any of those countries. Russia's experienced and battle-hardened military would be bolstered not only by the forced mobilisation of Ukraine's captive population, but by capture of Ukraine's defence industries, including potentially the technologies that have brought Ukraine success in striking deep into Russia and which could now be turned against the West.[12] For all these reasons, defeat of Russia is essential to prevent a broader, even more disastrous war.[13] And even before then, Ukraine's defeat would not only bring humanitarian catastrophe at home as Russia expanded its reign of terror potentially to the whole country, but also a renewed flood of refugees westward numbering potentially in the tens of millions, mirroring the mass movement of population at the end of the Second World War also fleeing Moscow's forces and the occupation regime that followed them.

The effects would not be limited to Europe. Under former President Joe Biden, the US pledged to support Ukraine. If that support is insufficient and Ukraine is defeated by Russia, that will shake the credibility of US commitments around the world. Washington's ability to defend its global interests could be severely compromised by actual and potential partners and allies being wary of placing too much trust in an unreliable US, leading more of them to find accommodations with Russia and China. And the United States's own power would be called into question. It is not just Russia that sees Ukraine as the front line of a bigger conflict with the West; that perception is shared across much of the world outside Europe and North America.[14] In that context, the fall of Ukraine could only be regarded as a major victory for Russia and a humiliating defeat for the US. The effects would be long-lasting and highly dangerous. Donald Trump's first national security advisor, H.R. McMaster, thinks the result of US credibility being undercut by failure to ensure the survival of Ukraine "could be cascading conflicts even more costly than the interconnected wars in Ukraine and across the Middle East".[15]

In fact it's not just the US that would suffer a catastrophic loss of credibility. The West as a whole would have shown that it is unable to defend the values it claims to stand for. That effect would be far more severe after years of fighting than if Ukraine had succumbed swiftly, as expected in February 2022. That could have been explained as a failure of foresight and analysis by many Western nations (despite no shortage of warnings of what Russia intended to do). But if the West has said that Russia must not win, and Russia then does so, that instead is a failure of credibility and commitment for the Western community of nations as a whole. The impact could be as great or more as that of the Suez crisis in 1956 or the US withdrawals from Vietnam in the 1970s or Afghanistan fifty years later.[16]

Russia seeks to roll back the power of the United States and the system it leads because those are the key obstacles to Russia's plans to expand its own power both in its former empire and globally. And both Russia and other challengers like China, Iran, North Korea and more will be encouraged by the idea that if the US fails to ensure the survival of a partner in Europe, it is even more likely to do so in their own neighbourhoods – and by Russia's demonstration that the US can be manipulated into abandoning its interests without a fight.[17] Those parts of the world that might be sitting on the fence waiting to back the winner in the conflict will conclude that it is not the US or the West. In addition, a conclusion to the war on Ukraine that involves ceding even part of the country to Russia would mean abandoning the principle that territory should not be seized by force. If Russia's claims to domination over Ukraine are successfully implemented through conquest, it tells the world that internationally recognised borders can be redrawn by means of military power anywhere. That would not just be an open invitation for Russia to continue its campaign of reconquest of the former Russian Empire because it has been blessed with success, but also for any other rogue state around the world that has designs on its neighbour's territory. China's neighbours would be the first to feel the result of this perception of a permissive environment for armed conquest, followed swiftly by large parts of Africa and Latin America as simmering disputes come back to the boil. The trend would be set towards a world filled with even more conflicts and proxy wars between global and regional powers as they cooperate or compete to replace the United States. That in turn means even greater arms races, flows of migrants and refugees, and disruptions to the global economy and trade, with a severe impact on ordinary people even in those countries that have managed to remain at peace.[18] Those global consequences have been recognised by friends and partners further afield, which in part explains the substantial support Ukraine receives from Japan. Japan not only shares a common neighbour from hell with Ukraine, but also lives in a rough neighbourhood to start with – and is nervous of the encouragement that North Korea and China will draw from seeing the US fail to deter Russia.[19]

Ripple effects would compound the damage. Victory would restore Russia's standing with China, and overcome disquiet in Beijing at the destabilising impact of Russian aggression. And China in turn would be encouraged to more assertive steps by the demonstration of US and Western weakness, probably at the expense of Taiwan. Europe would be divided between those countries further from Russia who accept a bad peace to avoid further confrontation, and those on the front line who recognise that this only compounds the danger to themselves. That could present the biggest challenge to European unity yet, at a time when unity of the EU and European NATO is essential for safeguarding Europe's future.[20] Even more dangerously, defeat of Ukraine would demonstrate to other countries around the world how important it is to possess nuclear weapons.

It is difficult to imagine any other country being permitted by the world to conduct the kind of campaign Russia has waged in Ukraine (and in Syria before it), still less with an overt agenda of exterminating the Ukrainian people. And yet, Russia's UN Security Council veto and the fear it has instilled through nuclear propaganda have given it a free pass to behave as it wishes, without fear of interference from the United States, while the rest of the global community looks on in either ambivalence or helpless paralysis. By repeatedly threatening their use, Russia has used its nuclear weapons as a get out of jail free card to escape the consequences of its actions in Ukraine; while Kyiv is ruing the 1993 decision to relinquish its nuclear weapons held over from the Soviet Union in exchange for security assurances from Britain and the United States (and, ironically, Russia). That juxtaposition sets a disastrous example. It tells other aggressive powers that nuclear weapons allow you to wage genocidal wars of destruction against your neighbours because other nations will not intervene. And it signals to those weaker neighbours that nuclear capabilities of their own may be the most effective deterrent for the aggressor. The result, almost inevitably, will be more nuclear weapons proliferation and the brinkmanship associated with them, leading to a vastly more dangerous world.[21]

What Else Could Be Done?

Before Ukraine is able to liberate its occupied territories and eject Russian invaders it needs to fight to survive. Meanwhile across the West, there's perpetual debate as to the likely end of the war, and which outcomes can and cannot be considered realistic. That has led to many proposals being put forward for how the conflict could, or should, be brought to a close.

But many of these proposals are unworkable and some are outright dangerous. The persistent calls for a "ceasefire" or "negotiated settlement" to end the fighting without a resolution of its underlying cause – Russia's ambition to eliminate Ukraine as we know it – will do no more than rewarding the aggressor while punishing the victim. That's because most ideas behind a supposed peace deal involve Ukraine the victim, not Russia the aggressor, conceding territory and accepting limits on their future defence and foreign policy choices. They offer peace through Ukraine ceasing to resist, rather than through Russia ceasing its attempts to destroy it.[22]

Early in the conflict, the Russian withdrawal from areas north of Kyiv allowed the world to witness the aftermath of atrocities carried out in towns like Bucha.[23] But for the subsequent two years and counting, other areas of Ukraine have remained under the same savage military occupation.[24] If Ukraine is eventually compelled to give up part of its territory to the invader, even with the possible incentive of eventual NATO and EU membership for the portion of the country that remains free, Ukrainian society may emerge from the war divided and resentful rather than relieved and ready for the future. The resentment, in cold and devastated cities where the human cost in numbers of dead and maimed soldiers is slowly becoming increasingly apparent, would be directed against the West and its broken promises and Ukraine's own leaders that held out the hope of victory only to have it dashed. That in itself will make restoring stability and prosperity to Ukraine more challenging, even before factoring in the likelihood of renewed Russian attacks when Moscow feels ready.[25]

Just as dangerously, whether or not a ceasefire was real and effective, it would provide Ukraine's Western backers with an excuse to conclude the problem is resolved and walk away. There is a years-long precedent for that in the shape of the so-called Minsk Agreements, a notional ceasefire formula that, like so many before it, tied Ukraine's hands while leaving Russia free to continue its aggression.[26] The abandonment of Ukraine's struggle would resemble the writing off of eastern Europe to subjugation and terror at the hands of Moscow during the early Cold War. And there is always a risk that Europe could find a figurehead willing to be the twenty-first century's Neville Chamberlain – this time accepting fig leaf promises of "peace" from Russia instead of Germany, but still at the expense of the people, then Czech and Slovak, now Ukrainian, abandoned to the aggressor.

Besides, consistent experience from Russia's other wars shows that just because Moscow signs a ceasefire agreement does not mean that it has any intention to cease firing. Russia has a strong track record of flouting the terms of ceasefires, and disregarding them altogether when it sees an advantage to be seized by doing so. And allowing Russia a way out of the conflict that does not involve undeniable defeat would suspend, not end, the war. A ceasefire would provide Russia with an opportunity to rebuild its military capabilities faster, including through pressing Ukrainians in any newly-occupied territories into the Russian army as was standard practice for the advancing Soviet forces in the Second World War and is today seen in Donetsk and Luhansk. And that, in turn, would only bring forward the date of a new offensive against Ukraine or against a NATO nation.

It is an entirely different kind of international agreement that would safeguard Ukraine's future, and with it the future security of Europe. Ukraine's strongest supporters point out that Europe has a ready-made mechanism for protection against Russia in the form of NATO, and so the best way to formalise support for Ukraine and deter Russia would be to allow it to join.[27] That idea encountered substantial opposition primarily from the US and Germany; and so, when in July 2024, NATO leaders met in Washington for their regular summit, it had already been decided that there would be no membership offered for Ukraine – despite a commitment to bring Ukraine into the alliance dating back sixteen years to the alliance's summit in Bucharest in 2008. Russia will have understood clearly from the summit outcome that NATO membership for Ukraine will not be a serious topic of discussion for as long as the war continues. That gives Russia a strong motivation to continue the war even if it eventually accepts that it has failed in its initial aims.

Recognition that NATO as a whole could not be persuaded to protect Ukraine prompted an alternative plan, consisting of a network of individual "security guarantee" agreements with partner countries designed to cement military assistance for Ukraine in place until it might, eventually, be allowed to join NATO. The first of these agreements was signed in Kyiv by the then British Prime Minister, Rishi Sunak, in January 2024. It was followed by a rash of others forming a web of overlapping commitments, that are probably the closest Ukraine can currently get to the kind of alliance support that would come with NATO membership.[28] Other countries following the UK in signing support agreements included Germany in February 2024, Belgium and Spain in May, and Japan and the United States in June. Each of them is bilateral; but together they form a multinational commitment forming a security framework around Ukraine that's more comparable to membership of an alliance. The result, in theory, should be to indicate to the Kremlin that Western support for Ukraine is a long-term commitment and not something that will evaporate if Russia waits long enough. That, in turn, should nudge Russia closer to amending its war ambitions.

The plan has to overcome suspicions both in Ukraine and beyond that the new "security guarantees" will be of little more worth than the ones the UK and France gave Poland before the Second World War, or indeed the Budapest Memorandum of 1994, which supposedly guaranteed Ukraine's territorial integrity.[29] But then, those doubts about how seriously countries will take their commitments when they are put to the test by confronting a nuclear-armed Russia also apply to their commitment to NATO, as we'll see in Chapter 5. And if the plan is over the long term to demonstrate to Russia that Ukraine will not be abandoned, the practical assistance that accompanies the guarantees on paper needs to be real and visible. They also need to be cemented in place as long-term commitments regardless of political change in Europe and beyond. A promise by one government that is torn up by the next would only confirm Russia's impression of the fickle nature of support for Ukraine, and once again encourage it to continue the war.

It remains the case that the best "security guarantee" would be providing sufficient aid and support to enable Ukraine to repel and deter Russia itself, through building still more capable and powerful armed forces of its own. But that means on top of helping Ukraine fight today's war, building a long-term defence plan that adapts to the potential inconstancy of aid from the

US and European partners, and ensures Ukraine can survive indefinitely and independently despite Russia's ability to rebuild and sustain its own war effort.[30]

It would be a mistake, though, to think of support for Kyiv as a one-way process where Ukraine consumes resources and provides nothing in return. Ukraine, through no fault of its own, is the unfortunate focal point of the broader confrontation between Russia and the West. The only alternative to European countries providing the aid that enables the front line of defence to hold there is to allow Ukraine to succumb, and then deal with holding back Russia on their own territory. Meanwhile, Ukraine's experience holds vital lessons for how other countries must prepare to defend themselves against Russia in any possible future in which Ukraine is no longer able to resist. That includes a demonstration for the front-line states of just what's required to withstand a land attack. The imminence of the existential threat from Russia led to a roughly four-fold expansion in the numbers of Ukrainian defenders under arms. No European country would be able to cope with that speed and scale of expansion, and even if it did manage to raise a citizen army, it would have nothing to fight with – even in Ukraine, many combatants are still purchasing their own equipment or relying on crowdsourced donations, two years and more after the full-scale invasion. Moreover while some front-line states invest in volunteer territorial defence reserves, most European countries would be unable to raise the volunteer battalions that saved Ukraine in 2014 and to some extent in 2022.

The fate of cities like Mariupol set a grim precedent for how similarly-sized capitals of NATO member states within reach of Russia might fare in open warfare. The centre of Lithuania's capital Vilnius is only 30 km from the border with Belarus, so the drive to defend the entirety of national territory reflects the choice countries like Lithuania face between stopping invading forces before they get to the capital, or potentially destroying it in order to save it.

But there are also positive lessons for Western militaries in how Ukraine has defended itself. The long-term static front line on the map in Ukraine has caused some observers to lose perspective when assessing developments in the war. It has obscured the fact that Ukraine has achieved major successes since the earliest phases of the war not primarily on land, where Russia's onslaught has been largely held back at immense cost to both sides, but at sea and in the air and in Russia itself. And the manner in which Ukraine has defended itself against Russian cyber and information warfare holds key pointers for other states that are already experiencing Russian attacks in this domain, regardless of being notionally at peace with Moscow.[31]

As discussed above, the greater the damage Ukraine can do to Russia and its armed forces now, the greater the likelihood that Russia will be deterred from attacking again in the future. But in order to bring about a more fundamental change of attitude in the Kremlin, the damage done would have to be sufficiently serious to be meaningful to the leadership when weighed against its pursuit of imperial power. That means more than massive casualties among Russian forces and severe damage to the economy. The impact would have to be even more fundamental for the country as a whole and for Vladimir Putin personally. It would require overcoming Russia's deep human and economic reserves and transcending its population's endurance and ability to tolerate extended hardship and adversity.

Meanwhile the balance of investment and risk argues clearly in favour of unstinting support for Ukraine. The costs sound high to European governments unaccustomed to investing in their security. But economist Timothy Ash calculates that annual support of $100 billion to keep Ukraine free and hold back Russia amounts to less than one-fifth of 1% of Western

GDP, and less than 10% of NATO's current defence spending.[32] And in any case, much of that investment would be in the donors' own economies, funding first arms production and subsequently peacetime industries like construction when the time comes to rebuild Ukraine. The risks, on the other hand, are potentially catastrophic. Some of the consequences of the worst-case scenario of a collapse in resistance by an exhausted Ukraine outlined earlier in this chapter would follow swiftly, and others would evolve over time; but almost all of them would be both highly damaging and, more importantly, irreversible.

And when it comes to Russia launching further attacks beyond Ukraine, the risk is that European and US vacillation over support for Kyiv would confirm to Moscow that the West lacks the will to defend itself. That equation is slowly changing, as more and more European states wake up, recognise the threat and start doing something about it. But it will be a close-run thing even with continuing US commitment to the future of Europe. That US commitment, and what could cause it to evaporate, is the subject of the next chapter.

3

AMERICA, DISTRACTED AND DIVIDED

"We have no intention of fighting Russia."

US President Joe Biden,
22 February 2022

At the end of the Cold War the US Army in Europe (USAREUR) numbered almost 300,000 troops, the majority of which were stationed in West Germany. Their mission was to deter the USSR, assure US allies, and protect the US's strategic interests in Europe. Over the following quarter-century, those numbers declined sharply, not only because the Russian threat was supposed to have gone away, but also because the US military was given so many other tasks globally. By 2014, USAREUR had one-tenth as many troops but deployed across a vastly greater area, from Estonia down to Romania with hubs in Germany, Italy, and Poland. Furthermore, it had no tanks or armoured artillery, and was in the process of having its attack helicopters taken away. And yet, the mission – to deter Moscow, assure allies, and protect American interests – was supposed to be precisely the same.

If those American interests are to be protected, and Russia is to be deterred, the US needs a robust long-term military force posture in Europe.[1] Any weakening of that posture will be an encouraging signal for further Russian aggression. US (and Western European) willingness to support Ukraine militarily is read in Central Europe, as much as it is in Moscow, as a measurement of willingness to defend NATO territory too. There are currently US service personnel stationed in all three of the Baltic states as well as in Poland. Those countries place great importance on the physical presence of US troops: the calculation is that if they are involved in responding to a Russian attack simply by virtue of where they are, this will automatically bring the United States into the conflict on the right side. The importance of that presence is highlighted by the way the dissenting voices opposing it were the same ones that argued for the abandonment of Ukraine and urged the US to force a "negotiated settlement" on Kyiv in the hope of satisfying Russia and averting future aggression.[2]

The US's contribution to European defence is not just the physical presence of troops. It also lies in capabilities that are beyond the reach of many European allies, such as signals intelligence, surveillance, space-based assets for communication and intelligence gathering, and strategic air transport. The United States is in effect the only NATO ally that is genuinely fully capable across all these domains, despite British aspirations (see Chapter 4). And while Europe could in time, given political will, start to build up capabilities of its own in some of these fields, there are specific areas where the US is indispensable – especially given Europe's delay in rebooting its defence industries. Those include not just high-end weapons systems and niche military inventory, but also crucial intelligence support, where US capabilities far outstrip those of individual European powers.[3]

AMERICA, DISTRACTED AND DIVIDED

Since the Second World War the US has defended Europe not through noble altruism but because it had a compelling strategic interest to do so. If at any point a US administration does not discern that interest – or wants actively to undermine it – then America's commitment to Europe is immediately in doubt. That is despite the fact that that commitment makes up only a small proportion of overall American military effort, with the bulk of US military power focused elsewhere than Europe. Many US taxpayers would probably be surprised, if they thought about it at all, how little of US overall defence spending is allocated to protecting Europe. Depending on the method of calculation, estimates range from as little as 4% to a maximum of around 15%.[4] They might also be surprised how much of their economy depends on Europe. The US and EU are by far each other's largest trading partners in goods and services, and the EU is the top trading partner for eighty countries worldwide, compared to the US with twenty. Those two factors combined mean that disruption of European trade – for instance, as a result of conflict spreading beyond Ukraine – would have an immediate and substantial effect on the US economy and the prosperity of individual Americans.[5]

Government trade figures show the US economy earns considerably more from doing business with Europe than from the entire Asia-Pacific region, including major trading partners like Japan, Korea, China and India. But only a few faltering attempts have been made to explain to US voters how Russia's challenges affect their security and prosperity despite being an ocean away. And in particular, there has been a sorry failure to explain to them that the great majority of "aid to Ukraine" is spent in the United States and secures American jobs. As a result, to too many people in the US, problems in Europe seem an abstract and distant distraction when there is no shortage of more direct and immediate issues to contend with at home.

And even to American strategic planners, Europe isn't the only continent of concern. The US has to manage the future facing not one but two major long-term adversaries, Russia and China, as well as a host of other challengers like Iran, whose proxies consistently seek to harm US interests in the Middle East and beyond. It is widely accepted that a sound defeat of Russia would demonstrate that military aggression does not pay and deter China, Iran and others from considering something similar. But as noted in Chapter 1, some parts of the US military and intelligence establishment appear not to believe Russia genuinely poses a military threat to Europe. Another line of argument fuelling suggestions that Europe should be left to itself is that the US lacks the capacity to deal with both China and Russia.[6] That line often overlooks, or deliberately obscures, the tiny proportion of US military power that is allocated to Europe and the fact that the forces the US would require are different in Europe and Asia. Deterrence and, ultimately, conflict in Asia require primarily naval and air forces, while Europe primarily requires air and heavy ground forces for its defence.[7]

Moreover the reasonable suggestion that China is the United States' most dangerous long-term adversary is too often accompanied by a refusal to understand that stopping and punishing overt Russian aggression now is the best way to deter Chinese aggression in the future; and that dealing with the Russia problem first will leave the US with a freer hand for standing up to China later, rather than having to manage two conflicts simultaneously. In addition, declaring an aim of ending Russia's war on Ukraine in order to focus on China provides China with a clear incentive to help Russia keep the war on Ukraine active for as long as possible. The argument that the US doesn't have sufficient stocks of munitions to provide them to Ukraine now while still being ready for China in the future is also sometimes belied by US military behaviour. The US has been willing to launch large numbers of extremely expensive SM-2 interceptor missiles to knock out Houthi drones in the Red Sea. One US naval officer told me that this profligacy had undercut his faith in the "saving it for China" argument. In the event of a conflict with Chinese warships, he said, "I expect to have enough missiles to last a week... I'm going to be firing them off like BBs [air gun pellets]. And here we are using them on drones."

While the US military is vastly more powerful than that of its closest allies, that doesn't mean that it can operate without the support of alliances and partnerships altogether. As former Supreme Allied Commander Europe (SACEUR) Gen. Tod Wolters points out, all US plans for defence and security in the Indian Ocean and Pacific assume at least some degree of support from European allies; but the US needs to consider carefully how strong that support will be if the US withdraws its own support from Europe.[8] Overall, it seems the looming China threat, as well as distracting the US from Europe, is one more reason for the US to cooperate with Europe in reducing the threat from Russia while there is still a window of opportunity to do so.

The US and its Possible Futures

Nevertheless, countries closer to Russia know that a major threat to their security derives from a change of regime in Washington as well as consistency in the Kremlin.[9] In 2024, the potential for Donald Trump to be re-elected as President of the United States was justifiably seen as potentially disastrous for Europe's defence against Russia. However, as we will see below, some of the most alarming trends in the US approach to defence cooperation with Europe will persist regardless of who is president.

In the US political system, military forces cannot be deployed without presidential approval, regardless of the country's treaty obligations. And there is serious concern, based on close observation of Trump, as to whether that approval would be given even in a case of clear aggression by Russia, let alone the kind of ambiguous situation Moscow would be more likely to try to create.[10] That much is clear both from Trump's own statements and the assessments of those who know him well. Trump's former Secretary of Defense, Mark Esper, believes that Trump "doesn't understand the importance of the alliance and how it's critical to our security as well, and wanted to pull troops out of Europe... One of the first things he'll do is cut off assistance to Ukraine...and then begin trying to withdraw troops and ultimately withdraw from NATO."[11]

In late 2023, US elected representatives passed a bill designed to prevent any US president from leaving NATO, in another attempt to limit the damage Trump can do if elected. But the wave of self-satisfaction that accompanied the bill obscured the underlying and bizarre reality: that the United States was taking measures to protect itself from the demolition of its cornerstone overseas alliance not by a foreign power, but by its own elected leader.[12] In addition, the measure won't prevent all the other means by which Trump, or any other president, could neutralise America's NATO commitment.[13] We'll look in more detail in Chapters 5 and 6 at how national leaders can simply decline to take part in NATO actions without formally withdrawing from the alliance. And even before the moment of crisis, the US could critically damage NATO's function and credibility by means such as recalling US troops and commanders from Europe, or blocking important decisions in NATO's network of headquarters.[14]

Trust in democracy depends on faith in its integrity. And that means that Russia can undermine that trust simply through the suggestion of successful interference in democratic processes, whether or not it actually happened. The British government's refusal to investigate whether Russia played a role in deciding the vote in the Brexit referendum in 2016, for example, leaves the possibility open to doubt and speculation, which in itself achieves that erosion of trust and confidence. But the same principle applies to hard security too. The strength of the NATO security guarantee depends on faith that it will be respected, and that countries will honour their commitments when the time comes. The calling into question of that response, including through not only the deliberate statements of former president Trump but the accidental actions of his successor Joe Biden, is also doing Russia's work for them by undermining the confidence that keeps Europe secure.

In fact, the entirety of NATO's power to deter rests on an immensely fragile foundation: confidence that when called upon, its members will honour their moral, not legal, obligation to come to each other's aid. But neither European leaders nor their armed forces and populations can have confidence that a Trump-led United States would honour its alliance commitments when needed.[15] Without that foundation of deterrence, and the conviction that NATO's most powerful member will act if an ally comes under attack, the Kremlin can be vastly more optimistic in its ability to challenge other European countries. And Trump has already promised to destroy that confidence by repeatedly calling into question whether he would assist NATO allies. In February 2024 Trump claimed that he had suggested to a foreign leader that he would encourage Russia to do "whatever the hell they want" to member countries he viewed as not spending enough on their own defence.[16] In 2020 Trump told European Commission President Ursula von der Leyen that the US would "never" defend Europe if it came under attack, that the US would leave NATO, and furthermore that Germany owed the US $400 billion for its defence.[17]

The equation is a simple one: the less Russia, or any other country, fears a US response to an attack, the greater the chances that they will carry one out.[18] Even if – as was the case in February

2022 – that turns out to be a catastrophic miscalculation by the Kremlin, it will matter little to the country that finds itself facing devastation as a result.

Europe, meanwhile, has also been looking for insurance against a renewed Trump presidency. During his first term, one approach adopted to limit the damage was to play to his weaknesses by using flattery as a political tool. Poland offered to host a "Fort Trump" to keep plans for a greater US presence there on track, and NATO officials up to and including Secretary General Jens Stoltenberg learned to present spending increases by NATO members to Trump framed as evidence of his own success in putting pressure on them. It is impossible to tell how much effect measures like this might have on a more determined Trump during a second term. And today, the perversity of the situation is illustrated by the way NATO too is taking steps to protect itself from decisions made by the elected leader of its biggest member. There have been moves for NATO to take over coordination of arms supply to Ukraine in order to pre-empt a US pull-out,[19] as well as long-term funding plans that similarly aren't dependent on the US.[20]

During Trump's first term in office, several of his most damaging ideas were never fully acted on, either because they were intercepted and blocked by more responsible figures around him – the so-called "adults in the room" – or because his chaotic approach to governance meant he lacked the patience and focus to push them through. Trump would bypass process and consultation to issue instructions on a whim, as when in the dying days of his presidency he arbitrarily ordered a massive US military withdrawal from a number of countries worldwide by means of an aide copying the format of an executive order.[21]

But in his 2024 campaign, Trump explained clearly how he would neutralise obstacles to his policies if re-elected. That includes a purge of government officials so he can surround himself with loyal administrators who do not challenge him. The result would be an administration with none of the brakes on Russia-friendly policy put in place by officials who actually understood Russia. Armed with experience and a better understanding of the federal bureaucracy, Trump would be far better able to overcome democratic checks and balances.[22] He would have an even freer hand than in his first term thanks to a judiciary that is compliant rather than independent. Trump-appointed judges have dismissed his criminal prosecutions on dubious grounds,[23] and a Supreme Court decision in July 2024 assured Trump in advance of immunity for crimes he might be planning to commit while in office, as long as they can be designated "official actions".[24]

If Trump, like Putin, surrounds himself with people rewarded with senior government positions on the basis of loyalty rather than competence, that raises the alarming prospect of not just a president, but an entire administration whose priorities are entirely out of kilter with US interests. And there are indications that contenders are already angling for those positions in a possible next Trump cabinet.

The distinctive social media output of former Deputy Assistant Secretary of Defense Elbridge Colby mingles sycophantic references to "President Trump" when endorsing Trump's disinformation with incessant arguments against defending Europe from Russia.[25] They are usually presented as a reflection of the need for the US to focus on confronting China instead, advocating the defunding of Ukraine in order to redirect resources to the defence of Taiwan, despite the fact that Taiwanese officials and civil activists argue the opposite – that successful defence of Ukraine is essential to deterring China.[26]

Colby pursues his campaign with almost comical dedication, with his Twitter account showing multiple strident appeals per day – in the process, consistently echoing and reinforcing

Russian narratives, including boosting its campaign of nuclear intimidation[27] and calling for the US to "withhold forces" in the event of a conflict between Russia and NATO.[28] If Trump wins the election and Colby succeeds in rejoining the circle of trusted associates, following through on any of the policies he proposes daily on social media would be potentially catastrophic for both global and US security.[29] The enthusiasm with which Colby's pronouncements are greeted by Russian state mouthpieces ought in itself to be sufficient evidence that they represent poor choices for the United States.[30] But it seems likely those policies would align with Trump's own instincts, given his proven sympathy for those foreign powers that seek to harm the US and the West as a whole. Trump has already threatened not to defend Taiwan against China.[31] And his former national security adviser John Bolton accused him of asking for Chinese President Xi Jinping's help to win re-election, encouraging Xi to build mass detention camps for China's Uighur minority, and promising to halt criminal investigations to give "personal favors to dictators he liked".[32] (Notably Bolton only did so when he had a book to sell, and has been widely criticised for saving the most important disclosures about Trump's term in office not for official investigations, but to boost sales.) In July 2024, Trump selected J.D. Vance as his running mate and therefore potential vice president. Vance too has been a consistent advocate for cutting aid to Ukraine and forcing Kyiv to submit to Russia's terms.[33] The nomination was welcomed by Russia's foreign minister and greeted with jubilation by the country's propagandists.[34] Once again, if a decision made in the country Russia describes as its "main enemy" causes such delight, it's a good indicator that it's bad news for that country itself.

The damage to US institutions could be long-lasting. Trump would be expected to reinstate discredited loyalists like former military intelligence chief Michael Flynn, who pleaded guilty to lying to the FBI about his interaction with the Russian ambassador. Military chiefs who resist Trump risk being replaced with more compliant generals. The chilling effect is already being felt well beyond defence and even government: even film distribution companies are reluctant to handle Trump-critical productions because they are "worried about Trump sending the Justice Department or Commerce Department after them and weaponizing the government against them".[35] And yet, viewed from outside the United States, the possible return of Trump seems to be accepted with a strange equanimity, indicating almost that Europe is more worried about the outcome of the US election than the US political establishment is.

Trump's conviction for falsifying business records in May 2024 left much of the rest of the world reacting with mild surprise to the realisation that the few criteria that determine who can stand for president of the United States do not include a stipulation that they should not be a convicted fraudster.[36] Regardless, Trump continued to be presented as a normal presidential candidate, rather than a repeatedly bankrupted pathological liar whom courts have found to be a fraud and a rapist and who incited an insurrection against his own country. Responsible US media – previously guardians of sanity in an increasingly polarised media landscape – treated the contest as one between two legitimate candidates with marginal differences of viewpoint, as opposed to a choice between a Democrat and a cult with a leader dedicated to joining autocrats around the world in setting fire to the system that has underpinned US security and prosperity. That instinct towards equivalence between the two led media to normalise many of Trump's most deluded or dangerous statements and overlook his age to focus on that of his original opponent Joe Biden.[37] When Trump encouraged Russia to attack NATO countries in February 2024, there was no mention of it on the next day's *New York Times* or *Washington*

Post front pages. Instead, the top stories were once again about Biden's age. And the potentially catastrophic prospect of the US abandoning Ukraine and Europe is framed as "taking a friendlier view of the Kremlin's security concerns".[38]

In part that equivalence seems to be driven by collective amnesia regarding what happened during Trump's first term. That has prompted foreign officials seeking Trump's support to treat him like a normal politician who wants to support US interests, as opposed to looking for the incentives that actually matter to Trump.[39] The months-long Trump-inspired hold on aid to Ukraine in 2023-4 was treated as an extraordinary event, with apparently no recollection that Trump had consistently blocked aid to Ukraine while previously in office, for personal political reasons.[40] The amnesia contributes to historical interpretations of Trump's actions that are unrecognisable from the outside. Marshal Billingslea, who served as an Assistant Secretary of State under Trump, explains that the reason Russia did not mount a full-scale invasion of Ukraine during the Trump presidency was because Trump's unpredictability was a deliberate strategy to confound Moscow.[41]

Another aspect of the collective amnesia gripping US media and, apparently, voters, relates to Trump's consistent working towards Russia's preferred outcomes, to the detriment of the security of the US and its allies.

It is often claimed by Trump supporters that he is "tough on Russia". In *Russia's War on Everybody* I examined the examples of "tough" behaviour they cite to back up this idea. In each case I found that they referred to decisions taken before Trump's arrival in power but implemented during his tenure, or initiatives taken by branches of the US government that he criticised or actively opposed once he discovered them. By contrast, the list of Trump's actions that favour Russia is long.[42]

Trump worked hard to undermine the US role in securing Europe. Actions like building a border wall, or mounting a disinformation campaign against Joe Biden's son Hunter, seemed diverse and discrete but all had one thing in common: they all served to block defensive measures against Russia. Funding for the wall came from sources including diverting funds earmarked for bolstering the defence of eastern Europe. And Trump successfully blocked defensive aid to Ukraine by linking it to a demand to cooperate in the campaign against Hunter Biden, based on disinformation that originated with an agent of Russian intelligence.[43] More direct assistance to Russia included passing classified information straight to its representatives – an action which in many other countries would alone have been sufficient to disqualify someone from ever standing for office again. And Trump's withdrawal of US forces from northeast Syria was a direct gift to Russia and a betrayal of US-allied Kurdish forces who were forced to switch sides and align with Moscow.[44] Russia's aspiration to see the US weakened and humbled benefited indirectly from other Trump decisions too, like the February 2020 agreement with the Taliban for US forces to unconditionally withdraw from Afghanistan – which set the scene for the chaotic and humiliating scramble to evacuate Kabul eighteen months later, causing immense damage to US prestige and credibility and great satisfaction to Moscow. And other initiatives undermining US security launched by Trump or his supporters also didn't end with his presidency. The year 2023 saw the steady rolling back of many of the institutional protections the US had put in place against foreign malign influence and disinformation, after its damaging potential became clear during the 2016 presidential election and beyond. Given how much Trump has benefited from Russian disinformation campaigns, dismantling the US's defences against Russian information warfare is a perfectly logical step even if he is not doing so under direction from Moscow.[45]

In fact, during Trump's presidency, the only reason greater damage was not done was the resilience of checks and balances within the US system of government. Officials at all levels of government continued to work on behalf of US national interests even when this was difficult or impossible to reconcile with instructions coming from the White House. This process was clearly visible from the outside while it was happening; so much so that the dedication for *Moscow Rules*, my book on Russia completed in mid-2018, was "to all those career US government officials who are working hard to build and deliver a sensible policy on Russia while hoping that President Trump doesn't notice". In some cases, this succeeded: Trump's strategically and logistically nonsensical order to reduce the US military presence in Germany was slow-rolled and then quietly dropped as soon as he was out of office.

It's still not possible to say with certainty whether Trump favours Russian policy objectives so consistently because he is consciously doing Moscow's bidding, or because his own instincts naturally coincide with those of the Kremlin, and Moscow – as in so many other cases – has been adroit at exploiting his personality defects. It is well established, for instance, that he is beholden to Russia as a result of decades of financial entanglement that long preceded any direct political support.[46] But the range of possible explanations doesn't alter the end result; if Trump were indeed consciously working for Putin, it's difficult to envision how he would do anything differently from what he already does now. That's why Russia's interest in assisting Trump's election in 2016 was so evident.[47] Today, Trump would have a clear interest in suppressing knowledge of any Russian influence on his election victory in 2016, and that may be why highly classified intelligence material on the subject has been "missing" since the end of his administration.[48]

Voters who are inclined to believe Trump's promises may care little for the security of people beyond the borders of the United States – or feel, quite reasonably, that it should be provided as far as possible by their own governments. But the impact of US withdrawal from the world would not take long to be felt at home. The effect of even close allies making arrangements for their security that do not rely on Washington would not be limited to the US losing the global diplomatic, political and intelligence support that it can currently rely on.[49] In many ways the return of Trump would rapidly accelerate the slow-motion self-immolation of American power and influence around the world.

If Trump once re-elected follows through on his anti-NATO instincts, the first casualty could well be Ukraine. Hungarian Prime Minister Viktor Orbán was confident after private discussions with Trump in March 2024 that he would end all US aid to Kyiv.[50] But that would also have a secondary impact: if the US scaled back its commitment to defend Europe, that would mean a further shift in European countries' assessments of their own vulnerability. They could become increasingly reluctant to send Ukraine their own vital military supplies – and that could accelerate defeat, with all the consequences we saw in Chapter 2. For instance with German Chancellor Olaf Scholz repeatedly justifying his hesitancy by pointing at Washington, the effect of US disengagement on Germany could be unpredictable. Pressure to step up and fill the gap could be countered by even stronger arguments from Berlin for appeasement, claiming that even the combined strength of Europe is insufficient to face down Russian ambitions without the United States, and thus a settlement must be reached with Moscow.

And the damage would not be limited to Europe. The US's other security alliances will face a crisis of trust. Countries like Japan, South Korea, the Philippines and especially Taiwan will inevitably wonder how reliable their own partnership with the US is, and at a time when their adversaries have been emboldened by the permissive environment signalled by Washington's retreat. In extreme cases, some nations might find the least worst option is to find new ways of working with Russia and China in an attempt at self-preservation. In the Middle East, lack of confidence in the commitment of US forces and coalition leadership could replicate the trend already seen in Africa where they are being replaced by a Russian presence. Even America's partners and allies will remember the assault he mounted on the US intelligence community during his first presidency, and his habit of disclosing intelligence and sources to adversaries. Source protection and simple prudence would suggest they may reconsider sharing intelligence with the US to the extent they do today, in order simply to prevent it being copied to Moscow.[51] In short, if Trump makes good on his promises, it will start a major contraction of America's global power and leadership.

There would inevitably be an economic impact too, as trade agreements and financial arrangements evolved to match a new security environment. This in turn would impact American companies and eventually the US economy and individual Americans at home. Isolationists may also underestimate the effects of instability elsewhere in the world on the US economy. The Houthi movement began with local aims in Yemen, but by 2024 was disrupting global trade by means of attacking shipping in the Red Sea. In some parts of the world, regional conflicts will erupt faster and their impact will be even greater without the current stabilising influence of the US presence.

As we will see in Chapter 5, the US is the only NATO ally that explicitly holds nuclear weapons to protect its allies as well as itself. That includes placing a number of aircraft-delivered nuclear weapons in Europe, in order to clearly link European security with US nuclear capability. In the event of a reduction in US commitment to Europe, these would inevitably be a prime target for withdrawal. That in turn would remove one of the deterring factors for Russia to consider before stepping up its campaign of nuclear blackmail, with the nuclear deterrent forces of the UK and France capable only of a full-scale "strategic" response to what Russia might choose to do to reinforce its demands.

No Good Options

All of this means that friends and allies of the United States will breathe a sigh of relief if Donald Trump is not elected president in November 2024. But that will in no way mean that the problem has gone away, just as Trump and his followers who reject justice and state institutions will not have gone away. With or without the presidency – or with or without acceptance of defeat – Trump-driven domestic political change in the US will impact the country's relationship with the world. An America that becomes increasingly divided will find it harder to maintain its vital international role, and understand that role's direct links to the US's own security and prosperity.[52]

The fundamental problem is that Trump doesn't have to be in power to wield a baleful influence on American politics, with tragic results for anybody relying on the US for support.[53] His capacity to interdict US state policy while out of office was dramatically illustrated by the block placed on aid for Ukraine for the better part of a year in 2023–24, by House Speaker Mike Johnson and Trump-friendly elements of the US legislature who prioritised domestic political point-scoring over the future of the global system that underpins US prosperity. That block led directly to Ukraine needlessly losing lives and territory, with the outcome of the battle for Avdiivka widely attributed to munitions shortages resulting from Johnson's imperviousness to increasingly emotional appeals to do the right thing.[54]

Core funding assistance allocated for Ukraine had run out by January 2024. Consequently the US came empty-handed to the next Ramstein meeting coordinating the sourcing and delivery of assistance and began calling on other nations to cover the deficits in urgently needed supplies like artillery shells and air defence systems.[55] As a result, Ukraine's lack of air defence resources facilitated Russia's devastating campaign against Kharkiv and infrastructure across the country beginning in March 2024. Opponents of the aid packages claimed that the funds were to be sent to Ukraine – and that Ukraine was a "corrupt regime" – while knowing full well that the bulk of the spending would remain in the US, purchasing new weapons and equipment and safeguarding American jobs.[56] That key point has been repeatedly overlooked, not only in US Government communications to its own population, but also by foreigners like David Cameron who appealed for the unblocking of funding for Ukraine on the grounds of its importance to Europe and "global security", rather than explaining why it mattered to America and Americans.[57]

The conclusion, unfortunately, has to be that even if Trump does not win the presidency, he will still undermine the next administration's foreign policy and limit what the US can do. And there is no doubt of the support he will have in doing so: polls show Republicans rating Donald Trump as a more reliable source of information on the Ukraine-Russia conflict than media sources and even the US military or the Pentagon.[58]

At the outset of both World Wars, Washington, with strong popular support, sought to remain uninvolved in the conflicts. Now, as then, strong isolationist voices in the US argue that wars far away are of no concern at home. Others bicker over which challenge needs to be faced, as if there is a choice – with Russia and China now taking the place of 1930s Germany and Japan. But neither previous effort at isolationism succeeded in the long term, and in fact only worked against US goals by assisting in failure to deter the aggressors in those wars. That's one of the reasons why after the Second World War the US cemented its leadership by stepping into key roles in international institutions like the UN, NATO, and their financial and economic underpinnings, like the World Bank and the International Monetary Fund. And since then, every subsequent US administration has recognised the value of those roles to the United States itself – with the exception of Trump, who in his first term pulled the US out of UNESCO, the World Health Organisation (WHO) and the UN Human Rights Council (UNHRC), as well as suspending US contributions to funding other UN activities. Trump also threatened to withdraw from the WTO, but had not managed to do so by the time he left office.[59]

But even the Biden administration, for all its vocal support for Europe, placed strict limits on what it is willing to do to defend it against Russia. A possible order from Trump for US forces not to move when needed is considered a worst case scenario. But under Biden, America's military commanders in Europe have already experienced stop orders from Washington preventing them from responding to the situation they saw unfolding. In February 2022, US European Command (EUCOM) began preparations for precautionary movements to respond to any deterioration of the situation beyond Ukraine that would follow on from the full-scale invasion. To do so, they would use all of the careful planning and hard work that had gone into ensuring military mobility across Europe in the previous decade (see Chapter 5). But commanders found they were prevented from putting their plans into action by something entirely different: a hold placed by the administration in Washington because of fears of "escalation". EUCOM's deterrence mission was compromised by a political intervention from its own chain of command that could not have been anticipated in any of its planning.

Throughout the war, the US has assisted Ukraine with weapons and materiel to allow it to hold back the invaders. Those supplies have been vital to Ukraine's continued survival. But that's been accompanied by extreme reluctance to provide Kyiv with specific capabilities that would be capable of carrying the fight to Russia. A pattern of initial denial followed by long delay and eventual release has followed a familiar and depressing routine for a succession of high-profile capabilities, including HIMARS artillery systems in June 2022, Patriot air defence complexes in December 2022, ground combat vehicles in January 2023, cluster munitions in July 2023, longer-range Army Tactical Missile System (ATACMS) ground-launched missiles in March 2024, and more.[60] US officials point out that technical aspects like logistics, training, support, infrastructure and delivery all impose real delays on provision of new capabilities to Ukraine.[61] And they are right — but that ignores the fact that the biggest delay has consistently been the political hold before that process even starts. The paradox is that while the US has been by far the greatest provider of military support to Ukraine by volume (throughout 2022 and early 2023 the US was the biggest single donor country),[62] it also receives the most criticism for not giving Ukraine what it needs precisely because it has the most to give.[63] The net result has been the US leading a coalition of the only grudgingly willing among Ukraine's supporters, with Germany repeatedly pointing to America in an effort to justify its own reluctance to supply arms.

Ukraine was further frustrated by limitations on how it could use the US weapons systems it finally received, and being prevented from using them to strike back at Russia. Although US policy was widely interpreted as a ban only on Ukraine using US-supplied weapons against Russian territory, consistent statements from American officials made it clear that Washington was opposed to strikes against Russia overall.[64] American attempts to dissuade Ukraine from its campaign of targeting Russian oil refineries in 2024 – part of a strategy to erode Russia's overall capacity to wage war – were widely condemned as further evidence that the US wished to place more restrictions on Ukraine than it did on Russia, which meanwhile continued its attacks on Ukrainian residential areas and life-supporting facilities like power plants.[65] The US policy amounted to protecting the sites from which Russia launches its long-range attacks on Ukraine, while also providing safe zones for Russia to gather its forces for an offensive, and from which it could pound Ukrainian defensive lines with no fear of retaliation.[66] As such, it was indefensible from a legal as well as moral and practical standpoint; there is no dispute that under international law, Ukraine had every right to defend itself by striking back at the source of the aggression – while Russia continued to engage in actions that contravene all legal and humanitarian norms while being protected from the consequences on its own territory.[67]

The prohibition on Ukraine striking into Russia was widely blamed for the ease with which Russian forces prepared their offensive towards Kharkiv in May 2024.[68] Not only was Ukraine unable to attack Russian military logistics or the buildup of forces to disrupt preparations, but they were also unable to construct defensive fortifications of the kind seen elsewhere along the front line because of Russia's artillery dominance firing from safe areas on Russian territory.[69] It was after this clear and cruel exposure of the implications of the US ban that international pressure mounted to the extent that it finally prompted a change in US policy.[70] Dissent with the US position from other coalition members became increasingly public and vocal, led – unsurprisingly – by the leaders of the Nordic and Baltic states, consistently pointing out Ukraine's rights under international law.[71] Endorsements of this position followed from France,[72] the UK,[73] and NATO Secretary General Jens Stoltenberg.[74]

Just as with weapons deliveries, public perception of US action is that it comes only when it's nearly too late to avoid disaster, and well past the time at which the decision would have had the maximum positive impact. The process has also been criticised for an apparent lack of urgency: the relaxation on US prohibitions in May 2024 took fifteen days to work its way through the administration from approval by Biden to delivery of the formal decision, at a time when lives and territory were being lost daily.[75] It should be possible to calculate another grim tariff: the number of needless Ukrainian deaths it took on each occasion to nudge the Biden White House into each incremental step along the path from protecting Russia to allowing Ukraine to defend itself. Easing restrictions on what Ukraine can do with US-supplied weapons in mid-2024 – even if two years late – was the only way to show the Kremlin and the world that the US believed in protecting Ukrainian civilians more than it believed in protecting Russian military assets.

The effect of easing restrictions on cross-border strikes was immediate and dramatic, and is credited with neutralising Russia's Kharkiv offensive. And yet, the easement was only partial, and still strictly bounded with conditions and limitations: Ukraine could strike at Russian forces preparing to attack, but not at the aircraft delivering deadly glide bombs to pound its defensive lines and front-line towns and villages.

At the time of writing, Russia appears confident the US-granted safe zones will remain reliable, as evidenced by construction of new airfields close to the border with Ukraine – in a zone that is well within range of Western-supplied weapons, but protected by the United States.[76] The US has repeatedly and explicitly justified these restrictions by a desire to avoid escalation. But consistently signalling weakness in this way simply confirms for Moscow that Russia itself can escalate without consequences. The limited and hesitant US response to the Kharkiv offensive in May 2024 gave Russia confidence to increase its terror attacks on Ukraine in early July, including missile strikes on a children's hospital.[77] Widespread outrage at that attack provided the US with yet another opportunity to relax its restrictions in order to shape future Russian behaviour by showing that atrocities incur adverse consequences; instead, the White House confirmed yet again that its policy of protecting Russia would not change.[78] But that policy provides another reason for partners and allies to be circumspect about the prospect of US support in a crisis. Other users of American weaponry must also now be seriously considering whether Washington might seek to place limitations on their use if they are needed for defence against Russia.

The Biden administration may have assessed that by depriving Ukraine of systems that could strike at long range, and then protecting Russia from them once they were provided, it could reduce the impact of the war by limiting its scope to Ukraine itself. If so, this was a miscalculation that instead raised the costs of the war by lengthening it, while also contributing to a palpable loss of US influence and authority. But US policy can also be interpreted as representing a cold hard calculus of return on investment in global security. While keeping Ukraine in the fight, Washington is also faced with the need to balance between challenges, with American military commanders responsible for protecting the security of two different continents competing between themselves for resources and attention. That raises the question of at what point US military support to Ukraine has achieved its primary goal of protecting US interests. In that respect, a temporary abatement of the Russian military threat through helping Ukraine gut Russia's army could be assessed as sufficient, without pouring in more resources to help deal Russia the salutary defeat that would actually change policy in Moscow and across the country. If that was indeed the calculation, its outcome is that the US has assisted in a temporary solution to a permanent problem, and meanwhile Russia is free to continue to pummel Ukrainian cities, murder its civilians, and exercise its reign of terror in the occupied territories.

And supporters of Ukraine have repeatedly been confronted with galling evidence that the US's priorities lie elsewhere.

Following the Hamas attack on Israel in October 2023, the US flooded weapons and equipment into Israel to help it conduct its punitive war on Gaza, while still denying Ukraine permission to protect itself against an aggressor by striking into Russia.[79] These weapons included thousands of heavy bombs, similar to those adapted by Russia into glide bombs and used to bombard Ukrainian cities with a tragic toll in civilian lives.[80]

In January 2024, the US and UK responded to attacks on shipping in the Red Sea by conducting airstrikes in Yemen. President Biden said that he would "not hesitate to direct further measures to protect our people and the free flow of international commerce as necessary".[81] Protection of shipping expanded into US-led multinational naval operations, demonstrating strong international commitment to keeping trade routes open.[82] That was in shocking contrast to the hands-off approach that the same countries had taken to Russia's months-long stranglehold on the Ukrainian economy in the form of a naval blockade in the Black Sea, eventually only lifted through Ukraine's own efforts.

Then in April 2024, Iranian drone attacks on Israel led once again to concerted action by the US and its allies. Coalition aircraft shot down a number of drones well outside Israeli airspace, aiding the defence of Israel in a way that had been repeatedly ruled out for Ukraine. And in addition the drone attacks led to almost immediate new US sanctions on Iran – after the same types of Iranian drones had been used against Ukraine for months with no response from the US.[83] The unavoidable conclusion was that the US had no objection to Iran building drones as long as they only deliver death and destruction in Ukraine.[84] Furthermore

Israel demonstrates that a country does not need to be a member of NATO to enjoy protection by a coalition of NATO states – again, of the kind that has been denied to Ukraine. The logic appears to be that for the White House, only Russia has the right to conduct aggression without consequences.

Don't Upset the Russians

The one aspect of US policy that has been utterly consistent is resisting decisive action against Russia for as long as possible. That consistency has led to serious consideration by responsible national security experts of whether or not former President Biden did in fact wish Ukraine to win the war.[85]

The Biden administration consistently communicated its aspiration to support Ukraine. Sadly, it also consistently and clearly communicated that it feared direct confrontation with Russia. This signalling took the place of any real efforts at deterring Moscow. For over two years, Biden claimed to "have Ukraine's back" at the same time as emphasising "flat assurances" from Ukraine that US-supplied weapons systems would not be used against Russia itself.[86] Half measures like these, combined with the lack of a clear commitment to Ukrainian victory and reliance instead on phrases like supporting Ukraine "as long as it takes", made Ukrainian victory less likely and thus dragged out the war, favouring Russia.[87] Ruling out NATO membership for Ukraine, supposedly on the grounds that a country cannot join NATO while it is at war, provided an incentive for Russia to ensure the conflict did not end. If this is a precedent indicating the extent of US willingness to defend other countries in Europe against Russia, it is a highly alarming one.

Withdrawal of the United States from the defence of Europe was a primary goal for Soviet "active measures" campaigns, as it is now for Russian ones.[88] Direct influence by the Russian intelligence services on individual members of the Republican Party would be fully in accordance with published Russian plans for subverting US politics as part of "practical steps to weaken Russia's opponents".[89] And US support for Ukraine has, naturally enough, been a key target for Russian disinformation and covert influence operations.[90] There has been recognition within the Republican Party itself that Russia had successfully "infected" party members, with the result that Russian messaging was delivered directly to the floor of the House of Representatives.[91] Notably, in efforts to stall the delayed bill on aid for Ukraine during April 2024, Representative Marjorie Taylor Greene tabled a series of nonsensical amendments some of which quoted long-disproven Russian disinformation.[92] Her amendment referring to Hungarians in Transcarpathia sparked particular scepticism, amid doubts that she would be able to spell Transcarpathia without external assistance, let alone find it on a map.[93] But as well as Republican politicians, counterproductive decisions by the Biden administration also fuelled speculation about how they are being steered, and by whom. There was alarm at the apparent influence on the White House of external foreign policy analysts who favour buying Russia off at Ukraine's expense.[94] And the US media sees a steady stream of reporting based on anonymous sources suggesting that Ukraine's situation in the war is hopeless and Russia's military victory inevitable, which leads to influential commentators redoubling their efforts to argue Ukraine should be abandoned.[95] Biden also appeared to be held back by concern that a decisive defeat of Russia would precipitate political change in Russia and resultant chaos, and it would be preferable to preserve the current Russia than an alternative that might be even more dangerous and unpredictable.[96] That narrative too has been a consistent theme in Russia's attempts to influence Western policy.

Incomprehension at Washington's sometimes inexplicable hesitancy has fuelled persistent suggestions that the US is reluctant to enable a convincing Ukrainian victory because of a tacit or explicit agreement with Moscow.[97] Specifically, according to veteran national security reporter William Arkin, the US committed to not getting involved directly in exchange for a promise that Russia would limit its attacks to Ukraine.[98] It is true that such an agreement would explain at a stroke many US actions that are otherwise completely baffling – even President Volodymyr Zelenskyy has noted that Putin's behaviour suggests he had had conversations before invading Ukraine assuring him that he would not suffer the consequences.[99] But that suggestion has been received with extreme scepticism elsewhere. When considering the possibility, former US Ambassador to NATO Douglas Lute told me "we're not that bad, and we're not that good" – meaning the United States is neither sufficiently evil to consider selling Ukraine out in this manner in the first place, nor sufficiently competent to keep it a secret if they did.[100] And when I asked an intelligence insider whether otherwise incomprehensible US actions were the result of a back door deal with Moscow, they replied succinctly "not this time".

Public perception of Biden as old and ineffectual posed a serious threat to his election chances. Yet presented with an opportunity to show strength and determination by taking decisive action in support of Ukraine, Biden repeatedly declined to act. There's no doubt that supporters of Ukraine – and of Europe – were better off dealing with Biden's hesitation than Trump's obstruction. But neither is an effective means of mitigating the threat from Russia. In fact there's an absurd contrast between high-profile US declarations of support for Ukraine and condemnation of Ukrainian successes, such as its attacks on Russian oil refineries. Even Biden's vague "as long as it takes" formulation morphed by the end of 2023 into "as long as we can" in the face of political hostage-taking in Congress.[101] The net effect is inimical for Ukraine and consequently potentially disastrous for Europe, but the internal logic of the Biden administration may have perceived it as a success that "escalation" was avoided because Ukraine did not enjoy sufficient success to pose a genuine challenge to Russia.

The closest the Biden administration came to advancing a clear and coherent explanation for its hesitancy in enabling a defeat of Russia was repeated references to a fear of Russian "escalation". In fact, as British long-term Russia-watcher Edward Lucas observes, the West led by the United States has repeatedly signalled that it is "more scared of Russia escalating than it is of Russia winning". That's because one result of Russia's decade-long programme of nuclear intimidation to lay the groundwork for its war on the West has been to make "Russian escalation" almost synonymous with the release of nuclear weapons.[102] The result is that with or without Trump, the highest levels of decision-making in the US have suffered from a pathological reluctance to confront Russia and present it with consequences for its actions. That constrains US options fatally, and has led to the US becoming more fixated on avoiding further escalation than on addressing the escalation that has already taken place.[103]

President Zelenskyy has been explicit about the effect. "Every 'don't escalate' to us, sounded like 'you will prevail' to Putin," he told the World Economic Forum in Davos in January 2024. "Nothing has harmed our coalition more than this concept."[104] But still, the US persisted in urging restraint even after clear and consistent demonstrations over more than two years that Russia accepts it is at war, and escalates at a time of its choosing, encouraged rather than deterred by US restraint. Furthermore, when faced with decisive action by Ukraine or its backers, Russia accepts the consequences accordingly without resorting to reprisals that amount to potential state suicide. Joe Biden's State of the Union Address in March 2024 stated clearly that Putin would not stop at Ukraine, and that "if the United States walks away now, it will put Ukraine at risk. Europe at risk. The free world at risk, emboldening others who wish to do us harm" – but the accompanying message that "there are no American soldiers at war in Ukraine. And I am determined to keep it that way" will once again have reassured Russia's planners.[105] Disturbingly, the US Intelligence Community's annual threat assessment released that month played down the likelihood of Putin having ambitions beyond Ukraine, but played up his nuclear threats and suggested they have to be taken seriously.

The way the fear of escalation seems to have been divorced from assessment of its likelihood matches reluctance to seize Russia's frozen assets to pay for the damage done by the war, partly over concern that Moscow might retaliate by seizing Western assets in Russia – ignoring the fact that Russia has already expropriated billions in Western bank holdings and corporate assets since the war began.[106] (Russia's decision to "nationalise" Boeing and Airbus aircraft that were leased to Russian airlines in February 2022 alone accounts for several billion dollars' worth of foreign property already stolen by the Kremlin.)

When questioning the extreme US caution over possible Russian nuclear use, colleagues and I are occasionally told that it is easy for us to criticise because it is not us that would bear the weight of responsibility for the devastating consequences of getting it wrong. That is a fair comment. But then we consider what our Russia-watching colleagues from the front-line states think on the issue – those with the most at stake because they will be directly in the firing line if they get it wrong. In a reversal of the usual pattern whereby the loudest voices are those with the least to lose, the Baltic states and Ukraine are by contrast the most exposed to the consequences of nuclear miscalculation. Yet it is they who have most consistently and forcefully argued the need to disregard Moscow's threats and take a firm line on deterrence.

For all the evident disagreements between a timid White House, a recalcitrant Senate, America's China hawks, and a Europe-facing component of the US's government establishment and military which remain fully focused on enabling Ukraine to evict the Russian invasion force, what matters is the actions, rather than the words of the United States.[107] Those actions point to only one conclusion: the assessment at the highest level of the US political establishment has been that enabling Ukraine to defeat Russia is not in the broader strategic interest of the United States.[108] Without a coherent strategy that included a clearly articulated vision for victory, the US and its allies that follow Washington's lead were left reacting to events, and in particular holding back from steps that would facilitate rapid and convincing Russian defeat. And that, in turn, meant the war became one of attrition, with all the advantages that gives Russia.[109]

Besides the grim, long-term consequences of that decision for the US itself, that assessment has undermined the faith in American commitment to Europe that was previously rock solid.[110] European leaders can no longer count on a United States that, differences and disagreements notwithstanding, is by default on their side. Trump's promise to transform both America's relationships with the rest of the world and the country itself raise a long-term prospect that for many has seemed unthinkable: that the world's liberal democracies would find themselves competing with three major autocratic powers, Russia, China and the United States. But with or without Trump, if the US is not willing to confront Russia over what it has done to Ukraine, how sure can Ukraine's western neighbours be that when it is their turn, Washington will honour its commitments – whoever occupies the White House at the time? As we saw in the previous chapter, once the US has encouraged Ukraine to resist and pledged its support, and then failed to deliver on its pledge, this sends a message around the world that American promises should be treated with caution. And that message will be heard most clearly in other countries that feel vulnerable to their powerful neighbours – such as the US's traditional partners in Asia including Taiwan, the Philippines, South Korea and Japan. What is worse, the US will have been seen to be reluctant to defend a core principle of world order: that borders cannot be changed by force. And that's the message that will be heard by dictators and aggressors worldwide.[111]

If Trump were to return to power, the end of US military assistance to Ukraine would be likely to be swift and definitive. The end of US military support to Europe would involve a far more traumatic, complex and expensive disentanglement for Washington, but also cannot be ruled out. But in any case, NATO and EU members that take defence seriously should by now have been seriously considering not only how to preserve Ukraine, but also how they would cope with an attack by Russia without US support in responding to it.[112] It is in the context of that new reality that European states must look to their own defences to deter Russia and, if necessary, repel it. Some countries are urgently doing so, but far from all. The remaining chapters of this book consider what is being done, where, and how fast – but more importantly, what that means for the future of Europe beyond Ukraine, and the people living in it. We start with the United Kingdom.

4

A FADING ROLE FOR A FADING BRITAIN

"We are not on the cusp of war with Russia."
Chief of the Defence Staff Admiral Sir Tony Radakin,
27 February 2024

"Too many of my colleagues in government are in denial about the scale of the threat... it's too hard to deal with."
Senior UK defence official,
September 2023

There's widespread acknowledgment that the UK played an indispensable role in early support to Ukraine, helping it withstand the initial Russian onslaught. The UK flew thousands of NLAW and Javelin anti-armour missiles to Kyiv in January and February 2022, and helped deliver urgent assistance from other countries like Estonia, at a time when much of the rest of the world was expecting Ukraine to shortly cease to exist.[1] That pattern continued after the full-scale invasion, with the UK setting the pace for other nations by shaming them into action – delivering high-profile weapons systems that the United

States and Germany were too timid to provide to Ukraine, and demonstrating that doing so would not trigger the Russian "escalation" that they so feared. A steady supply of less glamorous materiel has underpinned the major announcements. Late 2023 saw Ukraine using British-supplied Martlet missiles to intercept mass strikes by Russian drones. The multi-purpose lightweight missiles, originally developed for naval use, were delivered covertly early in the conflict along with StarStreak air defence missiles and launchers.[2] And equipment as prosaic as boots and running shoes, cold weather clothing and first aid kits has been supplied in vast numbers to Ukrainian servicemen cycling through UK-based basic training programmes. The UK also took the lead in establishing the network of "security guarantees" for Kyiv, trying to establish long-term commitments to Ukraine's security in order to disabuse Russia of the idea that the West would eventually lose interest in supporting it.[3]

But the determination to support Kyiv was in the face of the UK's own institutional challenges. When former defence minister Ben Wallace began insisting that Britain should supply Ukraine with defensive weaponry early in 2021, he reportedly met resistance not only from a hesitant Foreign Office but also from paralysing bureaucracy within his own Ministry of Defence (MOD).[4] Three years later, the impenetrability of MOD bureaucratic processes was still reportedly hampering efforts by smaller British firms to assist Ukraine.[5] Early support for Ukraine had strong cross-party backing in the UK, but also benefited from a fluke of political timing. Wallace's prime minister, Boris Johnson, could make potentially controversial decisions to do the right thing in support of Ukraine with little public attention at the time because of "Partygate" – a nonsensical scandal over whether he had broken isolation rules during lockdowns for the Covid pandemic – distracting the UK media and political establishment with the unintended consequence that he and the rest of the government could get things done while the media spotlight shone elsewhere. The situation combined elements of the existential and the ridiculous, seasoned with the kind of luck that may not be available in future. UK domestic attention was focused on what Boris Johnson had or had not done with a birthday cake: future prime ministers, who will have to take far more unpopular decisions, will not have the same luxury.

But after the first two years of the war, the UK's role as a leader and pacesetter in support of Ukraine became harder to maintain given its failure to energise its own defence and industry. The moral authority accrued by London started to erode, once it became clear that Britain's stocks of weapons systems and munitions were now exhausted and no significant effort to replenish them had been made. The relationship with Ukraine was still strong, and Volodymyr Zelenskyy, whose skill at delivering the messages international audiences like to hear has been a key asset in maintaining support throughout the war, could still massage British egos in early 2024 by highlighting the UK's role.[6] And, consistently throughout the conflict, the UK has said the right thing and called for Ukraine to be enabled to defeat Russia rather than merely survive.[7] But there were hints, of varying degrees of subtlety, that the UK was by now failing in its duty to its allies and itself, as when an open letter from three Baltic ambassadors to London noted that "NATO needs strong leadership, and we need the United Kingdom to be strong in this as well."[8]

Paying for Defence, or Not

A consistent British approach of only recognising as much threat from abroad as the government of the day would like to think it can afford is both a cause and an effect of a transformation in spending priorities. Between 1956 and 2023, defence spending fell from 7.6 per cent to 2.2 per cent – counted generously – of GDP. This was almost directly mirrored by a rise in healthcare spending, from 2.8 per cent to 8.4 per cent of GDP.[9] That doesn't mean a like for like replacement in funding, but it indicates how national defence has been supplanted in the country's political consciousness by the National Health Service (NHS) as a priority, to the extent that the NHS now consumes an ever-increasing proportion of British taxpayers' money amid constant complaints that it is underfunded. Politicians question the trend at their peril. Other political sacred cows like welfare and immigration similarly detract from the country's ability to invest properly in defence. Already a decade ago, the UK was spending more on social welfare benefits in London alone than on the nation's entire defence budget.[10] And recognition of immigration as a vote-deciding issue led the Conservative government in power until 2024 to token gestures like penalising people who wish to bring their spouses to the UK legally, or visiting students who bring benefit and revenue there, rather than the illegal immigrants arriving in vastly greater numbers at much higher cost than those targeted, but whom no British government is brave enough to tackle.

This is partly because while Britain may have published strategic documents available for perusal by those interested, it has not clearly articulated to voters a strategy for how to deal with the looming challenges of an unstable world, Russia among them. Even more so, there is no fostering of public awareness of just what role a military might have to play in meeting them – for instance why a capable navy might be important to an island that cannot feed or sustain itself without constant and reliable seaborne imports. That has led to a pervasive attitude among wide sectors of society – and the politicians that represent them – that the Armed Forces are an optional extra, to be paid for if there is enough left over from healthcare and welfare costs, rather than a critical insurance policy without which those social provisions could become entirely irrelevant.

That has led to a mismatch between the urgency of the challenge voiced by some parts of government, and the speed and responsiveness of others. In January 2024, then Defence Secretary Grant Shapps said that Britain was now in a "pre-war" phase, and should prepare for conflict in the next five years.[11] But over subsequent months there was striking unanimity among both current officials and former ministers that the UK was not only not prepared for conflict, but not even properly preparing for it.[12] Nor did it help that the urgency of the challenge appeared lost on Conservative prime minister Rishi Sunak, who earned a reputation for not just failing to understand the need for defence but manifesting a lack of interest in it and the people who defend the country altogether.[13] That was highlighted by his controversial decision in June 2024 to leave other national leaders commemorating the 80th anniversary of D-Day in Normandy to return to the UK for a non-urgent commitment – after originally considering not attending at all. But the impact of his disinterest was far greater than public contempt. Over the course of his prime ministership, it led to a distinctive situation in the UK where there was widespread recognition that there was a serious problem with defence – in Parliament, in the Armed Forces, in the MOD and some other parts of government – but at the very top level, Sunak and Jeremy Hunt, his minister responsible for public spending, were not willing to do anything about it.[14] The result was that the UK defence budget continued to be cut and the British Army to shrink while the UK urged its European allies to do the opposite.[15]

With the arrival of a new Labour government in mid-2024, John Healey, the new Defence Secretary, got off to a strong start, dispelling any doubt over British support for Ukraine by heading there almost immediately after his appointment and announcing additional military aid from the UK's shrinking reserves.[16] He also voiced strong support for defence investment and backing for the UK's Armed Forces. But while Healey may well point to those forces having been "hollowed out and underfunded for fourteen years" in an attempt to pin the trouble on the former Conservative government, the problems run much deeper than that.[17] Just days after his appointment, Healey headed to the Washington NATO summit alongside Prime Minister Keir Starmer. He may well have faced tough questions there over the gap between the UK's promises to NATO and its capacity to make good on them, since when NATO allocates the forces required for its ambitious new plans to defend Europe from Russia, it needs to know they will actually be available.[18] And the new government was unable to put a date on when it might be willing to increase defence spending to meet Healey's promises.

In the UK, there is a range of "Select Committees" made up of cross-party groups of parliamentarians, each of which is tasked with monitoring a specific area of government activity. In theory, these provide democratic oversight of government decisions; in practice, much of their time is taken up with investigating after the fact how government decisions went so badly wrong. On occasion, there is unanimity across different committees that things are seriously awry. The House of Commons Defence Committee is customarily fretful over the British government's neglect or mismanagement of defence matters, and has repeatedly warned that the UK's Armed Forces are simply not prepared for high-intensity war of the kind Russia threatens.[19] In 2024, they were joined by the Public Accounts Committee in savaging government plans. The Ministry of Defence had "no credible plan" to deliver promised military capabilities, a committee report warned, and meanwhile Britain's military strength was deteriorating, forcing greater reliance on its allies.[20]

For all the flaws in the analogy, it's useful once again to compare Britain's current situation with the run-up to the Second World War. Between 1933 and 1938 the UK's defence budget grew from 2.2% to 6.9% of GDP. That means that that 1933 starting point – widely recognised as historically low and inadequate – was already higher than where the UK started from in this decade. And now, the UK is spending only a fraction of what was thought necessary in the last "pre-war" era.

Only a few years later the UK was in the grip of war and spending closer to 50% of its GDP on national survival. The question, then, is whether or not the British government genuinely believes there is a threat of war. If it does, and its warnings are sincere, then it appears to have accepted that the risk of adjusting government spending to allocate more to defence is greater than the risk of catastrophic defeat and irreversible damage for generations to come. Critics of that approach suggest, quite reasonably it would seem, that when faced with the threat of attack by a determined enemy, it makes more sense to start with a calculation of what is needed for national survival rather than of what can be afforded according to peacetime fiscal rules – even at the cost of borrowing more, or eating into the currently sacrosanct budgets for welfare and healthcare.[21]

If John Healey wants to show he is serious about tackling the problems with Britain's defence, he could start by injecting a little honesty into MOD communications, whose consistent feature in the last stages of the previous government had been their detachment from reality. The UK's formal budget announcement in March 2024 claimed an increase in defence spending. But this claim was swiftly exposed as deceptive, as all independent analyses found that unlike all its major partners, the UK had in fact cut its defence budget despite being in what its own Minister of Defence had recently called a pre-war world.[22] The exposure of accountancy sleight of hand to pretend a cut in defence spending was actually an increase led to a concession by the MOD that the real defence budget "appears to show a dip, but cannot tell the full story".[23]

A succession of MPs from the ruling Conservative party joined with the opposition to berate the government for its failure to take defence seriously and fund it accordingly. Former ministers from the MOD and Foreign, Commonwealth and Development Office (FCDO) lined up to call for urgent reconsideration of the government's line at the time that defence spending would increase to 2.5% of GDP "when economic conditions allow", rather than in response to the clear and growing threat.[24] In a highly unusual revolt, two serving government ministers publicly joined the chorus of alarm.[25] Shortly afterwards, long-serving Armed Forces Minister James Heappey retired from politics altogether.[26] And then, once he had no political capital to risk, he was able to write publicly, and let rip about the government's systemic and long-term unwillingness properly to safeguard the UK's defence and security.[27]

That unanimous condemnation of government policy even from within the ruling party may have contributed to the announcement of a defence spending increase, not as part of the UK's formal scheduled spending round but during a visit to Poland by then Prime Minister Sunak. Sunak promised investment of billions in regenerating Britain's defence industries, replenishing stockpiles of weapons, and making good deficits in procurement.[28] Sunak claimed a total of new defence spending of £75 billion. This, he said, was "fully funded, without any increase in borrowing or debt", although since little evidence was provided of how this fiscal magic was to be worked, this led to suspicion that the plan was to make the grand announcement but leave the problem of how to pay for it to the next government.[29]

Once again, analysis of the spending plans from outside government immediately highlighted problems with the defence pledge's headline claims. Much of the promised funding was expected to be swallowed up by existing funding gaps rather than providing additional resources. And as well as the lack of explanation of where the money was to come from, the "£75 billion" claim was swiftly discovered to be fraudulent – or at least only justifiable if you tortured government spending figures well beyond the bounds of common sense.[30] By just the next day, government ministers had quietly abandoned the claim of a £75 billion increase.[31]

In fact it now seems almost routine for MOD announcements on spending, procurement or readiness to be swiftly shown to be deceitful. Seasoned defence commentator Julian Lindley-French observes that every recent "increase" in the UK's defence budget has seen the British Army reduce in size, so there is a danger that if the British Government "raises" the defence budget any higher the British Army could cease to exist altogether. And a senior military officer, commenting on the need to treat British government announcements on defence with extreme scepticism because of their general failure to tell the truth, told me: "it's appalling that we are now equating statements from Downing Street and MOD Main Building with those from the Kremlin and North Korea".

The comparison sounds ridiculous, but it can't be denied there are points in common. Colleagues of mine studying the Russian defence budget have noted a process of increased secrecy and obfuscation making it harder to arrive at reliable figures, while in the UK, a parliamentary inquiry in mid-2023 found that "the Ministry of Defence has become demonstrably less transparent over the past decade", and furthermore that British Government responses to requests for information were "unacceptably slow and... impeded our work". In fact, MPs found, the MOD's reluctance to communicate even with the statutory body that is supposed to ensure its democratic oversight meant that "debate about UK armed forces readiness currently relies on media reporting and corridor conversations".[32]

The lack of transparency and communication goes hand in hand with the UK's pattern of deceptive defence announcements. The result is a widespread cynicism about defence communications. Even commentators who were at one time staunch supporters of MOD policy under almost all circumstances have by now registered their disillusion with the Ministry's attempts at deceiving the public and its elected representatives.[33]

The practice of fiddling with the figures until they produce the desired result – a practice described by some unsympathetic policy analysts as "mathsturbation" – extends well beyond budget announcements presenting defence cuts as increases. In May 2024 the MOD claimed it was entering a "golden age of shipbuilding" based on a headline figure of "up to 28 warships and submarines in the pipeline", which turned out on closer inspection to amount to a hope to build six additional new support vessels for the Royal Marines, whose design process had not yet begun and for which no funding had yet been committed. And buried in the press release was the detail that these six ships – if ever built – would replace seven specialist vessels currently in service, not to mention the two frigates whose retirement was quietly slipped in to the last paragraph.[34]

In the same month, Defence Minister Grant Shapps – or whoever used to write his posts on Twitter – claimed that the RAF had "greater lift capacity today than at any point since WW2". That claim too was immediately and widely debunked as complete nonsense, not least because just in the previous year the UK MOD had retired its entire fleet of C-130 Hercules transports, a move broadly condemned as short-sighted at the time.[35]

Other encouraging figures regularly produced by MOD and government figures seem to bear even less relation to reality. The UK consistently claims that "the Royal Navy contributes 25% of

NATO's maritime strength"[36] – a figure that no outside observer can get anywhere near, no matter how many different ways of measuring "maritime strength" they try. Hoping that there was some innocent explanation for this apparently wildly optimistic figure, I asked the MOD at the beginning of April 2024 what it was based on. By the time this book went to press, I hadn't heard back. With the same hope, I asked a senior Royal Navy officer if they could explain it. They pondered the question at length, considering whether it was measuring strength by numbers of platforms, numbers of personnel, or even number of days on operations or exercise, before concluding: "As it stands it doesn't make any sense at all... I don't know where Grant Shapps is getting this nonsense from but it's bollocks."

Former Defence Minister Ben Wallace seems to agree. He described figures from the March 2024 budget announcements as "a shallow gimmick that assumes no one understands how defence departments work".[37] And even the claim that the UK has consistently met NATO's minimum spending level of 2 per cent of GDP is a tenuous one: in 2016 the MOD was found to have fudged the numbers in order to claim the threshold was still being met.[38] Sadly, the UK's attempts at sleight of hand over numbers, and pretence that smaller is better, are the defence equivalent of an overweight man sucking in his gut while standing on the scales – it fools nobody except those who want to fool themselves.

Readiness for War

Britain's defence planning has been based for decades on the idea that the UK would only go to war as part of a coalition – of which the primary member would be the United States. If that assumption of the US always being present as the backbone of military effort is no longer valid, it requires a major recalibration of the UK's basic criteria for military effectiveness. Jack Watling, a respected defence analyst at London's RUSI military think-tank, says the UK MOD argument that "gaps in our own capability are acceptable because we're part of an alliance" are like going to a bring-your-own-bottle party empty-handed because you assume everybody else is bringing something, and then finding there is nothing to drink.[39] And if Grant Shapps was correct that the UK's situation is "pre-war", the British Armed Forces have work at hand to undo the legacy of decades of relying on the assumption they would not be fighting a major war, or dealing with the impact of war on British soil.

The UK's "Exercise Agile Stance" is a long-term programme set up by former British Chief of Defence General Sir Nick Carter to "up [the UK Armed Forces'] game in terms of what our readiness looked like and be realistic about it", by exercising British forces' "ability to disperse from their bases in order to maintain survivability in the event of an attack". But the need to do this in order to survive is in itself an admission that the multi-decade process of concentrating military assets at a handful of major bases – largely on cost grounds – was prejudicial to their primary function of being able to fight a war.[40]

There's a similar impact of long-term assumptions in air defence. The UK in effect does not have air defences beyond fighter aircraft at just two airbases, with an April 2024 report finding that "UK GBAD [ground-based air defence] systems are not currently equipped to be able to defeat many kinds of air threat".[41] That's a reflection of the fact that despite Ukraine demonstrating that not just military targets, but cities need to be protected against strikes by extremely long range missiles and – if the enemy is close enough – waves of one-way drones, the risk of air or missile attack on the UK is at present negligible. Nevertheless Russia's long range bombers have routinely practised missile launch runs on their trips around the north of Norway to visit UK-adjacent airspace, and at present the UK is virtually defenceless against this kind of attack.[42] And it's not just the UK that needs protection: "the real air defence question", one military analyst told me, "is whether the [UK] force can protect key sites to deter their being targeted and then deploy sufficient air defences to protect its forces in the field".

That's especially the case because the demands already placed on the UK's forces mean they are stretched to their limit, leaving little or no bandwidth for additional tasks or roles. That applies to people as well as equipment. Stories of the working environment inside the Ministry of Defence "Main Building" or the UK's Permanent Joint Headquarters (PJHQ) paint a consistent picture of people pushed to operate full-time at maximum capacity and beyond. It's hard to imagine, given the existing pressures on personnel in key roles already during peacetime, how it would be possible to find spare capacity within the system and its human resources to actually fight a war on top of the already frenetic baseline of activity.

This grim situation gets grimmer if you factor in the overall decline in numbers of military personnel, especially since 2000. By January 2024, the British Army had shrunk almost 30% from 109,600 to 76,950, the Royal Navy and Royal Marines by almost 25% from 42,800 to 32,590, and the Royal Air Force had reduced by in excess of 40%, from 54,600 to 31,940.[43] The speed of decline is striking, and may even be accelerating: the British Armed Forces as a whole shrank by 4% in 2023 alone.[44] In a regularly-repeated comparison, the British Army is now the smallest it has been since the 1790s. That was an era when Britain's power and global influence relied heavily on sea power. The trouble is that now the UK has neither the large land forces, nor a powerful Navy.

An official review of how UK defence treats its people published in mid-2023 highlighted low morale and broken promises contributing to the haemorrhaging of personnel, and concluded that "it is a miracle that [defence leaders] are delivering the consistently high-quality outputs they are today".[45] But the problems with numbers, arising both from botched outsourcing of recruitment and poor housing conditions eroding quality of life and thus increasing outflow, had been well documented as they accumulated over years of underfunding and prioritising savings over resilience or effectiveness.[46] The Army failed to reach its recruitment target for soldiers every year in the decade to 2024. That's been widely blamed on the Army giving up involvement in public-facing recruiting – itself a damning symptom of overstretch and underfunding – and outsourcing it to a large contract services company, Capita. Since then, reporting of horror stories of incompetence by Capita has been almost routine, in particular the delays of months or years between applying to join the Army and actually being able to join – which led to exceptionally high rates of dropping out of the process out of sheer frustration with it, and the Army losing even highly motivated potential recruits as a result.[47] And yet, in March 2022 Capita's contract was extended.[48]

Outsourcing to private enterprise has been a major contributor both to the calamitous state of recruitment, and to the ongoing scandal over sub-standard and dangerous accommodation provided to service families. The regular failure to house service personnel and their dependents adequately or even safely leads to wry smiles at the constant mantra that people are British defence's "greatest asset", or "most important resource".[49] In early 2024, this mismatch of words and action risked being compounded still further by a disastrous proposed scheme for reducing the amount of housing space available to service personnel.[50] Overall, service members ask, it's hard to understand how after thirty years of the military shrinking rapidly, the UK still cannot properly house the size of the forces it has left.

Meanwhile the pressing need to bring in more people has led not to urgent focus on major disincentives like service housing, but to controversial decisions, among them relaxing security checks for officer candidates. British Army documents describe security clearance vetting as being "the primary barrier to non-UK personnel gaining a commission in the Army", meaning they should be waived in some cases; while critics point out that the checks are there for a reason, and "non-UK personnel" are the ones most in need of background checks before being trusted with sensitive or secret information.[51] This was one of a series of incidents that led to strident external criticism that the Army was demonstrating it had other priorities than being ready to fight a war.[52] In one of his public statements calling for urgent preparations for national defence, Chief of the General Staff Sir Patrick Sanders referred to a "burning imperative to forge an Army capable of fighting alongside our allies and defeating Russia in battle" – in effect a recognition that it wasn't capable of doing so before.[53]

The British Army's infantry is divided into categories which broadly correspond to the kind of transport they use to arrive at and go into battle: "armoured", "mechanised" or "light mechanised", plus "light role" as a euphemism for infantry units that aren't provided with transport at all.[54] Even where the army is provided with mobility, the majority of its fleet of armoured vehicles, including tanks, in service at the time of writing were built between thirty and sixty years ago. Successive procurement disasters led to major gaps in capability, and armoured vehicles like the FV430 series remain in service despite being now not only older than the young soldiers driving them, but even older than the generals commanding the Army. One British Army officer told me the severest capability gap was felt in the "close fight": while air power and MLRS rocket artillery systems could carry out long-range strikes against the enemy, once the fighting moved to closer ranges, he said, his soldiers would be "basically unsupported".

Although the army may eventually get tanks upgraded to Challenger 3 specification, there are to be only 148 of them – and the consistent track record suggests that number will be repeatedly cut before final delivery. (By contrast, as we will see in Chapter 7, Poland is aiming for a fleet of well over 1,000 modern tanks.) And of those 148, current orders suggest that only 60 will be fitted with modern active protective systems (APS) to deal with incoming threats.[55] The planned in-service date for Challenger 3 is 2030 (also the projected date for increased numbers of MLRS systems) – but as the numbers stand at present, even after the full replacement programme the UK will have a total number of tanks that is comparable with a week or two of attrition on a battlefield like those of Ukraine.

For other armoured vehicles, however, 2023 and 2024 saw long-awaited good news for the Army. The UK-German RCH 155 wheeled artillery system is to be ordered, filling the artillery gap, although timescales and numbers remain for the time being unspecified.[56] And Boxer multi-role vehicles are already arriving in service in numbers, at the end of a design and procurement process that started almost thirty years ago.[57] The Ajax family of vehicles has become a case study for long and expensive procurement delays and development challenges, but the first of them are scheduled finally to start to arrive in units in the course of 2024.

Meanwhile, the decision to deliver 14 Challenger 2 tanks and approximately 50 AS-90 self-propelled guns to Ukraine significantly hollowed out UK stocks, which in itself is an indication of how depleted they had become. The British Army isn't the only force to have sacrificed its own capabilities to bolster those of Ukraine: not just equipment, but also training programmes and manpower have been diverted to supporting

Ukrainian resistance. But the proportion of the UK's training and readiness absorbed by support to Ukraine is estimated at 75%, which no doubt has led to careful consideration of just how sustainable the impact can be.[58]

The Royal Air Force too has suffered from a reduction in strength without that being accompanied by a proportional reduction in what politicians demand is done with it. In 2024, the effort to provide support to Israel while under mass drone attack meant taking RAF Typhoons away from NATO's air policing mission in Romania rather than being able to mount a new deployment.[59]

Even exercises and public events highlight the mismatch between aircraft numbers and commitments, with an impact affecting other services too. The fleet of aircraft available for conducting parachute drops has been reduced to a total of 22 A400M transports. With one permanently detached to the Falkland Islands and a number of others unavailable for maintenance at any given moment, that raises questions over the purpose and viability of Britain's airborne forces – since an airborne drop of any size could require the use of the RAF's entire available fleet of parachute-capable aircraft.[60] Those limitations have already made themselves felt in practice runs for reinforcing the front-line states, with British Army paratroopers forced to use US aircraft for an exercise in Estonia because no RAF assets were available.[61] And June 2024 saw very public attention to the problem as the UK's participation in the 80th anniversary of D-Day was curtailed because there were insufficient RAF aircraft for the scale of commemorative parachute drop already planned.[62] Supporters of the RAF pointed out, quite correctly, that operational commitments had to take precedence over this non-vital event, but that didn't address the underlying question: if the RAF does not have the assets to cover events planned years in advance, like D-Day or an exercise in Estonia, what happens when they are called on to do something vital but unexpected, like support the defence of a NATO ally?

But of all three services, the Royal Navy may be the one that is under the most obvious strain to meet its current commitments, let alone step up in the event of major conflict.

On hearing that I was writing this book, a senior naval officer serving in Fleet Headquarters in Portsmouth contacted me out of the blue to ask whether I would be describing what they called "the disastrous state of the Royal Navy". They confirmed the media reporting I had already noted, and went further, calling the situation with readiness "pretty scary". "We are supposed to have a force of Type 45 destroyers," they continued. "Most of them are alongside in Portsmouth with scaffolding on. You only have to do a tour of Portsmouth to see we have practically no ships at sea."

The Royal Navy's most evident challenge is simply an insufficient number of ships and submarines for the tasks they have been set, exacerbated by an insufficient number of personnel to sail them or their Royal Fleet Auxiliary (RFA) support ships.[63] Real-term cuts in pay have led to an unprecedented situation where crews of RFA vessels, essential to Royal Navy operations, have voted to go on strike because of a proposed pay offer that fell well short of inflation.[64]

The shortage of hulls and crews has led to ever-increasing demands on those vessels and people actually in service. Early in 2024 HMS *Vengeance*, a Royal Navy submarine forming part of the UK's "Continuous At Sea Deterrent" (CASD) nuclear missile force, completed a record-long deployment.[65] Although this was presented as an achievement by some cheerleaders for the Navy, the crew going over six months without daylight or fresh air was also taken as an indication of the severe and unsustainable overstretch facing submariners. The reason for this overstretch, according to a Navy insider, is "because there are no other boats or people... The mental effect on these people is astonishing."

For over a decade the UK's flagship project, so to speak, in conventional defence has been its two aircraft carriers, HMS *Queen Elizabeth* and HMS *Prince of Wales*. The immense cost of the carriers project has been criticised for being out of proportion with British defence spending overall, and for diverting funds from other capabilities that are vital but less glamorous. That accusation seems to be supported by the limitations eventually being put on the carriers' use by not only there not being enough aircraft to fly from them (with the Royal Navy's fixed-wing air force long abandoned, aircraft and pilots are borrowed from the RAF and the US Marine Corps), but also there being insufficient support vessels for more than one of them to be engaged in operations at the same time.[66]

In theory, the Royal Navy has six RFA tankers available to support operations. In reality, half of those are in long-term reserve, and considered unlikely to return to service given the manpower challenges facing the RFA as well. The impact of deficiency in support vessels is clear in naval operations today, which leads to an obvious question of how much more severe the problem would be in the event of war. At the start of 2024, HMS *Diamond* was the only Type 45 destroyer actually in use, as the other five ships of its class were in the UK undergoing maintenance.[67] But the lack of Royal Fleet Auxiliary store ships – with the single vessel currently in service also undergoing maintenance – meant that Diamond too was dependent on a US supply ship and was unable to replenish its stocks of munitions during operations in the Red Sea.[68] In fact, for the rest of the decade the Royal Navy will be the only navy in the world that has an aircraft carrier but no seagoing store ship.[69]

Supporting shore-based infrastructure too has been starved of investment, including not just docks and maintenance facilities but accommodation in shore facilities which compete with Army housing for horror stories about their "truly awful" condition.[70] That's just one of the reasons why the Royal Navy and Royal Marines are facing an even bigger drop in recruitment than the Army, with intake down by over 20% in 2023 compared to the previous year.[71] The force already relies on reservists to meet its existing operational commitments, but it's an even greater challenge for manning the new Dreadnought class of submarine, scheduled to take over CASD duties from the ageing Vanguards currently in service. "There's a ticker board in Fleet Headquarters," I'm told – counting down the number of days to Dreadnoughts entering service – "but we will have boats but no crew. We need people through the doors now because the training pipeline is so long. And they're not coming in. So how will we mount CASD?"

Doing a Little of Everything

The constant demands to do too much with too little are a symptom of the mismatch between the UK's ambition and its willingness to pay for it. So too are the continued attempts to maintain "full-spectrum" military capability. In theory that should mean being able to undertake every kind of military operation, on land, in the air, and at sea, independently of allies. In pursuit of that aim, even through the decades of cuts, the UK has never quite given up a significant military capability – unlike other countries that have stepped away from attempting to fund and maintain aircraft carriers, submarines, or even tanks. But the result of trying to do everything as cheaply as possible is shrinkage of each individual capability, producing a kind of Bonsai defence force, attempting everything a world-class military would do but on a smaller scale, and consequently suffering a lack of capacity across the board.

Recognition of the limitations set by the UK's unwillingness to invest in defence has from time to time led to calls for abandoning the pretence at being omni-capable, and specialise on specific capabilities.[72] But the number of recent operations underwritten by US support shows that to some extent this is already happening; once again posing the question of just how much British forces' effectiveness will be compromised if for whatever reason that US support is no longer available.

Like so much else, the deficiencies have been made undeniable by observation of combat in Ukraine. The fighting there should have served as a reminder of two simple, irreducible facts about war. First, that it involves attrition – and a force that is so etiolated by decades of cuts that it has no capacity to absorb losses and continue is not a force that is relevant for conflict. And second, that success in conflict also requires being physically present where needed – and a force that is so reduced that it cannot be where it is required because there is simply too little of it to go around has similarly made itself irrelevant. To take the simplest of examples, technology can assist the process of taking ground, but that is of limited use without manpower to hold it. That's a variation of the stock response to promises that "cyber power" will compensate for reduced troop numbers – that "you can't cyber your way across a river".[73]

Nevertheless at some point during the process of running down the British military, the MOD adopted the philosophy that if a given asset was twice as capable, that meant only half as many would be needed. That's left those assets stretched thin across all the commitments the British government wants them to undertake. When the UK wanted to offer a contribution to US-led strikes in Yemen to protect Red Sea shipping, no suitable naval assets were initially available and the aircraft that did conduct strikes, flying from Cyprus, were from the same unit already tasked with operations over Syria and escorting

British aircraft over the Black Sea to protect them from Russian interference.[74]

The British government's consistent line on defence has been that technology means fewer (expensive) people are needed in the Armed Forces. But sophisticated technologies don't just need operators: they need people to keep them online and serviceable, and repair, replace or upgrade them as required. The result is that in overall terms a high-tech force can require additional personnel, not fewer. For all the transformative effects of use of UAVs in Ukraine, drones don't replace people – they still need men and women to transport, prepare and/or arm, deploy and operate them. The reality is that no matter how clever new technology is, it works with, rather than replaces, mass and the industrial and human capacity to produce it. Meanwhile, the high-tech Royal Navy is decommissioning ships for lack of people to sail and operate them.

And on the flip side, the fighting in Ukraine has shown that small and cheap attack drones can have a severe impact on an enemy force by destroying much more expensive targets as well as personnel. That means that the enemy's drones could pose a radical new challenge for militaries that, like the UK, focus on an inventory of small numbers of very capable pieces of equipment.

In short, without the ability to absorb losses, both of people and equipment, no country can fight for long. And without adequate stockpiles of munitions and other materiel, no defence is credible. Addressing both of those problems is a severe challenge for the UK: so much so that outgoing Chief of the General Staff General Sir Patrick Sanders bucked the trend by even before retirement, not accepting the official line that the British Army needs fewer people.[75]

Among the full spectrum of capabilities, the UK's nuclear weapons are by far the most expensive to retain. The cost of updating Britain's nuclear deterrent has been expanding rapidly, and in early 2024 was projected to account for over one-third of the UK's entire planned equipment budget of £289 billion for the ten years to 2033. (If you exclude the cost of the nuclear capability, the UK is only spending approximately 1.75% of GDP on defence.)[76] Whether or not that represents value for money is a recurring topic of political debate in the UK. In part, that's because of an enduring perception that the deterrent is really just an adjunct to the US's far more powerful nuclear forces, and the UK could afford itself the luxury of sheltering under the American nuclear umbrella. But if that umbrella looks like it may close – or even if the president holding it starts publicly discussing taking it away – the need for an independent nuclear force to deter Russia becomes far clearer.

The principle of "extended deterrence", under which the US serves as the nuclear shield for its allies as well as itself, has been the primary means of deterring nuclear adventurism or blackmail by Russia. But as we saw in Chapter 3, this principle too has been called into question in the context of a potential Trump victory. That's led to intense discussion over whether British and French nuclear weapons could serve as a substitute for those of the United States in protecting Europe.

As ever, deterrence is a function of the capabilities available and perception of the will and resolve to use them. The combined British and French nuclear arsenals are a fraction of the size of Russia's; and a promise to use them on behalf of allies, rather than for direct protection only of the UK and France themselves, would require a substantial shift in what those countries' publics have been told they are for. But with or without that shift, anything that calls into question the US's commitment to counter Russia's nuclear arsenal would only increase the incentives for Russia to use it – first of all, by stepping up its campaign of nuclear intimidation and blackmail to temper European resistance to its plans for further aggression. That means that of all the heated debates over which military capability the UK should retain and which it could abandon, for the first time in decades the one on nuclear weapons is among the least controversial.

Rebuilding the Force

The mechanism by which the UK institutionalised defence cuts as a routine has over time proved inimical to readiness and capability. Each year, the armed services are tasked with identifying "savings"; and over time, the peeling away of funded activities, equipment, infrastructure or personnel have accumulated to form severe deficiencies. Individual services will typically offer up a range of options for meeting prescribed targets for cost reductions. Some of those options may at times have been genuine "efficiency savings", although after decades of cuts the chances of identifying any more of these must be vanishingly small. And the reductions may be due to overall cuts in the defence budget, or to pay for newly identified priorities or unexpected costs due to the latest procurement disaster; but in all cases the impact on readiness is the same.

Individual reductions in capacity, capability, redundancy or resilience are accepted and institutionalised and become the new baseline, but they combine over time into major deficits that prove vastly more expensive to remedy than it would have been to maintain the capability by continuing to fund it. And serving military officers find themselves unwilling or unable to impede the slow process of hollowing out the forces because of the basic problem that standing up for defence and opposing spending cuts has long been incompatible with career advancement.[77]

Now, the UK is belatedly forced to take a hard look at its war-fighting capability as it grapples with the aftermath of decades of these cuts affecting personnel, infrastructure, training and equipment. Defence analysts regularly use the phrase "hollow force" to describe the British military, with the outward appearance of a highly capable and modern defence force hiding the reality of thinned-out stocks of weapons systems, munitions and vehicles, a severe deficit of personnel, and not enough money to train, arm, house and equip even those there are.[78]

According to the commander of the UK's Joint Forces Command in the previous decade, Richard Barrons, when he raised the need to rebuild national defence and resilience because of the growing threat from Moscow the response from government showed that "the implications of thinking about the revitalisation of a risk from Russia were unpalatable and expensive and denial – frankly – was cheaper".[79] One symptom of this approach was an unwillingness to sign long-term contracts for munitions in order to safeguard both a ready supply and the industries that produced them. The one-off orders placed instead, leading to finite stocks and the atrophy of the country's munitions industry, were described as a "gross strategic error" by the Chief of the Defence Staff of the time.[80]

As across Europe, British government announcements have now highlighted the need to revitalise domestic defence industries to support long-term rearmament plans. That has got off to a slow start: the UK's apparent lack of urgency has been criticised by parliamentary overseers, who noted that despite recognition of the vital need to increase production of 155mm artillery shells both for Ukraine and for the UK's own needs, it took nine months of negotiations between the British government issuing a "letter of intent" in November 2022 and a contract finally being signed in July 2023 – only after which could the supplier start even to prepare to ramp up production.[81] That's just one example suggesting that MOD procurement efforts are still operating at a peacetime tempo. In April 2024 it was revealed that more than half of a £900 million fund collected for Ukraine from other countries by the UK, intended for the purchase of urgently needed capabilities like air defence, drones and mine clearance equipment, remained unused because of bureaucratic delays in awarding contracts.[82]

It was only in February 2024 that the UK announced investment of £245 million to "procure and invigorate supply chains" in order to produce artillery ammunition.[83] The need for "invigoration" nods to the fact that defence production takes time to build from a cold start. And supply chains are another significant issue. Reliance on imports is a key vulnerability that affects not only the resilience of society if those imports are interrupted, but also plans for preparations even in peacetime. The UK no longer has some of the basic industries that would underpin a revival of defence production. If the domestic steel industry has been disbanded, for example, producers need to look to the UK's partners and competitors for the raw materials for a wide range of military products.[84] The UK's last factory producing TNT was closed in 2008, accompanied by unheeded warnings that this meant a complete loss of national capability for producing military explosives.[85] It was only in July 2024 that the incoming Labour government announced a plan finally to restart the domestic production of artillery barrels.[86] Meanwhile, however, the constraints of a peacetime mentality are still putting the brakes on ramping up defence capacity – as with planning permission for arms manufacturers being refused because granting it would "cause discrimination, harassment, and victimisation between people of different races or religions".[87]

Today, British defence policy refers to the Army's ability to field a division-sized warfighting unit. In fact the UK has committed to provide NATO with a Strategic Reserve Corps with corps troops and a sovereign division under command, while notionally also retaining an additional global response force to be ready for other contingencies. In the course of research for this book I couldn't identify a single outside assessment of the Army's current capacity that found this remotely plausible, and was told that 70% of the British Army's entire available "enablers" – units providing support functions – were required to sustain a single armoured brigade. Questioning of ministers and senior military officers by the House of Commons Defence Committee in 2023 found that while progress had been made towards improving readiness, a full and combat-ready division was a goal for the next decade.[88] In effect, the recent trend has been for the UK to enlarge its commitment to NATO, while shrinking its capacity to deliver it.

There has, unsurprisingly, been a crescendo of calls for a complete rethink of British defence spending, with a mushrooming of groups of retired senior defence and security chiefs lobbying for change. Each of these groups has stated in turn that the Armed Forces and reserves have fallen below the critical mass they need to be relevant, and must be completely overhauled if they are to "prepare genuinely for war".[89] Retired senior officers have been especially vocal on the current dire state of the British forces, whether or not they were willing to speak up while still in service.[90]

But serious concern at the state of the country's military also comes in independent assessments from the UK's friends and allies. When the respected Swedish Defence Research Agency (FOI) produced a survey of military capability across northern Europe in early 2024, it should have made uncomfortable reading for British defence planners. The report highlighted deficiencies across the board, with "forces [that] are partly hollow, spread thin across theatres, and have little redundancy, with serious questions surrounding the force's sustainability."[91] Major gaps in capability were noted in all the services: the report noted that the Army's main battle tank had not received a significant upgrade in the current century, and sending most of its heavy artillery to Ukraine left a gap until the late 2020s or early 2030s. In the air, numbers of serviceable Typhoon aircraft were declining and there was uncertainty over how many F-35Bs would eventually be purchased due to a failure by the former Conservative government to commit; and meanwhile the UK had no airborne command and control platform, after retiring its five E-3 Sentry aircraft in 2021 but only ordering three E-7A Wedgetails as replacements, which might start to arrive in late 2024. The report also politely challenged the UK's attempts to replace numbers with technology, pointing out that this approach "served somewhat to evade issues of mass and sustainability".

The UK's allies too have responded to the erosion of Britain's military capacity by becoming increasingly vocal in pointing out shortcomings. Even senior officers and defence officials from the United States, previously scrupulously tactful when discussing the capabilities of the relatively small and impoverished British forces, have been more frank in questioning the UK's aspiration to be a top-tier military power. In widely-reported comments in January 2023, an unnamed US general told then Defence Secretary Ben Wallace that the British Army was instead "barely tier two".[92] Retired officers, unsurprisingly, have been even more direct regarding the diminished capacity of the UK to contribute to coalition operations.[93] But early 2024 saw an unprecedented intervention by US Secretary of the Navy Carlos Del Toro, publicly urging the UK to invest more both in the Royal Navy and the British Army.[94]

As well as rebuilding their capacity, the British Armed Forces like others will need to make decisions based on observing Russia's forces and how they operate in Ukraine – and specifically, what does or does not need to change in their own composition and equipment as a result. Russia's full-scale invasion has driven home some lessons previously identified and others that are new: that there are no "safe areas" because the enemy can conduct strikes on targets throughout its adversary's operational depth with long-range precision fires; that dispersed operations are critical to survivability, including for aircraft and infrastructure such as headquarters, logistics and maintenance depots; that slack capacity is essential, not only to cater for attrition and munitions expenditure, but also for the training infrastructure required to expand forces when needed; that electronic warfare, UAV and counter-UAV capabilities need to be integrated across the force; and much more. Adapting any force to deal with all of those challenges makes for a long shopping list and an ambitious task: and very little of it will be feasible without the political will to fund credible defence, or the drive to push through change. But according to retired RAF Air Marshal Edward Stringer, the need for substantial change in the UK's forces has long been recognised, but "systemic inertia suppressed novel thinking – and still does".[95]

The new factor of hostile drones as a constant threat, causing high rates of attrition among personnel, artillery and armoured vehicles, has been widely acknowledged, and its potential impact on British forces considered both within and outside the military.[96] Some NATO armies are investing heavily in applying lessons learned from Ukraine in UAV operations. Estonia hopes to roll out hand-held drone detection systems to every infantry squad, and set up NATO's first specialist unit to operate "loitering munitions", or one-way attack drones.[97] Together with its neighbours and Poland, Lithuania plans to use massed drones to protect their border with Russia.[98] But if any similar initiatives are influencing British tactics or procurement, it's not discernible from public reporting. And in mid-2024, reservists undergoing training with the British Army told me they could not detect any updates to their training, or adaptation of operations and equipment, to survive in a drone-saturated environment of the kind they might encounter if facing Russian opponents.[99]

That's not to say that all future wars, even with Russia, will look like the current situation in Ukraine. That has become a war of artillery, trenches and fortifications like those of 100 years ago (plus drones) because of a combination of circumstances including Russia not expecting to fight a war in the first place, and thus not planning an actual opposed campaign. Future war with Russia could see instead shorter, faster, more mobile offensives which NATO would need to crush rapidly. In short, NATO militaries like those of the UK need to prepare for extended combat and high attrition using up vast stocks of fuel, ammunition, spares and people; but they need to do that as well as, not instead of, their current focus on brief manoeuvre operations. In any case, according to one assessment in 2022, at the height of fighting in Donbas, Russia was using more ammunition in two days than the entire British military had in stock.[100]

Ukraine has demonstrated that being in a war requires reserves not only of munitions, but of people. That fact is widely acknowledged by front-line states facing a direct land threat: in the UK, reservists make up approximately 18% of the whole force, while in Finland, as we will see in Chapter 7, the ratio is reversed and a small professional army is backed by a huge reserve ready for mobilisation.[101] The UK doesn't face a land invasion by Russia in the foreseeable future, but nor does that eliminate the possibility for an urgent need for more manpower. In theory the UK has a "Strategic Reserve", a force of former regular service personnel who have recently left the forces and can be recalled in a crisis or national emergency. In practice, there is no system for keeping track of these people. Another cost-cutting measure whose impact is now becoming clear was withdrawal of a small financial incentive for ex-regulars for keeping in touch and turning up to occasional musters, meaning that there is now little motivation for them to do so, especially if the reason they left the military early was because they were dissatisfied there.

And regardless of whether or not they would be happy to be recalled in an emergency, if they can't be found, it's not going to happen anyway.

The inability to recall reserves is just one symptom of the UK's need to relearn how to build a force ready for war through recruiting, equipping and sustaining sufficient numbers of personnel – alongside the redevelopment of the industrial base that's essential if they are to fight for any length of time. But to do so means its voters and its politicians alike need to step away from treating defence as an optional extra, or a luxury, and abandon the cosy notion that peace and security can be preserved without military power. The idea that freedom comes for free may be a severe challenge to the UK's efforts to renew interest in defence: in early 2024 a poll showed almost a quarter of British adults aged 25–49 saying that they would refuse to defend the country even if it were under imminent threat of invasion.[102]

All of this combined has led the UK's new government to commission a full defence review, led by widely respected external experts, to assess the scope of the problem before deciding how to fix it.[103] That's a sensible way round, even if it does have the inevitable effect of deferring difficult decisions – and the funding to pay for them – for at least another year while the review runs its course and presents its conclusions (whether or not the government then acts on them). There have been major UK defence and strategic reviews before. But it's vital that this new one should start with a realistic appraisal of both European and global threats to the UK, and with it an honest assessment of whether Britain's military power is sufficient to play the role it should in meeting or deterring them – with or without US support. Without that honesty, and clear communication to voters, there is little chance of investment in both conventional and nuclear defence being sufficient for the task. The key point is that if the UK's Armed Forces are not large, strong or capable enough to deter Russia from launching a small war, then Britain will have to fight a large one; hence defence spending now, and the willingness of the public to support it, is insurance against a far more expensive future.

Nevertheless, both for sensible operational reasons and because of a toxic organisational culture, a state of public denial from the upper echelons of the military and from the MOD persists. Initiatives by the incoming government also include attempts to redesign the MOD's organisational chart and procurement systems into something better suited to deliver defence capability.[104] But that may not be enough to bring about cultural change. Truths that are painfully evident to individuals at the operational level cannot be admitted to by their seniors and headquarters, especially when they reach sufficient seniority that their decisions and even their comments start to have political as well as military impact. The effective muzzling of senior officers is highlighted by the sudden transformation in their assessments the moment they leave office – they repeatedly launch stinging attacks on the UK's neglect of its defence as soon as they are safely retired and their pension is assured.

At that point they join the chorus of parliamentarians, policy analysts and the general public calling for fundamental change. But there's little sign as yet that those calls are having an impact on actual policy decisions. Rather than a clear plan for transforming the UK's military into forces ready to fight the kind of war Russia has demonstrated, current spending plans propose fixing the problems by means of incremental increases, rather than the overall reconsideration of defence as a spending priority that is required.[105] A question now asked increasingly often is how bad the UK's situation will get. It may be that unless and until the UK faces a disaster that finally focuses the mind of whoever is in No. 10, little will change. And that means that the UK risks continuing its fine tradition of starting wars catastrophically, at a tragic and needless cost in the lives of good men and women.

For the UK's new Labour government, the first task has been identified; aiding Ukraine to not only survive but destroy Russia's army faster than it can be rebuilt. But the British Armed Forces too need rebuilding; and the new government must show it is up to the challenge. As a result of all of the challenges listed in this chapter, British military power is for the time being seen abroad as continuing to decline, rather than being invigorated to meet the looming challenges. Consequently the UK will have only a marginal impact on deterring Russia from further aggression in Europe. That means that for their own future security, the British people now rely on NATO allies in Europe to do the fighting. How prepared those allies are for the task is the subject of the next chapter.

5

NATO AND EUROPE

HALF-PROMISES AND BROKEN PLEDGES

"We don't have any doubts that Ukraine is not the end of the game... what we are doing now is preparing for Russian invasion."

Senior European diplomat,
London, 25 January 2024

NATO's fundamental purpose as an alliance is summed up in Article 5 of the North Atlantic Treaty (the "NAT" in NATO), the clause that stipulates an attack on one NATO member state is to be considered an attack against all of them.[1] NATO's line, as voiced by British chief of defence Tony Radakin in February 2024, is that Article 5 means "any Russian assault or incursion against NATO would prompt an overwhelming response. The thousands of Allied troops currently stationed in Poland and the Baltic states could draw on the 3.5 million uniformed personnel across the Alliance for reinforcement."[2] The process is routinely presented as automatic. But in reality there are several ways the smooth process described by Radakin could come seriously unstuck.

First, this picture takes no account of just how many of those 3.5 million troops are ready, equipped, and able to move. But in addition, the actual text of Article 5 provides plenty of leeway for any member state that might wish to avoid confronting Russia and therefore decide that it doesn't want to move them at all. The Treaty doesn't contain the clear and direct requirement to support the victim of aggression that is ordinarily assumed; instead, it only stipulates the far more vague obligation for each member state to take whatever action it "deems necessary... to restore and maintain security". And even before deciding on a response, the process of invoking Article 5 at all could potentially be paralysed by the requirement – not codified but universally respected – for consensus. There has always been the risk that in a crisis, a spoiler state could dissent, and torpedo the entire Alliance's commitment to collective defence. That risk would grow substantially in the event of a new Trump presidency.[3]

The implication of all this is that while Russia is extremely unlikely to attack a NATO member state if it were indeed convinced this would trigger retaliation from the rest of the alliance, nevertheless there are circumstances in which Moscow could make a calculated assessment that it could target an individual country while ensuring through other means – political, diplomatic or subversive – that one or more major NATO allies could be effectively deterred from responding. When faced with the requirement to take "such action as it deems necessary", Trump – or any other national leader sympathetic to Russia – could simply declare that he did not deem it necessary for his country to do anything at all.[4]

In short, Putin and Russia understand that they can't defeat NATO militarily; but they may believe they can defeat NATO politically, by effectively making Article 5 redundant.

That means NATO unity is Russia's biggest problem but also its biggest opportunity. If the spirit of Article 5 is tested and fails, NATO's raison d'être immediately disappears and Russia has won. And that is the reason why one of the classic scenarios for how Russia might seek to do that – by moving 30 km into a Baltic state, digging in and threatening to use nuclear weapons if NATO responds – is once again under serious consideration. If NATO allies are persuaded they have a choice between surrender and nuclear war, Russia has achieved its objective.

In both France and the UK, a substantial proportion of increased defence spending is to go not to conventional rearmament but to the country's nuclear deterrent force. That means that they, at least, will be less susceptible to nuclear blackmail in the event of a US retreat from the defence of Europe. But countries like Germany are heavily dependent on the US's "extended nuclear deterrence" as a counter to Russian nuclear blackmail. If that extended deterrence is called into question, or indeed repudiated altogether, by a future US administration, even huge investment in conventional defence could be of only limited value in the face of more realistic Russian nuclear threats than we have seen to date. A single demonstrative nuclear strike on German front-line forces or on critical infrastructure or logistics points on Germany's own territory, carried out by Russia without fear of retribution, could leave any German government with no option but to opt out of the defence of Europe for fear of further attacks. That, in part, has led to the calls discussed in Chapter 4 for an independent nuclear umbrella for Europe that is not reliant on the United States.[5]

Previously focused exclusively on effective deterrence of Moscow, NATO settled into a new role and mindset over the decades of relative peace. Critics say that this reflected a norm of complacency, during a time when the threat and the actions taken to meet it were supposed to be much further away than

Europe's doorstep. Driven by the absence of any sense of urgency, procedure and paperwork seemed at times to be the organisation's primary outputs. NATO insiders time and again described a working culture dominated by the process, rather than the result, and the proliferation of highly-paid sinecures in a self-sustaining bureaucracy. A defining feature of NATO headquarters and institutions was the relaxed working hours, also reflecting a difference in cultures as well as in threat perception across the various countries that make up the alliance. For decades it has been described as perfectly normal that the only people at their desks on a Friday afternoon would be those from North America or northern Europe.

The cumulative effect, insiders say, was to stifle any efforts towards urgency and action; to the extent that in some wargames and simulations, as well as an opposition playing "Red", realism was injected by a third opposition player representing "NATO dysfunction". That may be a joke, but if so, it's a sadly plausible one.

SHAPE, the NATO headquarters organisation focused on military not bureaucratic command, also slowly evolved into a peacetime headquarters. After the end of the Cold War, most NATO countries wanted to demonstrate their good intentions towards Moscow by stepping down military preparations for conflict with Russia. These included identifying and planning for military targets, with the result that until the NATO summit in Vilnius in 2023, SHAPE reportedly had no authority to plan for attacking targets in Russia. In the event of conflict, key areas of planning would have had to start from scratch.[6]

The lack of focus on serious defence has been reflected in NATO's attempts to get its member states to take an interest in investing in it. NATO's Wales summit in 2014 registered a collective pledge that allies would increase defence spending to 2% of GDP – still a historically modest level. The aspiration was to reach this threshold over the course of a decade, which even at the time seemed a highly generous timeframe, bearing little relation to the urgency of the challenge. And yet, ten years later in 2024, far from all NATO's member states had met their commitment.

NATO, naturally enough, prefers to highlight progress made and the increasing number of member states that are making the grade. In the previous chapter we saw how the UK, among other countries, has in the past bent statistics to maintain the pretence of meeting the 2% mark. In 2024, NATO as a whole did the same, using selective accounting to suggest that its non-US members are collectively meeting it, by quietly dropping any mention of Canada.[7]

But that average also obscures the fact that many NATO members have still not met this baseline criterion, including larger allies like Italy and Spain, and Germany and France are just about reaching it.[8] It may be true that across the whole of the alliance, defence spending is now rising rapidly. But a significant proportion of that increase is down to individual nations like Poland forging ahead with urgent rearmament, while leaving less motivated allies behind.[9]

The focus on spending 2% obscures another, potentially far more useful, measure of defence seriousness that was also agreed on in Wales in 2014. While 2% focused on the input side of defence – how much was spent on it – the defence investment pledge at the time also undertook to measure and record the output side – what that spending actually produced in terms of usable defence assets and commitments. Those output measures included specific and meaningful targets to meet for each country, such as not only absolute numbers of warships, aircraft and personnel in hand, but what proportion of them are deployable and sustainable, which is a very different figure. Those output measures, however, remain confidential – with the sole exception of Denmark, who, in 2015, publicly released the metrics that they had submitted to NATO, partly in order to deflect criticism that they had fallen so woefully short of the spending target.

Overall, NATO allies should have left "spending 2% of GDP on defence" behind long ago as a meaningful measure of being ready for what is coming. Today, the measure has become symbolic for all the wrong reasons. Failure to meet this threshold is an indication of a nation's refusal to take seriously its duty to safeguard not only its allies but also its own citizens.

For NATO to function as intended, it is critically dependent on collective resolve. But the discussions in early 2024 over potentially deploying troops from NATO nations to Ukraine in support roles, first publicly mooted by French President Emmanuel Macron, brought into sharp focus the divisions between those countries prepared to take a robust approach to confronting Russia, and those terrified of that confrontation.

Opinions on the possible deployment of Western troops to Ukraine had long been a matter of private difference between the US and its allies. The UK and other countries were routinely sending special forces personnel to Ukraine while the US placed restrictions not just on the military, but even on diplomats travelling there. Washington was so sensitive on the issue that to enter or leave Ukraine, or even to travel beyond the city limits of Kyiv while there, US officials needed clearance not from the ambassador in-country but from the National Security Council (NSC) itself.[10]

But President Macron's suggestion of a coalition of the willing taking over certain tasks within Ukraine, such as training and demining, made the split very public.[11] The reaction from several allies was swift and alarmed.[12] The US once again emphasised that "the United States is not going to send any troops to Ukraine".[13] German Chancellor Olaf Scholz went further and declared, apparently without consulting them, that no European countries would send military contingents.[14] Even Britain showed alarming signs of switching sides to join the axis of timidity, with Foreign Secretary Lord Cameron ruling out a Western troop presence in Ukraine "in order not to give Putin a target" – as though those troops could only be there as Russia's passive victims.[15] The exceptions to the wave of protest were, as usual, Russia's direct neighbours. In exactly the same pattern as with Russian nuclear threats, it is the front-line states that would potentially suffer worst from any miscalculation, but they are the least concerned based on their long experience of Russian state behaviours.[16]

Another sign of that split with the front-line states was the debate over NATO choosing its next Secretary General, which provided another damning indication that the organisation had still not fully come to terms with the need to face down Russia.

There is a general trend of under-representation of central and eastern European states in top leadership positions on the continent. That's marked in the EU and even more so in NATO – where it is even less excusable, given the institution's vital focus on the region for defence.[17] Former Estonian Prime Minister Kaja Kallas, widely hailed as the perfect candidate for the job of Secretary General when it became vacant in 2024, withdrew her candidacy (but was later tipped to be the EU's new foreign policy supremo instead). That followed a rash of commentary from western European dignitaries objecting to her as a potential leader for nonsensical reasons – such as, according to former top Eurocrat Frans Timmermans, coming from "a country that is on the border with Russia".[18] German Chancellor Olaf Scholz reportedly also blocked Ursula von der Leyen, former German defence minister subsequently serving as president of the European Commission, from the post because she too was "too critical towards Moscow" – which argues that Scholz too had completely missed the point of NATO.[19]

Western politicians collectively decided that the next NATO Secretary General could not come from a country that knows Russia and was serious about defending the continent against it, and instead should be Dutch Prime Minister Mark Rutte, a candidate who spent fourteen years as prime minister of a country that had failed utterly to meet its NATO pledge on defence spending. That was despite obvious questions over whether he had the moral authority to call on other NATO leaders to do what he had manifestly failed to do himself, and his hardly being the right candidate to convince an incoming US president, whoever it might be, that the US's NATO allies are serious about taking on a greater share of their own defence.

The question of the balance between what would provoke Russia to escalation, and what would deter it from further aggression, has been a constant one for as long as the renewed threat from Moscow has been recognised in western Europe. It is because of that long-running debate that in 2021 I wrote the study referred to in Chapter 1 on what did, in fact, deter Russia.[20] In it I looked at historical examples from this century and the last one of where the West had been successful in dissuading Russia from aggression, and based on the consistent patterns that I found throughout those examples, I put together a list of do's and don'ts for the next time Russia needed to be faced down. That was published in September 2021; and included several recommendations that were directly relevant to the threat to Ukraine coming to a head over the subsequent few months.

Among the most important was avoiding appeasement and self-deterrence, and above all avoiding communicating it to Moscow – for instance ruling out Western troops deploying to Ukraine, and thereby easing decision-making in Moscow by taking Putin's worst case scenario off the table and reassuring him that Russia can continue to wage a war of destruction against its neighbour without undue concern for the consequences.[21] I identified as a key problem Western leaders "repeatedly announcing what they will *not* do to protect allies instead of what they will... thus sow[ing] the seeds of further aggression and armed conflict in the future". Sadly, the collective West chose to do more or less the exact opposite of what "What Deters Russia" recommended, and the result two and a half years later is me writing the book you are reading now, with Europe in a vastly more dangerous situation than it was then.

All of this meant that after Russia's 2022 invasion concentrated minds on the real threat, NATO had to rapidly change gear. Two years later, the renewed sense of urgency and focus was starting to take effect. NATO and its headquarters and subordinate commands have drawn up new plans for the defence of member states' territory. These "regional plans" are supposed to reflect a transition to defending the alliance's front lines, and stepping away from the previous situation where the most exposed member states might expect to be overrun before help could arrive.[22] They have been tested in NATO exercises, as well as multinational ones and bilateral drills with US forces in the region. Increasingly, exercises have practised harmonising and coordinating multiple different operations, in the way that would be essential in the event of full-scale conflict. In 2023, Exercise Trifecta synchronised and coordinated three major national drills (Poland's Anakonda, Sweden's Aurora and the US Defender) as well as smaller exercises from other states.[23] And NATO's Steadfast Defender exercise in early 2024 was the strongest indication yet of the alliance's new focus on addressing its primary function. The largest exercise of its kind since the Cold War, Steadfast Defender practised moving large numbers of reinforcements to and across Europe over a period of four months, involving operations at sea and in the air as well as on land over an area extending from Norway to Romania.

There's JEF and the EU, too

NATO isn't the only organisation that could bring forces together to respond to a crisis in Europe. The "Joint Expeditionary Force", or JEF, is a UK-led coalition of ten northern European nations: Denmark, Estonia, Finland, Iceland, Latvia, Lithuania, the Netherlands, Norway, Sweden, and the United Kingdom. The JEF was set up as complementary to NATO, but following Finland and Sweden's accession now forms a subset of NATO members. That is claimed to bring benefits in terms of planning, intelligence sharing and smoother transition between authorities.[24] But the JEF's more flexible range of responses, and broader focus than purely military threats, point to a continuing valuable role taking on challenges that may not fall within NATO's remit. In particular, the JEF won't be hostage to NATO's consensus-based decision-making process and could potentially respond far more swiftly and reliably to a crisis.[25] That's an immediate advantage in any situation where there might be doubt over whether NATO could arrive at an Article 5 decision, as described above.[26]

The JEF has its own counterparts to NATO's regional plans in the form of "JEF Response Options" (JROs) that member nations can draw on in response to a developing crisis. But unlike NATO, the plans have already been used. In October 2023 gas and communications cables under the Baltic Sea were severely damaged. Amid suspicion that the damage was deliberate, JEF Defence Ministers agreed the following month to activate a JRO for the first time, coordinating warships, aircraft, reconnaissance assets and specialist teams from all ten JEF nations across a vast area of operations to maintain surveillance of subsea infrastructure in order to detect and deter further interference.[27] The fact that the JEF could do this independently of NATO demonstrated one of its key advantages as a ready-made coalition of the willing that could step up in circumstances where NATO or the EU might not have the political will, or be able to muster the consensus, to do so.[28]

Attempts to present the EU too as a possible alternative alliance for combining defensive potential persist, although with less conviction now than before 2022.[29] There's greater recognition that the seriousness of the threat means this is not a time for European vanity projects, especially those that duplicate (and hence dilute) the vital role of NATO, but without the crucial function of tying North America into security arrangements, including the United States for as long as it is willing.

In particular, discussion of EU accession for Ukraine combined with the reality of the war has forced a realisation that the EU cannot possibly accept a new member that might be militarily overrun. And that in turn has prompted grudging recognition that the EU as an organisation and even as an idea is entirely dependent on the security cover provided by NATO.

The EU's aspiration to have an instrument of military power of its own has never quite gone away, however. The most recent plan is to develop a "Rapid Deployment Capacity" by 2025, with 5,000 troops capable of carrying out stabilisation and evacuation operations. It's possible this could fill a gap left by NATO shifting away from crisis management and out-of-area operations towards home defence on the territory of allies. But concerns persist over the potential double allocation of military capacity to both NATO and the EU, when soldiers – as ever – can only be in one place at a time, and over the proliferation of competing headquarters and chains of command.[30]

Where the EU has a much more significant role to play is in assisting member states in rebuilding their defence industries and trying to ensure they have the capacity to fight and survive a war. Any conflict between Russia and NATO that does not end almost immediately will turn into a competition not between military forces, but between societies, and their respective resilience, industrial capacity, and will to fight and win.[31] It's true that in long wars where vital national interests are recognised to be at stake – unlike the Western involvements in conflicts like Iraq and Afghanistan, for instance – the side with the larger economy tends to win.[32] And there's no doubt that overall, the West's economic power dwarfs that of Russia even without the heft of the United States to back it. But that advantage is undercut by not only a lack of resolve to mobilise those economies to defend themselves, but also the lack of an overall strategy both to help Ukraine and to protect Europe as a whole.[33] In other words, winning a war of attrition requires an industrial strategy within and between European states, and one has been painfully slow to emerge.

The lack of a munitions industry willing and able to make up the deficit when US aid was interrupted was one of the key reasons for the Ukrainian army's acute shortage of artillery shells in early 2024, directly blamed for losses of territory and lives.[34] In March 2023 the EU had approved a 2 billion euro plan to boost ammunition deliveries to Ukraine, planning to send a million 155mm shells within twelve months. That plan fell well short of its goal – not only because of industry bottlenecks and failure to invest properly in boosting production, but also, according to EU foreign policy chief Josep Borrell, because amid Ukraine's artillery famine European producers were still exporting shells under previous contracts to countries that were not at war.[35] That lack of capacity and prioritisation for a time made faraway South Korea a bigger supplier of shells to Ukraine – at the time, indirectly – than all of Europe combined despite the Europeans being Ukraine's neighbours.[36]

As late as March 2024, EU industry commissioner Thierry Breton was only laying out plans to "change the paradigm and move into war economy mode", including encouraging EU countries to buy more weapons together from European companies, and help those companies increase production capacity. But even those plans still needed approval from all the EU's national governments, some of which have historically been protective of their national sovereignty when it comes to military and weapons spending, and the European Parliament.[37]

The new plans by the EU to harmonise and coordinate defence industries have been welcomed by NATO officials, but in some cases warily and with the hope that they complement rather than complicate already long-standing NATO standardisation agreements.[38] That's not the only potential concern. The European Defence Industrial Strategy says that 50% of member states' defence procurement should be within the EU by 2030, and 60% by 2035. If implemented, that could present a major problem for EU member states that are currently buying equipment from the UK, US or Asia – or might wish to in the future, given the lack of European alternatives to high-capability assets like F-35 aircraft or JASSM-ER long-range missiles. And the plan would blow a hole in Poland's long-standing rearmament programme, which is heavily dependent on purchases from the US and South Korea (see Chapter 7).[39]

In any case, none of these plans presents a short-term fix for helping Ukraine or rebuilding national stocks and defence preparedness. If all goes well, senior defence investment expert Camille Grand points out, the European Defence Industrial Strategy (EDIS) and the European Defence Industry Programme (EDIP) might receive funding in 2028.[40]

As well as swift reinforcement of military capabilities in the short term, long-term rebuilding of Europe's defence industries is also vital.[41] But investment in that rebuilding is still being held back by peacetime approaches to budgets, timelines and priorities. Symptoms of the continent's enduring peacetime mentality range from the frustrating to the ludicrous. When Norwegian-Finnish munitions producer Nammo sought to expand its largest factory in anticipation of increased demand, the plans were put on hold because a new data centre for TikTok was using up all the spare power capacity in the area. "It can't be so that we lose the war because we store too many cat videos," its chief executive complained.[42]

France's minister of the armed forces has already suggested the French government might force firms to put defence orders before civilian ones if manufacturing of crucial components for rearmament does not speed up.[43] But the continuing lack of long-term reliable orders with European defence manufacturers reflects the short-term needs of backing Ukraine often still not being accompanied by long-term investment in rearmament for Europe's own national militaries. The push to supply Ukraine with 155mm artillery shells in 2023 and 2024 once again provides a case study. Orders were placed for Ukrainian requirements, but with the exception of artillery-heavy front line states Finland and Poland, most European militaries' artillery forces are so atrophied that they give no reason for manufacturers to think the level of orders will be sustained. The UK's lack of heavy artillery was detailed in Chapter 4: Germany, meanwhile, in December 2022 could field only thirty-six operational Panzerhaubitze 2000 howitzers.[44]

The issues with production of 155mm shells are just a symptom of a much broader problem. National defence industries cannot be activated at no notice. Europe is currently replicating Russia's own experience, where the massive budget increases of the early phase of military regeneration in the 2000s – those not swallowed up by corruption – went on resurrecting entire industries that had been neglected over the previous decades. It was only by the middle of the 2010s, a full decade after the start of increased funding flows, that the result started to feed through in the form of a steady supply of new and modernised weaponry for the Russian armed forces. And besides shells, there is an enormous range of even less glamorous items of military equipment that needs to be produced and stockpiled in readiness for a military confrontation. An expanding army rapidly consumes hundreds of thousands of items of uniform, equipment, footwear and so on – none of which can be conjured out of the air. Ukraine's semi-equipped emergency volunteer battalions at times resembled the UK's "Local Defence Volunteers" in civilian clothing with armbands in 1940, or Finnish solders mobilised in 1939 and provided with a utility belt, a capbadge to attach to their winter headgear to denote them as combatants, and if lucky a rifle – sardonically nicknamed a "model Cajander" equipment set after the prime minister who had refused to fund military resourcing ahead of the Soviet invasion. Even in much better prepared Finland today, reservists have been warned they may need to privately purchase some personal protection equipment. Overall, according to Belgium's former deputy chief of defence Lieutenant General Marc Thys, Europe is so far from having the kind of industrial capacity necessary to sustain credible deterrence that it will take five to seven years to regenerate it. "It's not a joke, we're in deep shit," he added.[45]

Europe and Readiness

As long ago as 2016, a study by the RAND think-tank found that for the UK, France or Germany, even just generating one war-fighting brigade would be "a major endeavour that probably would leave the forces with little spare capacity for any other contingencies", and even then there would be "questions... regarding the capabilities that those forces might have at their disposal or their aptitude for the kind of warfare that fighting the Russians might involve". And all three countries – most of all the UK – have seen further reductions in their force generation capacity over subsequent years.[46]

Availability of forces is one problem; how they may perform in actual combat is another. In March 2024, warships from NATO nations joined the mission in the Red Sea intended to protect civilian shipping from Houthi drone and missile attacks. The deployment provided case studies of testing European military assets under operational conditions, and the results were not encouraging. Although the UK's HMS *Diamond* was widely reported to have performed well (leaving aside questions of the sustainability of intercepting drones with vastly more expensive missiles), other vessels found that using their weapons systems under operational conditions highlighted serious problems.

Belgium despatched one of its only two available frigates to join the mission, the *Louise-Marie*. The thirty-year-old vessel previously owned by the Royal Netherlands Navy took almost two months to prepare for deployment, and even then was anticipated to be present primarily to "show the flag" rather than use its main weapons systems, designed in the 1980s long before today's drones were a threat.[47] Tasked in January 2024, the frigate finally joined the Red Sea mission in mid-May, after training for the deployment while transiting the Mediterranean revealed major defects with the ship's ageing missile systems.[48] The German frigate *Hessen* made it to the Red Sea earlier, where it narrowly avoided downing a US MQ-9 drone – only because guidance malfunctioned for both of the two missiles launched at it.[49]

The Danish frigate HDMS *Iver Huitfeldt*, designed specifically for air defence tasks, also encountered multiple serious and dangerous failings as soon as it was engaged in live firing. The ship's most capable radar system was put out of action in the middle of a hostile engagement by a software conflict with its combat management system – a problem that according to a leaked message from the vessel's captain, had "been known for years without the necessary sense of urgency to resolve the problem". Perhaps even worse, when the 76mm deck gun was fired, about half of the proximity-fused rounds exploded just after leaving the muzzle. The same leaked message noted that "all shells... are more than 30 years old, they have been retrofitted with a '2005 proximity fuze'... which appears to be unsuitable for actual combat".[50]

This may well have been an isolated incident – at least others have not been publicly reported in such detail. But the alarming implication of all three nations' experience is that the military equipment of other NATO allies, when called upon to fight off a Russian attack, might also prove to be "unsuitable for actual combat" – with potentially disastrous results. Russia too has had more than its fair share of embarrassing equipment failures; but it has also had years of war experience to learn how to work around them.

The Netherlands provides a case study of capability gaps on land too. The country has an ambition to recreate a heavy infantry brigade, but is hampered by the fact that it long ago decided the tanks that would be essential to support it were a luxury it could do without. A force of close to 1,000 tanks at one point during the Cold War has shrunk to a purely token capability of just 12, which are leased from Germany and form one of five companies within a joint German-Dutch tank battalion. The limited integration of military units was a face-saver for both countries, but the sudden pressure of scrutiny and needing to show operational relevance has highlighted serious deficiencies in the cooperative arrangement.[51] The Netherlands' own tank force was scrapped entirely in 2011, which means that recreating it a decade and a half later will be costly. The Dutch defence budget, like others, has seen a substantial increase, from about 15 billion euro in 2023 to 21.4 billion in 2024. But that doesn't include the cost of acquiring or running tanks, so for the time being the country's land forces will continue to have to plan to fight without them.[52]

Meanwhile, however, the Netherlands has recognised the crucial role played by long-range precision strike weapons in Ukraine and plans to invest accordingly. In February 2024, the US approved the sale of up to 120 Joint Air-to-Surface Standoff Missile-Extended Range (JASSM-ER) air-launched cruise missiles (ALCMs) to the Netherlands for integration with the Royal Netherlands Air Force (RNLAF)'s 52 F-35 aircraft. JASSM-ERs have been priority purchases for front-line states Finland and Poland too, as we will see in Chapter 7. But the selection process for the RNLAF highlighted once again European dependence on US weapons systems. Alternative French and Anglo-French missiles were considered, but rejected because they were still in development.[53] And for any of these types of weapons to remain effective depends on upgrades ensuring they are resilient against Russia's electronic warfare countermeasures.

Since February 2022 military readiness has been the subject of intense scrutiny across Europe, including finally recognising the absurd situation that the UK had no more than a week's worth of artillery ammunition to keep it in the fight, and the German Bundeswehr just two days.[54] But the defensive readiness of countries as a whole, as opposed to just their armed forces, is now belatedly coming into focus. When Sweden's FOI defence research agency carried out the 2024 survey of twelve European countries' defence capabilities referred to in Chapter 4, it covered more indicators than straightforward military numbers, including economic, social, demographic, political, morale, legitimacy and political factors. It repeatedly highlighted deficiencies and in many cases, the gap between rhetoric and reality.[55]

As we will see in Chapter 6, in many ways the excess capacity and redundancy that is required for genuine resilience militates against economic sense. The same goes for defence readiness: large stocks of everything are needed, ideally in order to make sure they never need to be used. And war leads to both military and civilian casualties – in large numbers – so health services need to have capacity in reserve to cope with them. Some countries have made efforts to alert civil society to the need to be prepared for conflict, and be more explicit and transparent about national security risks and what they mean for individual citizens. In March 2024, Polish President Donald Tusk called on younger generations across Europe to "mentally get used to the arrival of a new era" where war is no longer something from the past, and "literally any scenario is possible".[56] But most European leaders are still not being honest with their populations about the strategic situation in which Europe finds itself.

Some countries will need more than just honesty. Without expansion of their armed forces, a number of European allies will reportedly struggle to provide the troops stipulated by NATO's new operational plans while continuing to meet their own national defence requirements.[57] But there are questions over whether that expansion will find sufficient willing recruits. A regular survey of willingness to fight in defence of your own country conducted around the world shows consistently strong support in Russia's neighbours, but in the most recent survey (conducted between 2017 and 2022) just 36% of Dutch 16- to 29-year-olds said yes.[58] That may have changed since the invasion of Ukraine, and the growing recognition across European societies of the reality and urgency of the threat.[59] But another complicating factor may be the widespread penetration of Russian narratives of innocence throughout not only the societies of NATO nations, but the armed forces that are drawn from them. In February 2024, a full two years after the start of Russia's invasion of Ukraine, I received an email from an intelligence officer whose job is briefing the command of one of the forces that would be on the front line of NATO's efforts to withstand a Russian attack. Alarmingly, they rehashed a standard repertoire of Russian propaganda narratives about how none of this was Moscow's fault – and everything stemmed from the "humiliation" and "punishment" that NATO and the West had supposedly inflicted on Moscow after the end of the Cold War (in fact, the very opposite of what happened in reality, as detailed in my earlier book *Moscow Rules*.) And the email concluded with the question: "Has NATO aggression not caused this Russian foreign policy we are now seeing?"

But even if the forces are available and motivated, they also need to be capable of moving to where they are needed. That means overcoming major obstacles to that movement across Europe even in peacetime, before Russian missile strikes make the challenge still harder by targeting the transport and logistics infrastructure needed for reinforcements to arrive. The "military mobility" strand of the EU's Permanent Structured Cooperation (PESCO) defence cooperation initiative aimed to smooth out some of these problems. Sometimes described as a "military Schengen", the project was supposed to tackle two key problems: paperwork and infrastructure. It aimed both to ease the bureaucratic load by reducing the number of document checks, clearances, and applications with advance notice that were previously required to cross borders, and to address key bottlenecks that would slow movement at points like ports and railheads.

One essential step for ensuring mobility across central Europe was mapping of transport infrastructure. Military movements require far more information than is provided by a standard road map – for instance, road widths and bridge carrying capacities need to be known in order to assess whether heavy equipment can pass, either under their own power or on transporters. For much of NATO's new area of responsibility after it accepted new members in central Europe, this information needed to be reviewed or generated from scratch for allied forces arriving in the region. In one mobility exercise in the late 2010s, practising getting reinforcements to where they needed to be, US Army

Europe discovered the hard way how expensive incorrect mapping can be. A trainload of armoured vehicles was sent through a railway tunnel in central Europe – but wrong information on the height of the tunnel meant several million dollars' worth of equipment was snapped off the top of the vehicles one by one as they entered it.

As with so much else, PESCO's primary mechanism for getting things done, "discussions in expert working groups", did not proceed with the urgency that was appropriate to the challenge. It was only in January 2024 that Germany, the Netherlands and Poland started to plan a "military corridor" for speeding through reinforcements – almost a decade after the urgent need was highlighted by military commanders, including the former commander of the US Army in Europe Lt-Gen Ben Hodges, who campaigned hard for better mobility. And for now, rules and procedures for who can go where still vary from country to country. In some host nations US forces have enjoyed relative freedom of movement: but when this assumption is transferred elsewhere and leads to US forces in, for example, Estonia, turning up unannounced at bases or borders, even under the friendliest of circumstances it leads to misunderstandings, friction and delay.[60]

Germany and France

The way different understandings of how to meet the Russia challenge pull European leaders in different directions comes into clearer focus when considering the EU's two neighbouring heavyweights: Germany and France.

Germany is a world-class economic power, but that status depends entirely on the benign international order that has allowed it to flourish since the Second World War. Nevertheless since the Cold War Germany has felt it has had the luxury of ignoring the costly and inconvenient need for defence.

Many German politicians who previously sought to mollify Putin into a constructive relationship have, like Emmanuel Macron, realised the limitations of this approach.[61] And polls show that many Germans would like in principle to see a more capable German military. But far fewer wish to see their country more involved in international crises. In addition, almost three-quarters oppose a military leadership role for Germany in Europe.[62] Germany's federal minister for foreign affairs, Annalena Baerbock, can put her name to joint letters with her French and Polish counterparts recognising that Russia will not stop at Ukraine and hence European defence has to be sufficient to deter Moscow.[63] But that doesn't always translate into German action.

Nevertheless Germany would play a critical role in the defence of Europe with or without a presence on the front line. The country is of vital importance to EU and NATO logistics simply because of its location. Germany's sea, air, rail, road and river links would all be essential to NATO efforts to move to the scene of a crisis in central or eastern Europe – not to mention the network of major US bases and facilities hosted there. That makes Germany a prime target for Russia in the event of open conflict; and even before it, Berlin is within the range of Russian missiles stationed in its forward bastion of Kaliningrad.

In one respect Germany's role in future conflict would be comparable to the one it played during the Cold War, when it provided host nation support for the vast numbers of troops from NATO allies – including not just the US and UK but contingents from Belgium, the Netherlands and others. Its role was to guarantee freedom of movement for those contingents, and protect their infrastructure as well as its own. But the key difference is that Germany too was contributing to its defence, with a conscript army numbering at times half a million, or 1.4 million with mobilisation of reserves.

Germany's willingness to cooperate in the defence of Europe was put to the test in early 2022, when the urgent shipments of munitions from the UK to Ukraine ahead of Russia's invasion had to be flown on a circuitous route to avoid German airspace. There are conflicting accounts of the reason why; but whether it was because of German fears of upsetting Russia and "escalation", or merely impenetrable bureaucracy, the effect was in practical terms the same: Germany presented an obstacle to urgent action that had to be worked around. In a future crisis where speed of movement is vital, NATO allies will have to hope that Germany will be part of the solution not part of the problem.

In 2022, the incoming chief of the German Army, Alfons Mais, realised that the force he had inherited "has more or less nothing. The options that we can offer politicians to support the alliance are extremely limited."[64] The dramatic announcement of a *Zeitenwende* or a "turning point" in Berlin's attitude to defence in February 2022 was supposed to fix that. But the optimism that accompanied the announcement has long since faded, and the expansive promises of increased defence spending have come up against the reality of the budget hole it had to fill, and the immense cost of making good on decades of underspending.[65] Rearmament, and even the ability to meet NATO's defence spending targets, are further challenged by peacetime rules that impose a "debt brake" limiting government borrowing.[66] The combined effect could have severe impacts on German ambitions to rebuild capable armed forces, with doubt even cast on whether Germany can afford the F-35 aircraft it has ordered if there is no radical change to its constitutional finance rules. Plans are already being revised across the board. The original aim to increase the number of Bundeswehr soldiers from the current 183,000 to 203,000 by 2031 has been declared "unattainable", with the military facing similar long delays in the recruitment process to those experienced by the UK (see Chapter 4).[67]

Decades of cuts have left gaps in personnel, materiel and infrastructure that will cost far more in reconstruction than if they had been maintained. For instance, in the previous decade the German Army eliminated its short-range air defences altogether – a decision that can only be explained by the idea that the military would never actually have to fight a war, and so had no need to be defended against threats from the air.

This is a symptom of what some outside observers think is an essential lack of seriousness in Germany about security against external threats. At the turn of the century, according to former staff members, the German intelligence services did not employ a single Russian speaker. A quarter-century later, when the nature of the threat could not be clearer, the German government was reportedly still "keen to play down" the discovery of a Russian plot to murder one of the country's most prominent arms industry executives.[68] Long after Germany's allies decided to remove hardware and software manufactured by China's Huawei from sensitive communications networks over espionage fears, Germany continued to provide Huawei communications apps to hundreds of thousands of soldiers and other federal employees.[69] And the lack of security consciousness was a direct contributor to an embarrassing scandal in March 2024 when senior German military officers took no precautions to protect confidential discussions on the potential use of Taurus missiles in Ukraine, leading to their being released publicly.[70] As if wishing to confirm that online security is somebody else's concern, the press conference by Defence Minister Boris Pistorius addressing the leak was also hosted online, with an access password of "1234".[71] Lessons were not learned, and two months later a whole series of classified Bundeswehr meetings were also found publicly accessible online, with the military only becoming aware when approached by media for comment.[72]

The long-running saga over requests for Taurus for Ukraine starkly illustrated the constraints on German decision-making. The missiles are comparable with the British Storm Shadow and French SCALP weapons that have proven immensely valuable in Ukraine's struggle to survive, but despite willingness to provide Kyiv with substantial amounts of other equipment like air defence systems, tanks and helicopters,[73] Germany under Chancellor Olaf Scholz doggedly refused to offer Taurus. To justify the decision, Scholz put forward a succession of claims that were swiftly shown to be false – for instance that German servicemembers would have to be deployed to Ukraine to operate them, or that Germany can only take its lead on what to supply from the United States, not from France or the UK, let alone acting on its own initiative. And then, at the height of the controversy, it became known that production of Taurus had stopped altogether because Germany had not placed any orders for it – two years into a major land war nearby.[74]

In one respect Germany does attempt to meet its NATO defence commitments. Germany was the first NATO member to deploy an eFP battle group in the Baltic states, as lead nation in Lithuania, with its contingent starting to arrive at the beginning of 2017. Now, they are also the first to commit to providing a brigade for this mission, planned as a permanent standalone German deployment, not on rotation or as part of a multinational force. But that commitment too has highlighted the deficiencies in German military power, and the enormous expense of putting them right.

The first troops of what should eventually become a brigade arrived in Lithuania in April 2024, but it is not scheduled to be at full strength until 2027.[75] In theory, the brigade there should be backed by a heavy tank division in Germany as fast reinforcements. In practice, the Bundeswehr has had to pull from across the whole force to bring together this brigade alone, and even then one of its tank units despatched to Lithuania has no tanks at all after they were sent to Ukraine. The hope is that they will receive replacement Leopard 2s delivered directly to Lithuania in 2026, if they are manufactured in time.[76] That has added to the expense of the commitment – to the dismay of some politicians, the cost of creating and arming the brigade has been estimated at 11 billion euro,[77] and operating and maintaining its Lithuanian base at 800 million euro a year.[78]

France, meanwhile, joined the club of European countries boosting their defence budgets in April 2023, planning to spend 413 billion euro over the period 2024–2030, a more than one-third increase over the previous funding period.[79] That's a major change from the previous decade and Emmanuel Macron's first term as president, when the Chief of Staff of the French Army resigned in protest at inadequate funding for defence.[80] And by early 2024, France was driving hard to push its allies into a more proactive, less passive approach to Russia, not only providing aid like SCALP and AASM air-launched missiles, Caesar howitzers and a wide range of munitions and equipment, but also as we saw above, being unafraid to mention the possibility of more direct support for Ukraine.

In part that is because of a remarkable change in attitude towards Russia by French President Emmanuel Macron. In the previous decade, Macron used to insist on the notion that "we" were "pushing Russia away from Europe".[81] In 2021, I compared his approach with that of Boris Johnson, saying that while Johnson had already been through the experience of seeking a better relationship with Russia and come away disillusioned and wiser, that experience still lay in the future for Macron – and I hoped that the cost of that experience would not be too high for France or for Europe.[82]

Belatedly, Macron too has completed this journey, and the change has been spectacular. In early February 2022, he had formed part of the diplomatic procession to Moscow trying to cajole Vladimir Putin out of his plans to invade Ukraine, and at a meeting which spawned countless memes he offered Putin "security guarantees" from the far end of an immensely long table. And even after the invasion and the accompanying evidence of Russian atrocities in Bucha and elsewhere, Macron told the European Parliament in May 2022 that the West should not "humiliate" Russia. But by June 2023, Macron was calling for the defeat of Russia for the first time (as opposed to just "preventing a Russian victory"), and apologising to eastern Europe for his and his predecessors' earlier dismissal of their concerns. And finally, in early 2024, Macron was ready to state that "nothing should be ruled out" in order to bring about that defeat, including the possible deployment of Western troops to Ukraine.[83]

The dramatic change of attitude has been explained by Macron being "mugged by reality" and "radicalised by disappointment" – that like so many before him, he had been duped and played by Russia in general and Putin in particular.[84] But the result is that by 2024, Macron is one of the foremost exponents of standing up to Russian threats and – especially – not reassuring Moscow by ruling out any form of escalation from the Western side. Defence and deterrence planners call this "strategic ambiguity", which is a fancy way of saying you're not telling your adversary what you're going to do. That would seem to be a pretty basic idea when it comes to trying to dissuade somebody from attacking you – but as we have already seen, France's repeated reminders that it had options at its disposal that Russia would find distinctly uncomfortable, like positioning French military forces directly in Ukraine, unfortunately made France's allies distinctly uncomfortable too.[85]

But Macron and his ministers have been consistently willing to put pressure on Russia by emphasising that they choose not to be as fearful of escalation as their more hesitant allies. In doing so, Macron has voiced a principle that has long been understood by the front-line states: that manifesting weakness in the face of Russia's intimidation and threats is equivalent to choosing defeat.[86] A repeated French response to Russian attempts at nuclear fear-mongering has been a simple reminder that France has a nuclear arsenal too – a distinct contrast to the fearful approach taken by the United States. And Macron has clearly linked the outcome of the war on Ukraine to its implications for European and French security in an effort to win over his own domestic voters, in a way that many other European leaders have as yet failed to do.

Macron's conversion seems, for the time being, to have suppressed the deep-seated fantasies of a special relationship with Russia that long influenced French policy, underpinned by instinctive anti-Americanism.[87] On arrival in office he was part of a long succession of Russophile French ministers and heads of state, and as late as the start of 2020, Macron was convinced that European security depended on "re-engaging Russia", and despatched envoy Pierre Vimont on a tour of Europe to sell this vision. Sitting with Vimont on a stage in the French Embassy in London, I and colleagues firmly but mostly politely dismantled the French arguments of the time on both moral and practical grounds, leaving Vimont with the final resort that we must keep talking to Russia and hope for the best. Now, Russia has succeeded in removing even that hope in Paris: in April 2024, French Minister of Foreign Affairs Stéphane Séjourné was able finally to admit that "it is not in our interest currently to hold discussions with Russian officials because the statements and the summaries issued about them are lies".[88] That ability to respond to reality, combined with willingness to invest in defence forces and not rule out options for using them, for the time being makes France one of the most useful European contributors to the security of the continent as a whole.

Not all states share France's new determination or recognition of urgency. For some countries, public support for defence spending is held back both by a perception of distance from the problem and the luxury of reliance on larger, more powerful neighbours. That is a problem facing the governments of Canada and Ireland in particular.

Canada has announced major investment in the joint US-Canadian North American Aerospace Defense Command (NORAD), with C$38.6 billion allocated to modernising the capabilities Canada contributes.[89] Together with an order for 88 F-35s announced in January 2023, measures like this mean Canada's defence budget is on track for substantial increases, in addition to the over C$13 billion allocated in funding and military assistance for Ukraine.[90] But the "renewed vision for Canada's defence" declared in April 2024 notably extended plans for rearmament over twenty years, meaning that responsibility for implementing them would pass to other governments, probably as soon as Canada's federal elections in 2025.[91] Furthermore, besides the 2% of GDP pledged to be spent on defence, NATO allies have also pledged to spend at least 20% of that amount on equipment and related research and development (a response to the problem of some militaries counting huge military pension bills as a major part of their defence spending). NATO defence spending data released in March 2024 showed Canada spending 1.33% of GDP on defence, and of that just 14.37% on equipment. When countries' performance in meeting both commitments is plotted on a graph, Canada and Belgium are the only NATO allies that fall in the so-called "quadrant of shame" where neither target is met.[92] Plans for purchase of new submarines announced during the Washington NATO summit that same year may have been timed to blunt criticism there of Canada's hesitancy on defence spending, but if so had little effect given that they did not include any detail on how much would be spent on them or when.[93]

Canadian media have compared the government's reluctant approach to spending on munitions and military equipment with its willingness to allocate billions in capital grants and tax credits for other industries.[94] Defence-friendly commentators suggest the relative paucity of defence investment is not because Canada cannot afford it, but because it does not face consequences for not doing so and allowing neighbours, allies and partners to shoulder the cost.[95]

Meanwhile Ireland is facing a growing realisation that its policy of neutrality does not offer protection.[96] Dependence on the UK will always be a sensitive topic in a country where independence from it is such an integral element of the national mythos. And that makes honest debate doubly challenging. Former Taoiseach Leo Varadkar countered claims of "freeloading" by, counterintuitively, referring to partnership agreements with NATO and the EU under which they protect subsea cables in Ireland's maritime space rather than any capacity that Dublin itself might have. He also suggested that neutrality and having "lots of friends" was in itself a protection, and highlighted that Ireland is one of the few countries whose international aid budget is bigger than its defence budget.[97]

But the country has no capacity of its own to defend its airspace, and little to deal with subsea threats in its maritime areas of responsibility (its two small maritime patrol aircraft are unarmed and have no subsea capabilities).[98] That has exposed Ireland to harsh criticism as a relatively wealthy country – its GDP per capita is the second highest in Europe – but one that has shown little inclination to protect itself or its vital interests, relying instead on the capabilities of neighbours and partners further afield.[99]

Between Canada and Ireland, there's also Iceland, in a category of its own within NATO. With a population of just 380,000 and no military forces at all, Iceland contributes to shared defence through providing host-nation support to US and NATO operations. That is a vital function given Iceland's strategic geography, sitting in the centre of the "Greenland-Iceland-UK gap", a stretch of ocean that would be key to containing Russia's navy in the event of conflict.[100] The country hosts US air operations from Keflavik airbase and a number of radar sites around the island, and in addition provides specialist personnel to fill "soft" but vital roles in NATO structures like political or strategic communications advisers. Nevertheless it is even more dependent on partner nations for its security than Ireland.

Ireland notwithstanding, there's a belated but growing recognition across the continent that immediate action is essential to prevent more widespread war with Russia – or to prevail in it if it is already too late to prevent it. The further-sighted understand that Europe is involved in a global contest that it cannot afford to lose, as it risks fundamentally losing control of its own destiny by ceding it to other powers that are more willing to make use of the forces at their disposal.

That's been reflected in a rash of public appeals and open letters from retired diplomats, civil servants and military officers across Europe.[101] There have also been warnings and urging from those national leaders that understand the threat. "I beg you, colleagues, we need to get serious about European defence", Polish Foreign Minister Radosław Sikorski told the European parliament in November 2023.[102] Where these warnings are being heeded, Europe may finally be emerging from what veteran *Le Monde* reporter Sylvie Kauffmann calls "twenty years of naivety, complacency, arrogance or sometimes simply negligence."[103]

But a deeper change in mindset requires a recognition among Western Europe's political leaders, as well as in civil society, that the security and prosperity the continent has enjoyed since the end of the Cold War is not automatic but is underpinned by US defensive support – and today, protected by Ukrainians fighting on the front line.

The broad consensus regarding the threat from Russia that we saw in Chapter 1 ought logically to prompt European leaders to do whatever they can to head off that threat. Instead, many countries west of Warsaw are still measuring their defensive capacity by incremental improvements over decades from what they had before 2022, rather than undertaking urgent fundamental transformation of the kind demonstrated by Poland (see Chapter 7). This suggests that they still hope Russia will be somebody else's problem – either their more easterly European neighbours, or ideally a United States still committed to European security. Recognition of Europe's new strategic reality doesn't come easy to politicians who have spent their careers not having to be concerned about defence. To them, it feels strange and unnatural to have to think about facing direct threats without American protection. It would be far too easy to slip back into comfortable complacency, pointing at the evisceration of Russia's old army in Ukraine and turning a blind eye to Moscow building a new one. And across Europe, far too few national leaders have explained to their voters that the freedom and prosperity they take for granted must be protected – and that protection is a long-term, expensive commitment that they will have to vote for. Many European governments are nervous about further borrowing to fund defence, at a time when levels of public debt are already high following the Covid pandemic.[104] But the only alternative is to raise taxes – and that's what some countries have already done because it is the only responsible option. As put by the then Estonian Prime Minister Kaja Kallas on raising taxes to cover defence needs, "I'm committing political suicide, but I don't have a choice."[105]

Optimists continue to point to the size of EU states' GDP relative to that of Russia, disregarding the fact that it's not the size of your economy that wins wars, even wars of attrition, but what you do with it. Western militaries are not set up for long wars – but just as they cannot choose whether or not to be at war with Russia, they may also be unable to dictate the nature of that war and how long it lasts.[106] Ideally, European armed forces should be capable of conducting large-scale, mobile, combined-arms manoeuvre operations with an emphasis on winning swiftly to avoid a longer war of devastation. That emphasis would rely on a full scope of military capabilities, available in high quantities. But without major re-investment, some countries' militaries would find their stocks and reserves exhausted long before the fighting finished, and then find themselves in the same perilous situation as Ukraine was in early 2024 – limited in self-defence by shortages of munitions and losing people and territory as a result.

All of this points to the inescapable fact that defence spending has to increase to keep the continent and its people safe. There was another choice available: assisting Ukraine in deterring Russia through defeating it, by providing Kyiv with prompt, full, and unrestricted support. But European leaders – and, especially, Washington – chose not to do so; and consequently, they are now faced with the far more expensive alternative.

6

READINESS AND RESILIENCE

"If we could just somehow fill into a glass and distribute around Europe [our] willingness to defend your own country…"

Elina Valtonen, Foreign Minister of Finland,
29 September 2023[1]

Meanwhile, a possible future overt invasion is not the only threat Russia poses to Europe. A semi-covert campaign of attacks, sabotage, subversion and disruption is happening already today.

Despite the challenges facing Western unity and preparedness that we've discussed in previous chapters, Russia would still have to think long and hard before launching another conventional military operation against a European state because of the risk that NATO (and, for the time being, the US) could still perform its function and deliver it a crushing defeat. But Moscow has learned that that doesn't apply to any of its efforts that don't cross that line into undeniable armed attack. That still leaves Russia a huge range of options for waging war by other means, such as information warfare, terrorist attacks, targeted assassinations, cyber and ransomware campaigns, subversion, culture wars, energy cut-offs, economic blockades, psychological pressure and malign influence and much more.

Campaigns like this were well understood during the Cold War. But just as in conventional defence, decades of supposed peace have led to collective amnesia on the challenge and how to deal with it. As a result, over the last decade the West has grappled to understand and deal with the threat, and that in turn has led to a proliferation of terminology to describe it – so-called "hybrid threats", "grey zone warfare", "sub-threshold attacks", "liminal operations" and many more mix-and-match variations of those terms.

I detailed the human impact of these covert attacks, as well as the way anybody can become a victim of them, in *Russia's War on Everybody*. But recent years have seen an intensification of Russia's efforts, as well as a change in their nature and, interestingly, who is carrying them out.[2] Russia's methods have evolved. The murder gangs that roamed Europe in the previous decade, including targeting Sergei Skripal in Salisbury, were made up of Russian military and intelligence officers. Today, those identified as preparing or carrying out attacks are no longer Russian serving officers themselves, but freelancers hired for the occasion, including online.[3] That seems to indicate that Russia is reaching further to deliver effect. It also may be a result of the wave of expulsions of Russian spies masquerading as diplomats that had taken place over the preceding years. But either way, it demonstrates that Russia retains the ability to tap into organised crime networks well beyond its borders, and can always find unscrupulous individuals to attack their own countries on Moscow's behalf.[4]

Paradoxically, after February 2022 the rest of Europe had been experiencing a rare period of relative quiet while Russia's intelligence services tasked with delivering death and destruction were fully occupied in Ukraine. But a spate of reporting on intercepted Russian sabotage operations in mid-2024 suggests that that period may be coming to an end, and Russia has either rebuilt the capacity to conduct operations in Europe, or is sufficiently satisfied with its progress in Ukraine that it is redirecting its efforts further afield.[5]

There are few parts of Europe that are not targets. In Lithuania, Moscow has used organised criminal networks to arrange attacks on Russian opposition figures. The Estonian security services have noted intensified Russian efforts to recruit local citizens to target their own government, and say they have successfully intercepted far more significant attacks than those carried out to date.[6] But Russia has also reached far beyond its neighbours, right across the continent to arrange the murder in Spain of a former Russian military officer who flew his helicopter across Ukrainian lines to defect.[7] British suspects alleged to have committed arson attacks for Russia have been charged under the UK's new National Security Act, which came into force in late 2023 – none too soon, since previously a wide range of hostile actions against the UK on behalf of foreign powers were perfectly legal.[8]

The objectives of some interdicted sabotage attempts appear clear. In Norway, Russian intelligence agents have been reconnoitring targets like critical and vulnerable infrastructure and military installations, with "a clear goal of uncovering Norwegian emergency preparedness routines", according to the country's PST security service. Eviny, a major energy company in western Norway, is tracking abnormal activity around its power lines and thirty-nine power plants, with the active help of "vigilant residents".[9] In May 2024, a cache of explosives and detonators was found deliberately buried close to a NATO oil pipeline near Heidelberg in Germany.[10] Also in Germany, alleged agents for Russia were arrested after being detected plotting attacks on US military bases, including the major Grafenwöhr facility, used among other things for training Ukrainian soldiers to operate US Abrams tanks,[11] and an arson attack at a weapons plant was assessed to be intended to disrupt shipments of arms and ammunition to Ukraine.[12] One of the highest-profile Russian plots intercepted to date was a plan to murder the CEO of German arms manufacturer Rheinmetall, an enthusiastic supporter of Ukraine, along with other defence industry executives across Europe.[13]

But in other cases, the aim is less obvious. Beyond targeting logistics, military targets and high-profile individuals, covert operations to date have included a range of arson attacks or attempts, including against Ukrainian-owned warehouses in the UK, a paint factory in Poland, homes in Latvia and, perhaps unexpectedly, an Ikea outlet in Lithuania. Some threats work on a purely psychological level, aiming to cause destabilisation by means other than physical attacks. Estonia has been subjected to hundreds of bomb threats against schools, with its security services assessing that their aim is to "create psychological and emotional tension by targeting the most vulnerable – threatening the safety of children".[14] The tactic was replicated against Slovakia in May 2024, when over 1,000 schools received bomb threats.[15]

Poland has been a particular focus of attention for Russia.[16] In part that's explained by its location – not only constituting an eastern frontier of NATO and the EU, but also playing a key role in logistics for support of Ukraine today and, potentially, movement of reinforcements eastwards in the event of conflict elsewhere in the future. That means that the country's transport links will be of obvious interest to Russia. Poland has disrupted at least one network of agents set up for reconnaissance and sabotage of the country's rail network,[17] and other arrests include a man reconnoitring security arrangements at Rzeszow airport, which Polish authorities linked to a possible plan to assassinate

Ukrainian President Volodymyr Zelenskyy who was due to transit through there.[18]

But in addition, as in other countries, Poland has suffered attacks that seem to have no objective other than simple destruction. That includes an arson attack that destroyed Warsaw's largest shopping mall among a spate of other fires around the country attributed to Russian sabotage.[19]

Reported instances of sabotage, as always, are likely to represent only a small fraction not only of incidents under investigation by the authorities, but also those that pass entirely unnoticed. Researching beyond current media reporting reveals broader patterns of intervention that never make the headlines.[20] But the sudden spate of media coverage of Russia's campaigns in the first half of 2024 raises the problem of how exactly governments should explain the threat to their citizens. Heightened awareness risks every minor incident at a defence plant, logistics hub or government official's home being blamed on Russia, in the same way that during the same period, every routine maintenance issue with a Boeing aircraft in 2024 risked making headlines because the company itself was under intense scrutiny.

April 2024 saw two incidents in rapid succession, a fire and an explosion respectively, at two key munitions producers, Scranton Army Ammunition Plant in Pennsylvania, and the Glascoed facility in Wales. Although it's not been suggested publicly that these were anything other than accidental, their timing during intense efforts to increase shell production for both national needs and supplies to Ukraine inevitably sparked speculation that Russia could be to blame. Shortly afterwards a Canadian journalist contacted me to ask if munitions plants there receiving new contracts to boost production, like IMT Defence in Ingersoll, Ontario, were now more likely to be targets for Russian sabotage attacks.[21]

Full and proper public awareness of the threat, and what is needed to counter it, but without crediting Russia with omnipotence is a fine balance but a vital one. That problem cuts both ways, though. A series of Ukrainian attacks deep inside Russia has led to the GUR military intelligence service being credited with fires, explosions and incidents there which may have had nothing to do with them – after all, even in peacetime Russia is not short of man-made disasters.

Recruiting proxies to carry out sabotage is just one of the ways Russia is already attacking Europe beyond Ukraine. There's a similar pattern of Russian activities steadily growing in scale before suddenly coming to widespread public attention in Russia's active electronic warfare disrupting flights around the Baltic Sea region and beyond.

This is a major problem over an expanding area of Europe that dates back years and is becoming increasingly serious. The impact is on time and positioning services – the nuts and bolts of satellite navigation systems – which go offline altogether or, potentially worse, feed pilots misleading information. For instance, systems reliant on satellite connections cannot keep accurate time, and ground proximity warning systems have to be disabled because if GPS is telling them the aircraft is somewhere completely different to where it really is, they are liable to sound urgent alarms about flying into a mountain that isn't there.

Outages have become routine over wide areas of central Europe and the Black Sea. Cockpit footage shared by the Flightradar24 flight tracking service shows clocks going backwards, and safety systems becoming unavailable one after another as the aircraft enters the affected area.[22] That doesn't mean flying in Europe is unsafe, since airliners are still able to use a number of fallback systems, but it does mean that some of the built-in redundancy of systems to ensure safety is no longer available. It imposes costs too. Unavailability of GPS will put paid to plans for increasing the efficiency of flights by fully replacing "beacon to beacon" flying along routes determined by the location of land-based navigational aids with GPS-based routing. And where some of the smallest airports are fully reliant on GPS-based services instead of using navigation aids, landing becomes impossible and flights have to divert or even give up altogether and return to their starting point.[23]

I asked two pilots with two different airlines how the outages affected them on a daily basis. In sharp contrast to excited commentary by policy analysts viewing them as a manifestation of "Russian hybrid warfare", both pilots were entirely relaxed about it; one called it "a potential minor irritation that we have a checklist for and is very easily handled indeed", and for the other it was just a "non-event". That's a good indication of just how normalised the unavailability of services that had previously been taken for granted has become.

Nevertheless airlines are understandably cautious about bringing attention to an issue that some passengers might see as compromising their safety, and that caution has probably contributed to the public remaining largely unaware of the problem. In the UK, the issue only came to widespread notice when media highlighted Russian jamming of satellite signals for an aircraft carrying Defence Secretary Grant Shapps in March 2024, and then a month later the impact on "British holiday flights" was widely reported.[24] But far from being something that just affects British air passengers passing through, the problem has long been the norm for aircraft in the area. And for the region's countries and airlines, the economic costs and disruption resulting from flight cancellations and aborted landings are high and increasing.

When the pattern of disruption was first noted in the previous decade, it was believed that the impact was a side-effect of Russia using its electronic warfare capabilities for its own military exercises. That effect extends beyond Russia – GPS outages for aircraft are also common in the vicinity of Israel and around Cyprus. But the evident negative impact on NATO countries, and Europe's failure to respond beyond protests, meant that there was every incentive for Russia to step up the programme and make it deliberate. It is yet another example of hostile action from Russia becoming gradually normalised because nobody is willing or able to deal with it, which in turn encourages Moscow to do it more. In the case of GPS jamming, the disruption and the areas affected have both been steadily growing, as has interference affecting maritime traffic too. But in April 2024, vessels in the eastern Baltic Sea region reported a new sudden wave of GPS outages, indicating that Russia's efforts had stepped up a gear and were now significantly affecting surface shipping.[25] And Russia has also reportedly been using electronic warfare means to target satellites in lower earth orbit – again, with minimal repercussions.[26] Direct interference with satellite broadcast systems has seen ordinary citizens in some parts of Europe find their intended television viewing replaced with Russian propaganda.[27]

If nothing continues to be done to deter Russia, the logical next step is for Moscow to attempt to block GPS for European road traffic too. This has already repeatedly been done in Russia's own cities – but if Russia were able to replicate the effect across other countries, with millions of navigation systems dependent on GPS location services it could sow widespread chaos. A small foretaste of what that might mean can be seen in northern Norway, where Russian jamming of GPS is already not only disrupting air traffic on a daily basis, but hampering the work of police and emergency services. With their dependence on satellite navigation for search and rescue and ambulance flights as well as everyday operations, the Russian jamming presents a direct threat to public safety, and there should be no surprise if it is eventually a factor in avoidable civilian deaths.[28] The same impact expanded over far more densely populated central Europe would have consequences that were immediate and potentially disastrous.

Another Russian line of effort that has been expected, but not yet materialised, is sponsoring violent terrorist groups to carry out attacks in European capitals. That was a consistent feature of Moscow's campaigns during the Cold War.[29] There can be little doubt that Russia will have considered resuming the practice, and that if it does so, it can tap into large disaffected populations in multiple European states – whether immigrant or home-grown – who would be only too happy to be sponsored, organised and equipped to cause damage in that way.

Immobilising Europe

We saw in Chapter 5 how NATO allies are belatedly taking steps to ensure military forces can move rapidly across Europe when they need to. But it is not only NATO that has been at work. A distinctive feature of much of the current Russian campaigning is how if applied at sufficient scale, it could be used to stop not just Western troops moving, but anything else as well.

In 2020, I wrote a study for the Swedish Defence Research Agency on the ways Russia could immobilise Europe before a conflict.[30] It was part of a report on "anti-access and area denial", or A2AD, the term fashionable at the time for ways of preventing enemy forces moving into or within an area of potential or current conflict. Much of the rest of the report focused on the area of greatest concern at the time – the way Russia, among others, was developing a wide range of missile and artillery systems that could make movement by NATO forces by air, land and sea dangerous and costly. But my chapter looked instead at how Russia could potentially do this without firing a shot. I listed a range of methods Russia could employ to block military movements without actually going to war, like GPS jamming, sabotage of transport links, hiring "activists" and local proxies to disrupt transport and logistics with demonstrations and blockades, cyber disruption of rail and road traffic management, and more. I said that when Russia felt it was ready to confront Europe, all of these methods would be encountered well before the first missile was fired. What is alarming in 2024 is that so many of the methods I described are now already in play across Europe and in the United Kingdom.

These methods for sowing chaos included the gradual expansion of GPS jamming described above, but also operations that look a lot like preparations for disrupting ground transport in order to prevent NATO troops moving East in a crisis. Russia has stepped up a Europe-wide campaign of sabotage and reconnaissance of key logistics links. According to Czechia's transport minister, Martin Kupka, Russia has carried out "thousands" of attempts to interfere with the country's logistics, including hacking attacks on signalling systems and on the networks of the Czech national railway operator. Rail companies in Latvia, Lithuania, Romania and Estonia have also suffered cyber-attacks attributed to Russia-linked groups.[31] And these are in addition to the long-running campaign of cyber reconnaissance that has seen Russia's hacking teams trawling the computer networks of Western logistics and transport firms delivering aid to Ukraine for any intelligence that might translate to a battlefield advantage.[32]

The campaigns include physical attacks as well as hacking. Some incidents, like those in Poland described earlier in this chapter, have been identified as deliberate sabotage of railway networks, and others remain officially unexplained despite security police investigation – as with repeated derailments of the Malmbanan railway line in northern Sweden.[33] Similarly, the long-running blockade of the Ukrainian border by Polish farmers has extended at times to attempts to interfere with logistics hubs and access roads to railheads and sea ports.[34] While the evidence that Russia has encouraged or facilitated the protests is circumstantial, there's a clear incentive to do so and it demonstrates what Russia could achieve if it were able to mobilise well-timed protests – again, as predicted in the Swedish report.

Suspicious activity has spiked at sea too. The Baltic island of Gotland has long been recognised as vital for controlling sea and air traffic in the region; so much so that reinstating its defence was one of the first priorities when Sweden started to rebuild its military in the previous decade. Now, the island is a focal point for activity by Russia's "shadow fleet", a collection of suspicious vessels with mystery owners, suspect insurance, and registration in places like Eswatini, which as a landlocked country is not a traditional seafaring nation. Their primary role at present is allowing Russia to avoid sanctions on oil exports, but the fact that they are fitted out with communications equipment that is "by no means standard or necessary for merchant vessels" has led to suspicion this is not their only purpose.[35] What role these vessels could play in a crisis remains, at the time of writing, publicly unclear. But as Ukraine has demonstrated, when implemented by Russia activities of this kind need to be seen not as an end in themselves, but also as potentially setting the conditions for eventual armed attack.

Some means by which Russia could have been preparing for attacks or open warfare are now starting to be closed off. Countries across Europe are gradually realising the potential challenge of land and property in strategically significant locations being in Russian hands. In Finland, purchases in areas that are militarily sensitive are now subject to Ministry of Defence approval, following growing alarm in the previous decade at a pattern of suspicious land acquisitions by Russia-linked interests in the vicinity of important military or civilian infrastructure. One typical example of otherwise inexplicable behaviour that could form part of preparations for direct action involved an individual from Moscow purchasing land directly adjacent to an important military telecommunications mast, then building a large storage unit there and leaving it empty.[36] Another more spectacular case involved the discovery in 2018 of something closely resembling a covert warfare base on a private island in the Åland archipelago.[37]

But Finland's cautious approach is far from universal. In Norway, background checks on private buyers of property are not routine, and it took media investigation to uncover a pattern of Russian officials purchasing a block of properties in the vicinity of the Defence Headquarters and National Land Operations Centre, and with a direct view over the important Bardufoss airbase.[38] And in the UK, the relaxed attitude to asset purchases by Russians has resulted in the Loch Striven Oil Fuel Depot, a major site in Scotland storing fuel for NATO warships and aircraft, being entirely surrounded by a Russian-owned estate.[39]

But a broader lack of understanding of the nature of Russian subversion has led to doors being left open to Russian influence or espionage. While senior government officials ordinarily undergo security checks to ensure that they have not been subverted by foreign powers, elected politicians often face no such scrutiny – and can have far greater effect in skewing a country's policy decisions to favour Russian interests. This aspect of the challenge goes far beyond government and politics. Russia sees all sectors of society as targets or vectors for espionage or malign influence, including universities, business, and particularly the media – and in most countries, few of these are subject to scrutiny that is appropriate to the threat. It was only in 2024, for instance, that the UK started to consider reinstating security vetting for key researchers engaged in academic work on dual-use technologies with possible military applications.[40]

And that insider threat lies behind perhaps one of the greatest challenges of all to NATO or its member states responding to a

Russian military challenge, up to and including stopping NATO reinforcements moving across Europe when needed. Of all the different methods identified by the Swedish report – railway sabotage or GPS jamming before open warfare begins, or missile strikes on ports and railheads once the fighting is under way – by far the most effective doesn't involve explosions at all. The most reliable way of preventing movement by the armed forces of any given country is through causing a legitimate order not to move to be given by that country's own chain of command or political leadership. And that is precisely the reason why Russia devotes so much effort to trying to convince both publics and politicians across Europe and North America that responding to what Moscow does is dangerous, escalatory and irresponsible. As we saw in previous chapters, the fear is that a new US administration could see US forces in Europe not only told not to respond to a Russian attack, as was the case for US European Command in February 2022 (see Chapter 3), but even pre-emptively withdrawn altogether, leaving Europe's armed forces and civil societies to face the threat with their own resources. Insider threat means that the US or any other country lying between it and Russia could take a political, not military, decision that troops were not to move toward the sound of the guns.

All of these challenges together mean that European states face a continuing threat both in peacetime and in the transition to open military conflict. But beyond the front-line states, there are few signs of countries seriously addressing the likely disruption if Russia continues and expands its current operations. Still more alarmingly, there's little discernible preparation for the significant stepping up of campaigns of subversion, sabotage and destruction that would precede a Russian military move. To look for the ways states could insure themselves and their citizens against hostilities up to and including war, we need to look to those European countries that have never lost sight of the threat; first of all, Finland.

Resilience: How To Do It

While as we will see in Chapter 7, Finland's armed forces are highly capable, the country's plans for defence go far deeper than military readiness.

Former military intelligence chief Pekka Toveri says that "Finland doesn't *have* a defence force, Finland *is* a defence force."[41] He's referring to Finland's approach of "comprehensive security", where vital functions of the economy, infrastructure, security of supply, civil defence, and overall societal resilience are the collective responsibility not just of state authorities, but also of businesses, NGOs and citizens.[42] It is an approach that in previous decades was known as the "Strategy for Securing the Functions Vital to Society", which is still not a bad summary of what it seeks to achieve: in short, ensuring that the country, government at all levels, civil society and individuals are robust enough not to collapse in the face of an attack.

This security mindset permeates the country's civic and social planning. Important bridges are constructed by default with points to attach explosives to blow them ahead of an advancing enemy. While evacuation routes and facilities have been updated based on lessons from Ukraine,[43] every building in Finland over a certain size, including all apartment blocks and public facilities, has long been required to have an emergency shelter for its occupants[44] – and even when the shelters have a tendency to be colonised by residents as basement storage space, they remain available to be cleared if needed. In the capital, Helsinki, there are shelter places available for 145% of the city's population, under plans that were drawn up in 2003. In other words, unlike many other countries Finland never lost sight of the challenge from its neighbour, and was planning for building bomb shelters while much of the rest of the West still thought it was enjoying a honeymoon with Russia.

Now, those long preparations are proving their worth. Finland reacted immediately to Russia's full-scale invasion by allocating additional funds to the Finnish Defence Forces (FDF) for procurement. But preparations for war also involve ensuring ongoing capacity: "production reserve agreements" have been activated, under which civilian companies are obliged to keep extra capacity in reserve to ensure the defence forces can sustain operations without being hostage to industry bottlenecks. That covers everything necessary for sustained warfighting, from food supplies to machinery.[45] The country has stockpiles of at least six months' consumption of major fuels and grains, emergency reserves of medicines and medical supplies, and has also begun storing military equipment, ammunition and spare parts on the territory of neighbours and fellow NATO members Norway and Sweden as well as further afield, keeping them in ready reserve but also at a greater distance from their only real threat.

According to Lt-Gen Mikko Heiskanen, deputy chief of staff for armaments and logistics in the Finnish Defence Forces and effectively head of Finland's war economy, the country has not yet moved to a war footing. In May 2024, Heiskanen said that Finland was at step three out of nine on its escalation ladder. For instance, although it had significantly increased production of ammunition after 2022 – now making five times the shells it did just five years ago and still increasing – it was still not working factories 24 hours a day. Importantly, the emphasis in both military and civil preparedness is on ensuring the country is prepared to weather a potential long-term crisis, rather than a temporary emergency.[46]

And Finland has demonstrated its readiness to take drastic steps to protect itself, accepting that this will cause economic disruption and inconvenience to its citizens. In 2015, Russia tested migrant dumping across the Finnish and Norwegian borders as a tool to impose costs and social tensions on its neighbours. When Moscow repeated the tactic in 2023, this led to Finland closing its border crossing points with Russia altogether, pointing to Russia's seeding of migrant flows with professional criminals that it intended to activate later to destabilise their target countries. At a stroke, this firm step neutralised all the advantages Russia perceived in cross-border migrant dumping, and its attempts largely ceased. The intense discussion of the legality of the government's approach to protecting itself against weaponised migration provides an ongoing case study of whether Finland is ready to prioritise national security over Europe's peacetime human rights norms.

Finland's whole-of-society approach to defence and crisis preparedness is reflected in the country's élite National Defence Courses. These run four times a year, typically with fifty participants about 40% of whom are women. Those fifty are made up of members of parliament and personally invited individuals in positions of leadership in various sectors of the economy and critical infrastructure, branches of government, the media, scientists, academics and influential cultural figures. In fact, representatives of the armed forces make up the smallest group among course members, and the broad-based course selection criteria have helped foster the country's holistic approach to defence, essential for genuine implementation of its concept of comprehensive security.

Each course lasts three and a half weeks, with intense twelve-hour days including presentations, discussions, site visits, table top exercises, and a three-day visit to a military base.[47] That's a long time for parliamentarians, government officials and senior executives to step aside from their jobs – but both the importance and the prestige of the course are widely recognised, making it rare for the personal invitations to join it to be declined. The élite cachet, and the inbuilt networking function, helps build a sense of community as well as a shared realisation of the importance of national defence – and consequently, willingness to support its funding in parliament and in public debate.

The courses aim to provide a total overview of Finland's foreign, security and defence policy, to improve collaboration between different sectors of society in an emergency and to promote networking between individuals working in those sectors – all to strengthen Finland's implementation of comprehensive security. As well as foreign, security and defence policy, the course content covers topics like the structure of the economy, infrastructure and security of supply, border and internal security, macro- and microeconomics, social and health care, education and culture matters, cyber, information, and hybrid influence, climate change and its economic and security implications, and mental and psychological crisis resilience. On-site visits include organisations considered vital to national security – not only various units of the Finnish Defence Forces, but also the police, the security and intelligence service, and the national broadcaster.[48]

The courses have been running for over sixty years, and more than 10,000 Finns in various key positions have attended them to date, with many more attending the week-long Regional Defence Courses which focus on preparedness, civil defence, security of supply of the economy, communications and transportation at regional and local administrative levels. That produces a solid network of people who not only understand how the country works, but also how to cooperate to keep it working when under attack. That in itself is a significant enabler for the country's comprehensive security approach; but at a deeper level, it has helped to embed and normalise that approach across society.

That common acceptance of roles and responsibilities in a crisis can seem at times to obscure the fact that what to many in Finland feels like normal and unremarkable state behaviour is radical and extraordinary for many other countries. The basic presumption of competence in civil defence, and the responsibility both of the state and of civil society to look after each other, show the conceptual gap between Finland and countries like for example the UK, to be discussed shortly.

But this presumption and all the security and resilience measures that underpin it – and, crucially, the fact that they were never dismantled like those of other countries during the decades after the Cold War – mean that Finland has long been recognised as an example of best practice in Europe for ensuring national resilience. That recognition was made explicit in March 2024 when the European Commission tasked former Finnish President Sauli Niinistö with drawing up a report on how to enhance civil defence and preparedness across the whole of the EU.[49] At a joint press conference, Commission President Ursula von der Leyen referred to the "specific mindset" in Finland that treated preparedness as a whole-of-society concern, and called for it to be adopted more widely.[50]

In collecting and compiling recommendations, former president Niinistö is faced with an interesting challenge. The Finnish resilience mindset is the product of a society, history and even geography that are far from typical for Europe. Finland's strategic culture, and the set of beliefs, attitudes and threat perceptions largely shared across its relatively homogeneous society, have evolved over decades if not centuries; and the prevailing culture of common values and national priorities are an immensely valuable national asset that is not shared by many other states. It predisposes the comprehensive security approach to function as intended, since in the words of one Finnish military academic, "in Finland even the worst people want the country to be secure and systems to work".[51] It will hardly be possible to transplant the attitudes that underpin successful comprehensive defence into other nations overnight, and Niinistö's report will have to recognise that what works for Finland may simply be unachievable for many other states.

Nevertheless, Europe has to start somewhere. Many Finns, including both government officials and private citizens, respond to praise of their defence forces and civil defence preparations with modest commentary that not all is perfect and the systems have their own flaws. Downplaying the country's achievements is a common reaction. That may be in part because Finland can at times be among the most Nordic of Nordic societies in its respect for modesty and disapprobation of showing off. But also, Finns look at their country's strong civil defences as a normal and natural state of affairs, and nothing to get particularly excited about. Sadly, looking across Europe, Finland's situation is far from normal. Finns may see room for improvement in their country's defensive systems; but that does not alter the fact that on a continent where most other countries have been content to abandon these defences altogether, Finland presents probably the best available example of how to do it right.

Like Finland, neighbouring Sweden never fully dismantled its civil preparedness systems or the mindset that went with them. The country's 350 government agencies, plus regions and municipalities, are all obliged by law to plan and prepare for war. But in addition, Sweden's 1.2 million companies all have a part to play in total defence, even if only a small one – which could be limited to a duty to maintain services in order to the greatest extent possible to preserve normality in society.[52]

The whole-of-society approach to civil defence is baked in to social attitudes. Civil preparedness is taught in schools; Sweden is talking about war with 10-year-olds. Sweden has 65,000 purpose-built bomb shelters, and other spaces that can be utilised, like car parks inside mountains or parts of the Stockholm metro built for this purpose. Their total capacity is 7 million people – Sweden's total population of 10 million does not all live in areas considered likely to need shelter. (By comparison, a review in Poland found in 2024 that less than 4% of the population could count on a place where they could shelter, leading to an urgent investment programme to provide bomb shelters and other security measures in Warsaw.)[53] Approximately 400,000 Swedish associations, communities, and small voluntary organisations understand their role, as well as the eighteen voluntary defence organisations which together command approximately 350,000 volunteers. In Sweden, Latvia and other countries, local authorities do not need to wait for instructions for dealing with a challenge in the form of the "little green men" that seized Crimea in 2014. The law says that if you are a local official witnessing a hostile action, you should respond as though the country is at war.

Nevertheless Sweden is working hard to reinvigorate its system to adapt to the current threat environment. The crisis preparedness instruction booklet issued to all residents in Sweden, and titled "If Crisis Or War Comes", dates from 2017 and was scheduled to be republished in 2024. And Sweden's chiefs of the armed forces and civil defence saying explicitly during 2024 that war is possible was not in itself new, but the stepping up of the messaging was a deliberate kick-starting of awareness among the population. This was part of an effort to start a national conversation about individual responsibilities at country, regional and local levels. This includes explanations for what to do to engage positively in the process of building resilience: although the threshold for useful engagement is supposed to be set as low as possible, Sweden has seen a substantial rise in numbers of volunteers for Home Guard or volunteer defence organisations.

But Sweden's experience also highlights a new challenge facing European states seeking to ensure civil resilience in the 21st century. So much of that resilience depends on mutual trust and a shared understanding of citizens' social contract with the state and with each other. Sweden has seen a radical shift over the last decade from being a relatively homogenous society where this could largely be taken for granted, to one suffering polarisation as one of the disastrous after-effects of mass immigration from societies with radically different values.[54] Where gun crime and civil disorder have soared, and policing by consent is no longer possible in some areas of major cities, Sweden now faces the same challenges as other countries with far less cohesive societies, like the UK: not only increased difficulties in calling on residents to meet their civil commitments, but also potentially a substantial insider threat ready to be mobilised.

Resilience: How Not To Do It

At the other end of Europe from Finland, the UK also demonstrates the other extreme of civil resilience planning, by not conducting any visible planning at all.[55]

At the end of the Cold War, Britain rushed to disband organisations and capabilities that would have tried to ensure the country could continue to function in the event of it turning hot. The Royal Observer Corps, whose role had evolved from tracking enemy aircraft during the Second World War to being prepared to monitor and report on potential nuclear attacks, did not survive to the end of 1991. By the middle of that decade, the Home Office had abandoned the entire concept of civil defence, and in just five years the UK had gone from being well prepared for transition to war, and continuity of state and government during it, to having no evident preparations at all. Police and fire services, and critical utilities like water and telecommunications, were no longer obliged to maintain training and reserve capacity for the country being under attack, emergency food stockpiles were sold off, and backup regional government offices closed down and abandoned. Successive British governments had decided that there would never be war again – or if there was, it would be somebody else's problem.[56]

That attitude has persisted throughout the three decades of nominal peace. Investment in preparedness has been the rare exception, not the rule. The 9/11 attacks in the United States triggered a temporary spasm of awareness of the need to prepare for major disasters and mass casualty incidents as the result of deliberate attacks. But the specialist hardware bought for fire and rescue services at the time, like mass decontamination units and urban search and rescue equipment, is now twenty years old and reported to be at the end of its useful life.[57]

Defence planners point out that a significant part of readiness consists of maintaining very large stocks of very boring things that may never be used. For civil resilience, that includes capacity in healthcare, including simple measures like availability of hospital beds in an emergency. Here too the UK's situation is dire. The National Health Service (NHS) is widely assessed to have no capacity to cope with a major crisis because it is already in one. A study by experts from the RUSI military think-tank of how the NHS would cope with war makes grim reading: it concludes that there is no capacity for either military or civilian casualties, and supplies of beds, blood, transport and trained personnel would be immediately overwhelmed.[58] And all of that would be the result just of dealing with incidents far away from healthcare facilities themselves, even before hospitals themselves are targeted. Russian practice in Ukraine and elsewhere, most recently at the time of writing with a strike on a children's cancer hospital in Kyiv, shows beyond doubt that the most vulnerable civilians will be a deliberate target for attacks in order to maximise disruption and civilian suffering.[59]

In all these aspects, the UK is dealing with the consequences of assumptions in both military and civil defence planning that it would simply not need ever to fight a major war. Historically, the

NHS would not have had to plan for military casualties to the same extent because of a substantial military medical establishment designed as an integral part of the UK's warfighting capacity. But the years of peace dividend and relentless cuts to defence capability saw this disbanded, and in part replaced by reliance on reservist doctors and nurses. The problem with that, of course, is that those reservists' day jobs are in the NHS, where they will be equally desperately needed. Just as with assets like aircraft, warships and tanks, personnel too may be exquisitely trained and capable, but still can't be in more than one place at a time.

The need for more people is clear. In January 2024 the head of the British Army, General Sir Patrick Sanders, called for a "citizen army" as part of a shift in the UK's national mindset, to be prepared for war and for the need for resilience that would come with it. This was widely misinterpreted as a call to reintroduce military conscription.[60] But while Sanders has been openly critical of cuts in military manpower – part of the belated but growing chorus of senior military officers speaking out about the defence crisis while still in uniform – his emphasis was more on understanding the requirement for national mobilisation in the face of a severe threat. He called on the UK's "pre-war generation" to prepare for the possibility of war, emphasising that this was a "whole-of-nation undertaking".[61] But Sanders's call has to contend with the reality of generations of British citizens with no concept of what it means to be at war. There is, as yet, little recognition that missile attacks, shortages, restrictions on freedoms and travel, loss of income and property, and the constant risk of sudden death for yourself or your loved ones are not just something that happens thousands of miles away, but could now hit home.

Unsurprisingly, Sanders's wake-up call met with resistance from within government. A spokesman for then Prime Minister Rishi Sunak responded by saying that "hypothetical scenarios of a future potential conflict were not helpful"; a brutally honest admission that official UK government policy at the highest level was not just to treat the threat as hypothetical but to prefer not to think about it anyway. Slightly more surprisingly, just a few months later the same Prime Minister reversed course and himself launched a plan for "national service" as part of his failed campaign for re-election. "National Service" was the UK's former term for mandatory conscription, in place until 1960. But while the need to bolster national defence has met broad acceptance as described in Chapter 4, Sunak's outline idea was widely condemned as even more incoherent and insubstantial than other recent UK defence announcements.

With apparently no consultation with the MOD or the armed services, questions were raised over why the Prime Minister was considering an ambitious and radical new departure for UK defence rather than addressing its already well-known problems and deficiencies.[62] The proposal for twelve-month placements with an armed service, with an alternative of voluntary work in critical services, threw up a wide range of further questions with, presumably, answers to be provided by the Royal Commission that Sunak indicated would consider the issue.

The utility of twelve-month individual attachments to highly technical services like the Royal Navy or Royal Air Force was queried as they would not have time to acquire useable skills, let alone the proposed placements in "cyber defence". Even in the community sector and civil resilience, the value of unskilled and potentially unmotivated eighteen-year-olds was not immediately clear. And there was no detail as to how the British Army, whose numbers fell to under 73,000 in mid-2024, would find the capacity to deal with tens of thousands of augmentees, all requiring the use of facilities, training areas, accommodation, manpower, and administrative capacity within the MOD that are already under severe strain. Uniforms, equipment, weapons and pay would all add substantial costs, and it was unclear how new joiners would be transported and fed by a British Army that has been stripped of its vehicle fleets and whose Army Catering Corps is a distant memory. Rough calculations based on the Armed Forces' current costs (which is still more detail than had been released by the British Government) showed that the scheme would cost many times more than the claimed cost of £2.5 billion (and it was not specified what would be cut elsewhere even to cover that sum).[63] The widespread conclusion was that Sunak's national service plan was more to do with a search for a pre-election novelty than a genuine ambition to improve the UK's military and civil defences.

Today, the UK's efforts to respond to the heightened threat across Europe mostly highlight how little has been done to prepare to meet it. In May 2024 the British government belatedly launched a website on emergency preparation, containing sparse and rudimentary advice like checking domestic smoke alarms and making sure children know how to call the emergency services. But the section on preparations for possible evacuation made it plain that central coordination or pre-planning was not to be expected, and individuals were expected to make their own arrangements for finding safe routes and shelter.[64] For the British government it seems a website telling people to look after themselves – which will in any case be immediately unavailable in a power outage – is a helpfully affordable alternative to actually having a civil defence system and plan.

Total defence is sometimes misconstrued as giving everybody a weapon and waiting for an invasion. But as conceptualised by the states most at risk, it consists instead in preparing everybody for resilience, even if not resistance. This resilience mindset means all government institutions considering what needs to be done if war begins tomorrow – or two years from now. It means thinking about how to respond to missile bombardments like those that have rained on Ukraine. That remains beyond the comprehension of many western European populations – and yet, in an open confrontation with NATO this would be likely to be one of Russia's first actions. Germany's Bremerhaven and other important sea ports, for example, will be prime targets because they are choke points for reinforcements heading East. But no country – including the UK – should think itself immune from strikes on sea ports, airports, national and NATO command centres and more. That means that although the threat to the UK is different from that faced by Finland or other front-line states, distance doesn't lend the luxury of being able to ignore the problem and pretend that the country is immune and untouchable.

Effective civil defence means stockpiling, training, and central coordination. It means citizens accepting that something has to change in their everyday lives if they personally, their families, their employers, their village or town, and their country is not to be caught unprepared. That starts with individuals knowing how to prepare a 72-hour emergency bag and where to evacuate or find shelter if needed, and continues through more active steps like public and private employers training and exercising in crisis preparedness – including releasing staff to maintain their training in defence or maintaining critical services.

It means, crucially, not assessing the functions of the state by purely economic measures. A simple example is, again, numbers of hospital beds. It is uneconomic to have a reserve of them, but if there is no spare capacity, where will the sudden flood of military and civilian casualties on the outbreak of war be treated? Reserve capacity of civilian services, just like armed defence forces, is an investment in national survival. It costs money even if not used, but the cost of not having it is infinitely higher.

That money has to come from somewhere – and so, voters have to be convinced to back governments that will tax them in order to spend it. That can be a hard sell. Estonian diplomat

Kaimo Kuusk thinks it may help if taxpayers know whom to blame: he recommends calling the additional costs a "Putin tax". But the challenge for countries that have not yet embraced comprehensive defence goes beyond increasing budgets. It calls for a fundamental shift in defence strategies, integrating private sector capabilities, modernising military infrastructure, and ensuring supply chain resilience. And for the state to continue to function, confidence in its resilience needs to be maintained. That in turn is dependent on a functioning economy. It follows that businesses need to be resilient in response to threats, as opposed to shutting up shop or evacuating from the country.

For countries like the UK and others that believe distance from the problem lends them safety, this shift in mindset seems at present impossibly remote. The widespread and misguided outrage that met just the suggestion of some kind of state service in the UK, even before considerations of its feasibility or funding, made it clear how many people there see no connection between international security and their own lives, or that the freedoms they enjoy might at some point be challenged and need to be defended. The UK does not enjoy the luxuries that a country like Finland does, of fundamental social consensus based on a shared national understanding of the threat, and decades in which to build a system to deal with it. That means, alarmingly, that the only thing that may cause attitudes to change in time is precisely the kind of strategic shock that comprehensive defence systems are designed to survive, but which the UK would have to face unprepared. In the absence of a strategy for national resilience, the UK's current next available course of action is to hope for the best.

7

EUROPE'S NEW LEADERS

"We were naive to think we could live like in a fairy-tale, happily ever after. We can only live happily ever after if we fight for it."

Former Latvian president Vaira Vike-Freiberga,
Riga, October 2016

"We know what happens if we don't fight – if we fight, we may die, if we don't, we die anyway."

Former commander of the Land Forces of a Baltic state,
Stockholm, December 2019

Europe is divided between those countries with historical experience of Russian domination, and those who have no knowledge of what that entails.

That's one good reason why the clearest recognition of the challenge to Europe's security from military aggression comes from the front-line states – who also risk being next in line as Russia's targets. Countries like Finland and Poland, their security priorities dictated by geography, have set the example of political will either to implement a crash programme of rearmament and military expansion, or to build on capabilities that were never abandoned during the lean years for defence. And as we saw in the previous chapter, the states of northeast Europe also show the way for dealing with subversion, hybrid threats, and all the ways Russia and other hostile powers cause damage without going to war – or, in the worst case when war cannot be avoided, means of giving their country and its citizens the best possible chance of survival.

Those countries know what is at stake, not only from the example of Ukraine, but from their own histories within living memory. In the post-Cold War era, they share a history of consistently sounding the alarm for Europe over Russia's intent – and consistently finding that Europe ignored them or wrote them off as disruptive trouble-makers hindering good relations with Moscow. Today, the warnings have given way to specific calls to action and plans for defence, together with ongoing energetic diplomatic campaigning to make them happen, as when the ambassadors of the three Baltic states in London penned a joint open letter laying out the urgent task of defence for NATO, but also hinting in passing that the UK could and should be doing more to protect itself and its allies.[1]

In the 1930s, the Baltic states' inability to find allies abroad or to stand alone doomed them to savage Soviet occupation, at an even higher and more tragic cost than Finland, which was able to fight and prevail. Today, that historical experience drives national determination to fight rather than submit. But the Baltic states also recognise that that fight has to be for the entirety of their countries. They are unable to trade land for time by retreating; not only do they lack the depth of territory to retreat to, but the experience of murderous atrocities committed against Ukrainians under even brief Russian occupation has re-emphasised the message that populated areas cannot be abandoned to Russian troops. Instead, all three countries have stated the need to be able to contest a Russian incursion from its very first moments. As noted above, Lithuania's capital, Vilnius, is after all only 30 km from the border with Belarus – already used by Russia as a forward location for invading northern Ukraine.

That's also an understanding that assistance from NATO, if not present before Russia attacks, will arrive too late. Former Estonian Prime Minister Kaja Kallas has pointed out that NATO's previous assumptions for defence of the Baltic states involved them being overrun, and then potentially liberated after six months – which the experience of Ukraine demonstrates is more than sufficient to inflict horrific destruction on the countries and their inhabitants.[2] That recognition lay behind a joint decision by the Baltic states in early 2024 to construct a line of defensive fortifications along their borders with Russia and Belarus. Fixed defensive lines might run counter to decades of military fashion, but their value – like so many other aspects of warfare that were thought to have faded into history – has been proven beyond doubt in Ukraine.[3]

Meanwhile, as discussed in Chapter 4, doubt in future US commitment to European security has led to the resurrection of multiple possible scenarios under which Russia challenges NATO by attacking the Baltic states.[4] That in itself is a tragic mark of how swiftly European security has degraded. For a brief few years after the arrival in the Baltic states and Poland of NATO's "enhanced forward presence" (eFP) battalions, made up of contingents from multiple NATO nations, there was no discussion of possible Russian attacks there because Russia's options had been closed off. An established NATO presence well before it was required meant that there was no possibility of interfering with those countries without the rest of NATO becoming immediately involved – which are the only circumstances under which Russia would consider it. Now, the so-called "fait accompli" scenarios are once again considered among Russia's most likely next steps.

All this creates a strategic situation where these three countries could become acutely vulnerable to hostile Russian intent if Moscow turns its attention their way after Ukraine. Advocates of appeasement would suggest that this argues for a conciliatory approach to Moscow, and avoidance of conflict. But with their long experience of working with Russia and its rulers, local political leaders know that attempts to placate their neighbour would be counter-productive. Instead, Kaja Kallas and Lithuanian Foreign Minister Gabrielius Landsbergis have emerged among the clearest and most fearless voices in Europe pointing to what must be done to protect the continent as a whole.

That includes constant recognition that Ukraine is fighting for Europe, and the more Ukraine can do to neutralise Russian military power, the safer Russia's other neighbours will be. Kaimo Kuusk, who previously served as Estonian ambassador to Ukraine, summarises the countries' shared interest: "Helping Ukraine is a chance to solve the problem we have faced for 250 years."[5] That also drives smaller coalition partners beyond the Baltic to also be among the most enthusiastic in aiding Kyiv. Denmark has approximately 8,000 active duty personnel in its army, for a population of around 6 million people. But it's not only proportionally among the biggest donors to Ukraine, it is also one of the countries that has donated entire sectors of military capability to be used there. At the beginning of 2024, Prime Minister Mette Frederiksen announced that *all* Denmark's artillery – including systems on order that had not even entered service with Danish units – was to be redirected to Ukraine.[6] Czechia, a nation of 10 million people, has also been consistent in its backing for Kyiv. The country hosts the highest number of Ukrainian refugees per capita (almost 500,000, or 5% of its pre-war population). It was the first to send tanks for the defence of Ukraine, long before larger countries summoned up the courage to provide limited numbers of Leopards, Challengers and Abrams.

As well as the moral clarity of its leadership, Estonia has set out practical suggestions for how Europe can overcome its instinctive reluctance to take defence seriously and ensure that Ukraine prevails. In late 2023, Estonian officials put forward a funding plan for backing Ukraine, based on a ruthlessly logical cost benefit analysis – a mathematical calculation for how much had to be spent to convince Russia that it did not have the long-term advantage, and would not prevail in an extended war of attrition.[7] The logic was based on the simple fact that wars end when the losing side decides that it will get a better outcome through stopping fighting than from continuing; so the objective was to persuade Russia that this was the case by turning the tide in the war and demonstrating long-term commitment to Ukraine.

That objective depended, like so much else, on eroding Russia's military forces faster than they can be regenerated. Estonia calculated that the cost of maintaining the necessary level of attrition was within 0.25% of GDP for each NATO member – a figure far less than that already spent by Estonia and other leading backers of Ukraine, and vastly less than the sums spent by the EU on tackling the coronavirus pandemic or even on targeted relief for high energy bills. Crucially, the plan's backers observed, the price tag would be infinitely smaller than the cost of the strategic loss of Ukraine in this war – and Europe would bear that cost if Ukraine fell.

Overall, Europe's smaller nations have assumed leadership roles based not on their economic capacity, but rather their willingness to recognise the urgency of the moment and take steps to meet it. It was Czechia that in early 2024, at the height of Ukraine's artillery famine, mounted an initiative to source an additional 800,000 shells from around the world.[8] Estonia also declared in late March 2024 that by shopping around, it too could source a large supply of shells for Ukraine[9] – prompting questions as to why much larger countries such as France, Germany or the UK had been unable to do so beforehand. In fact, the Czech and Estonian plans for scraping the global barrel for shells were only necessary because unlike Finland, whose preparations were discussed in the previous chapter, much larger European powers had failed completely to recognise the need to invest in their own munitions industries years beforehand.

Northern Europe and Military Preparations

Smaller states across the Nordic and Baltic region have responded to the threat from Russia to the best of their abilities given small populations and economies. The Latvian parliament voted to restore conscription in 2022. This was both to increase the number of active duty personnel in the face of the Russian threat, and to overhaul the reservist system and ensure that there was a greater pool of recently trained reservists available in the event of a crisis. Latvians can choose to serve eleven months in the regular forces, or five years in National Guard units with at least 28 days' training a year, or complete an officers' training course while at university.[10]

As of 2024, building Latvia's reserves into an organised, trained and well-equipped military force was still a work in rapid progress. Approximately 28,000 active reservists would know where to report, but had not necessarily yet been trained as formed units. Another 80,000 reservists at lower levels of readiness might have served in excess of ten years ago, so their integration into current defence planning was still ongoing.[11]

But a key element of Latvia's defence preparations, in common with other states in the region, is the recognition that in a crisis junior commanders and citizens will have to act on their own initiative. An understanding that command, control and communications will be disrupted drives a default expectation of resistance; according to one former senior officer, "battalion commanders do not have to wait for an order to start a war". Another consideration shaping Latvia's current defence posture is the choice that had to be made between two concepts of defence: focusing on an "iron fist" of a small number of heavy military forces, or developing a "hedgehog" principle of total defence that would not match Russian military capability, but would be too costly to attack and, like a hedgehog, impossible to swallow. The "iron fist" approach stemmed from NATO operating concepts, but limited Latvia's defence options to fighting for time for NATO reinforcements to – hopefully – arrive, and presented a potential choice between the Latvian army staying in Latvia or surviving.

Latvia would no longer be fighting alone. Canada has been the lead nation for the country's NATO eFP battalion since its inception, and as with the UK in Estonia, defence relationships are being cemented over time as a significant proportion of both countries' deployable militaries cycle through the two Baltic countries. Canada's contingent of approximately 1,000 soldiers in Latvia is scheduled to more than double to 2,200 by 2026. But the country is still focusing on total defence, and preparations for comprehensive defensive systems and resistance and sabotage operations in regions and cities, in order to deter Russia through being a visibly hard target.

Neighbouring Estonia has also made vigorous use of its small resources to bolster defence. The Estonian Defence Force has only about 4,000 active-duty soldiers: but has reorganised for potential expansion, setting up a new division headquarters in 2023, and in time of crisis would draw on its much larger reserve made up of former conscripts. Reserve officers also bring a wide range of additional skills to be placed at the nation's disposal when required; there are probably not many countries where a former prime minister continues to make best use of his experience by serving in the reserves as a lieutenant specialising in civil–military relations. In addition the Kaitseliit, the Estonian Defence League, provides a volunteer national defence reserve numbering up to 18,000.[12]

And like Finland, Estonia was early to recognise the need for long-range precision strike weapons to defend itself against Russia, long before their value was proven beyond doubt in Ukraine. Estonia requested supplies of HIMARS in December 2021, at a high cost for the nation's limited defence budget.[13] By 2024, early procurement decisions like the HIMARS request were starting to feed through into weapons, equipment and ammunition beginning to arrive in Estonia. And at the same time, rapid EDF enlargement was starting to bring noticeable results.[14] Like other front-line states, Estonia was ahead of Western Europe because it recognised what was at stake and took resolute action early. But the country also demonstrates how defensive preparations in a democracy are hostage to the need to maintain political popularity. In June 2024, both Permanent Secretary of the Defence Ministry Kusti Salm and the head of the Defence Forces, General Martin Herem, announced that they would be retiring early.[15] Salm explained that he was leaving his post because of the government's refusal to follow recommendations on war preparations, in particular increasing ammunition stockpiles – and so, he said, at present "Estonia's defence and security policy is crossing our fingers".[16]

Norway, meanwhile, had by contrast long been criticised both at home and abroad for its reluctance to fund its armed forces. It seemed extraordinary that Europe's richest country, with enormous financial reserves notionally set aside for a future crisis, was not spending more on defence now that the crisis had actually arrived. But in April 2024, Norway announced a twelve-year plan to modernise and expand its armed forces, including re-equipping with capabilities that had proved their value in Ukraine. The plan included boosting defence spending to 2% of GDP to be spent on defence in 2024 and to 3% by 2036, enabling expansion of the army over and above that already planned, and funding of new frigates, submarines, helicopters, long-range surveillance drones and satellites, air defence capabilities and long-range precision weapons. Norway's Home Guard reserve defence force is also to be enlarged and re-equipped, and long-range drones capable of surveillance across the country's vast area of maritime responsibility would be procured in cooperation with allies.

Norway is building up its forces in the northernmost Finnmark region, in the expectation that hostilities with Russia would involve a land incursion across the border there. The reinforcements include a new Ranger company stationed right on the border and armed with light anti-aircraft and anti-armour weapons, whose task would be to delay invading forces.[17] And the new defence plan referred specifically to lessons from Ukraine in prioritising the ability to protect national infrastructure against missile and drone attacks.[18]

In previous decades Sweden took full advantage of the perception of a peace dividend, ruthlessly cutting its once-mighty military and reducing it to a small force focused on international peace operations. But its attempts to reconstitute a defence force started relatively early for Europe, thanks in part to the clear vulnerability of key points like the strategically vital island of Gotland, which had been fully demilitarised and thus presented a standing invitation to Russian intervention.[19]

Sweden moved to reintroduce partial military conscription in 2017, and later liability for civilian duties in the emergency services.[20] The current phase of Swedish military expansion

189

means far more young people are available for conscription than are required, meaning both that the armed forces can be highly selective and that conscript service carries a degree of prestige rather than being a universal experience.[21]

And, like Finland, Sweden resolved decades of debate over NATO membership almost overnight – and as of March 2024, is a full member of the alliance. Non-alignment had been a fundamental element of Sweden's national identity for over two centuries, making the eventual leap to NATO an even more dramatic shift in the nation's international posture. But as with Finland, the undeniable threat ensured widespread public support for the transition to membership and the hope of firm guarantees of mutual defence.[22] Now the country faces the simultaneous challenge of continuing to rebuild its own capability for self-defence, while also ensuring that it can be integrated with NATO for mutual support.[23] But Sweden's political leaders have stated the challenge clearly, including the implication that Swedish citizenship includes an obligation to defend "Sweden, our values and our way of life – with weapons in hand and our lives on the line."[24] This has included calls to speed up preparations, both for the military and in civil defence, with stark warnings of the urgency of being ready for war.[25]

Overall, the sense of urgency is a common factor driving defence preparations across the region. It's led to both economic and political prioritisation of defence, to an extent which military commanders in other parts of Europe find their governments are unwilling to match. Romania, which shares a 600-km border with Ukraine (divided into two sections by Moldova), hosts a number of NATO defensive operations, including Air Policing detachments of quick-reaction aircraft rotating from allied nations. And yet, according to Romania's Chief of Defence, the country is unable to shoot down Russian drones straying into Romanian airspace from their attacks on Ukraine not only because its armed forces have not been provided with the weapons systems to do so, but also because Romanian law prevents the armed forces from conducting "military operations" in peacetime – and for the time being, the law considers Romania to be at peace.[26]

Finland, Building on Firm Foundations

As we saw in the previous chapter, Finland presents the opposite case: laws are designed to facilitate national defence, rather than prevent it. But as with civil preparedness, Finland's conventional military defences benefit from long and consistent preparations.

Finnish defence planning and arms procurement decisions during Europe's "peacetime" reflected a sober appreciation that it was unlikely to last, and as a result Finland is far better prepared to mount a credible defence posture than any other European state of its size.[27] Finland maintained a strong artillery force throughout a period when this was considered outmoded by many other European militaries, but has now seen the decision vindicated by the crucial role played by artillery in combat in Ukraine. Recognition of the need for modern, capable defence air power drove major investment in placing an order in December 2021 for 64 F-35s, one of the largest fleets in Europe. The Finnish Air Force also invested early in long-range strike capabilities that have also proven invaluable in Ukraine. In the previous decade, Finland acquired precision-guided JDAM bombs, JSOW glide bombs, and JASSM missiles – comparable to the UK's Storm Shadow used to devastating effect by Ukraine – for its F/A-18 Hornet fleet of combat aircraft. And in 2020, the US approved sales to Finland of the JASSM-ER extended range variant, which can reach targets almost 1,000 km away as compared to JASSM's 370 km, to be integrated on its new F-35s.[28] And as well as investments in hardware, the Finnish

Air Force has worked hard to maintain operational capacity – including the ability to conduct dispersed operations for survival, in contrast to the UK and other NATO nations who as we saw in Chapter 4 concentrated their assets at a very small number of superbases. All this was despite cuts to Finland's defence budget of 10% in the period 2012–2015, with spending only restored to its previous level in 2022.

Another key lesson from Ukraine seen in previous chapters was the importance of a trained ready reserve of manpower to provide defence in depth. Here too Finland sets an example. The Finnish Defence Forces' conscription and reserve system should generate a wartime strength of 280,000 troops with an additional 870,000 reservists – in total, almost one-third of Finland's entire working-age population, both male and female. But even those not in formal military service have options for voluntary training in defence and national security. The National Defence Training Association, or *Maanpuolustuskoulutusyhdistys* (MPK), supports both the FDF and civil resilience by offering training and skills development in either military or security duties. The "security" side includes emergency preparedness and basic safety skills, like first aid, firefighting, search and rescue, and aid to the civil population such as evacuation, mass accommodation and provisioning.[29] About 50,000 citizens take part in the voluntary courses each year, and in 2023 the MPK hit a record high of 115,876 training days provided – which statistically translates to an average of over 300 Finns in voluntary defence training on every day of the year. The number of women taking part is steadily growing: in 2023 they numbered 14,600, or almost one-third of the total.[30]

As we saw in discussions of resilience in Chapter 6, Finland's defence in depth is fully backed up by capacity in its defence industries, also carefully protected during the years of notional peace. In late 2023, the Finnish government announced that it would invest over $130 million over the next three to four years to double the country's production of artillery and mortar ammunition.[31] Finland's Nammo munitions company is also receiving EU funds to boost production of shells and propellant.[32] The ability to scale up domestic production validates Finnish government decisions of almost a decade before, when the Vihtavuori munitions production plant in central Finland – now owned by Nammo – was threatened with closure but was recognised as a strategic asset.[33]

Thanks to long-term planning for security of supply, stockpiles of raw materials and production lines were ready to be put to use.[34] All this means that today, the country is on track to become one of the largest artillery producers in Europe, with the aim both of securing Finland's own stockpiles and maintaining capacity to support Ukraine for years to come. And as we saw in Chapter 6, Finland has also moved to activate wartime production reservation agreements, pre-established contracts with over 1,000 Finnish companies designed to ensure the supply of necessary goods and services for national defence during crises.[35]

Finland's defence posture thus rests on long-term and consistent planning and political consensus across parties and generations. What has changed, and suddenly, is the formalisation of defence alliances with other partners to augment Finland's traditional self-sufficiency. Finland held back from applying for NATO membership for decades: and then, after the full-scale invasion of Ukraine in February 2022, took just eighty-one days to upend years of consistent state policy and apply.

This was accompanied by a spectacular shift in public opinion. Since the 1990s, attitudes toward joining NATO reflected in polls had remained fairly stable, with only minor blips marking major events like Russia's war on Georgia in 2008, or its seizure of Crimea and the beginning of the war in eastern Ukraine in 2014. In part, that was because overall the pros and cons of full membership of the alliance had remained stable too, and were much the same in 2021 as when I had surveyed them for the UK Defence Academy in 2009.[36] Even as late as January 2022, a poll showed only 30% of Finns in favour of joining NATO.[37] This changed almost overnight after Russia's move on Ukraine demonstrated the threat to its neighbours beyond any doubt. In late February 2022, a poll showed 53% of Finns now in favour of applying for NATO membership.[38] Two weeks later the figure was already 62%.[39] Public debate also transformed radically: social science studies subsequently found that after the invasion, much of the strong, vocal and predominantly left-wing sector of society that had previously opposed NATO membership and been critical of the alliance simply shut up.[40]

Joining a military alliance is not the only long-held taboo that has been broken. The fact that NATO is at least in theory a nuclear alliance too is causing ongoing debate in Finland, where historically negative attitudes towards nuclear weapons are weighed against the way their utility as a guarantee of security has been fully demonstrated by both Ukraine's fate after abandoning them, and the effect of Russia's nuclear threats on coalition partners.[41] Incoming President Alexander Stubb started his new term in March 2024 with a very untraditional acknowledgement that Finland needs real nuclear deterrence for its security. While a discussion of that kind would have been practically impossible before February 2022, and there is still at present no intent to host nuclear weapons on Finnish territory, the current political leadership wants to make it clear that in Finland's new situation no means of protecting the nation's security should be ruled out.

That is just one aspect of recognising the US as the primary security provider for NATO. Already in the previous decade, far-sighted Finnish defence analysts were describing how US forces could be introduced as a security guarantor into the traditionally self-reliant Nordic military space.[42] In late 2023, both Finland and Sweden signed bilateral Defence Cooperation Agreements (DCA) with the US, similar to those already signed by other NATO member states across central Europe. The agreement opens fifteen defence sites in Finland to US troops; most of them in the west of the country, but two, the Karelia Brigade in Vekarajärvi and a Border Guard garrison in Ivalo, lying 100 km or less from the Russian border.[43]

Compared to dramatic developments with NATO and the US, the steady progress of Finland's cooperation with the UK-led JEF has been uncontroversial and far less prominent in Finnish domestic debate. Finland joined the JEF together with Sweden in 2017, with a clear understanding of its role as a "gap-filler" for dealing with situations that NATO, the EU or both felt lay outside their area of responsibility. As we saw in Chapter 5, with Finnish and Swedish accession to NATO the JEF no longer includes non-NATO members; but defence and security officials in both countries still see the organisation as a useful additional mechanism for activating international cooperation in the face of threats that might not trigger an effective or speedy response from NATO.

Finland's prioritisation of national readiness and defence comes at a cost. The country is still admired for its world-beating education system, welfare and healthcare provision.[44] But some Finns point to declining standards in all these areas in difficult economic conditions as indicators that their nation's enviable position, repeatedly designated "happiest country in the world", may not last.[45] Nevertheless, even with further tough spending cuts foreseen in other sectors, public support for defence preparations remains strong.[46] It is an indication that as in the other front-line states, strong defence is understood as a fundamental necessity rather than an option or a luxury.

Poland and Crash Rearmament

That recognition has also driven defence priorities in Poland. But Poland sets a different example to that of Finland. Rather than maintaining a stable system through peacetime, Poland like other countries further West de-prioritised defence of national territory during decades of peace and NATO "expeditionary" operations. But the country is now making up for lost time, pushing through an immensely ambitious programme of growing and rearming its armed forces with levels of investment that outstrip almost all NATO allies.

Poland's new government elected in October 2023 is continuing the defence investment plans of its predecessor, with a 2024 state budget and emergency fund totalling over 60 billion euro. And new orders for weapons and equipment continue to be signed, including with domestic producers. There is broad consensus in Polish politics about the need for defence spending, even though other issues remain deeply divisive. This includes political cooperation on defence between the new coalition government and Poland's president, aligned with the previously ruling party.[47]

That political consensus is largely replicated across society. Support for defence initiatives is strong, with polls showing 66% viewing increases in the size of the armed forces favourably, and other figures indicating high levels of motivation to defend the country.[48] Due to the professionalisation of the army since 2009, the percentage of men and women with any military experience at all is falling. In 2022, only 24% of those surveyed were currently or had ever been in military service, as against 39% in 1999. But polls show strong support for mandatory conscription (52% in favour in 2022, as compared to only 35% in 2008), with particularly strong backing for universal basic military and defence training from young people (88% among 18-24-year-olds).[49]

That public support will be essential for implementing current plans. Poland is aiming for a reserve force 4 million strong, and is on course to have more tanks in service than Britain, France, Germany and Italy combined.[50] At the end of 2022, the army had 166,000 soldiers, numbering in addition to professional servicemembers 31,000 full- and part-time volunteers in the WOT Territorial Defence Force, and 16,000 further short-service soldiers enlisted under the quirkily-named "Voluntary Compulsory Military Service" (DZSW) scheme.[51] But the 2024 state budget accounts for over 221,000 active-duty personnel across all services, and a substantial increase in the military pay bill. There has been a learning curve for Polish forces too. Like several of their NATO allies, they have had to retrain and redirect their efforts from peace support operations to full-scale warfighting – reportedly needing to relearn how to conduct offensive operations from scratch. But once again, early recognition of the threat meant that Poland had a head start: this process began in 2014, long before countries west of Warsaw awoke to the threat.[52]

Although a military modernisation programme was already under way in Poland, Russia launching a full-scale war against a neighbour kicked it into high gear. A Homeland Defence Act was already making its way onto the law books; but almost immediately after the Russian invasion it was substantially amended to cover crash rearmament. The ambition to spend 2.5% of GDP on defence by 2026 was replaced with 3% by 2023, and the size of the Polish Army was to be eventually doubled from 150,000 to 250,000 professional soldiers plus an additional 50,000 in the Territorial Defence Forces. The reserve system was to be overhauled, and a new provision for one-year voluntary basic military service introduced. Perhaps most significantly of all, the law laid the groundwork for paying for it all, with funds from a wide range of state and private sources going into a new Armed Forces Support Fund over and above the defence budget.[53]

But since then, defence spending has far outstripped even the 2022 plan. According to NATO figures, the Polish defence budget increased by a full 75 per cent between 2022 and 2023, from $16.6 billion to $29.1 billion.[54] That means that spending has hit 4.23% of Polish GDP – more than double the NATO target of 2%.

This political consensus on the urgency of rearmament has seen Poland's defence officials go on a spending spree around the world. European companies are competing to fill an order for submarines, announced in November 2023. But as well as weapons systems familiar to European militaries, including American Abrams tanks, Apache attack helicopters and Patriot missile launchers, major orders have been placed with South Korea. The numbers are on a completely different scale not only to Poland's smaller neighbours to the north and south, but even to notionally top-tier militaries like that of the UK. In 2022, Poland signed a framework agreement for purchasing 1,000 K2 main battle tanks and 672 K9 self-propelled guns from South Korea, to add to its existing inventory and equipment sourced in the US. The figure for that tank order alone is more than seven times as many as the total number of overhauled Challenger 3 tanks the UK eventually aims to have in service.[55]

In the air, the picture is the same. Poland had already ordered 32 F-35A fighters in 2020, with deliveries scheduled to start in 2025. Then, in September 2022, Poland purchased a total of 48 South Korean FA-50 light combat aircraft, with the first batch arriving in 2023.[56] Poland's Air Force is planning for further expansion, and the orders already placed for F-35s and FA-50s on top of the F-16s already in inventory leave room for additional future purchases.

Like Finland, Poland is investing further in capabilities that have proven their importance in combat in Ukraine. This includes large orders of the Pilica+, Narew and Wisła air defence systems for short to medium range and protection of mobile assets. In February 2024, Poland announced a purchase of almost 500 HIMARS launchers, at a total cost of $10 billion.[57] Then in March the same year, while President Andrzej Duda and Prime Minister Donald Tusk were visiting the White House, the US announced approval of a further potentially huge additional package of weapons sales for Poland. This included over 1,000 air-to-air missiles, and more than 800 JASSM-ER missiles. While the numbers approved are a cap rather than a figure for confirmed delivery, they reflect Poland's ambition to overhaul its capacity to deliver long-range precision strikes after observing the critical importance of this capability for Ukraine. The number of JASSM-ER's approved are more than ten times the number of these missiles already in Polish inventory.[58]

And, like the Baltic states, Poland too has observed the effectiveness of fixed fortifications in the fighting in Ukraine and is now planning to spend billions of euro on defensive preparations on its eastern border. Officially titled "Tarcza Wschód" – "East Shield" – but nicknamed the "Tusk Line" by some Polish media after the current prime minister, the project will include new physical infrastructure, like bunkers, minefields and anti-tank obstacles, but also electronic elements such as satellite monitoring, thermal imaging cameras and anti-drone systems.[59]

Poland's government has argued that homegrown military production will boost its economy, as well as support the planned huge increases in the size of the armed forces.[60] Poland does produce weapons domestically like Krab howitzers, Piorun anti-aircraft missiles and Rosomak infantry vehicles, and is hoping that more Polish systems can be sold for construction under licence in other countries that may not have a developed arms industry of their own. The domestic defence industry has geared up across the board: explosives plants are reportedly operating at maximum capacity, the Lucznik factory in Radom is planning to produce up to 100,000 rifles per year, and the Huta Stalowa Wola facility producing howitzers and armoured personnel carriers expects to double its rate of deliveries in two years.[61] Poland also operates the last factory producing TNT, essential for filling artillery shells, in Europe or North America – which is itself an indication of how defence industries have atrophied across NATO.[62]

At the same time plans for boosting Poland's tank stocks by manufacturing Korean equipment locally have been moving slowly. As of early 2024 only 180 of the planned purchase of 1,000 K2 tanks had been fully contracted, to be delivered from Korea. The remainder, in a K2PL version adapted for Polish requirements, were to have been constructed in Poland along with K9PL self-propelled howitzers; but protracted negotiations over financing and technology transfer already threaten the 2026 start date for production planned by the previous government.[63]

Many of the details of the new defence contracts are, unsurprisingly, not public. That has led to concern over their implementation and affordability, especially after the plans for local production of Korean tanks have not progressed as swiftly as hoped.

Creating a special armed forces fund in addition to the core defence budget has allowed innovative approaches to funding some of the major purchases, including through syndicated loans from foreign banks.[64] But that hasn't dispelled doubts over the eventual financial impact of the rearmament programme, or the urgency of spending on arms sometimes outpacing long-term planning. In February 2024, the incoming defence ministry team found that the previous government had awarded over 500 contracts as urgent operational requirements, meaning they were not subjected to tenders or competition. This also meant they had not gone through the normal full pre-purchase analysis process, which contributed to a number of "ad hoc" purchases of equipment without providing for the essential infrastructure and training facilities for personnel in order to actually use it. Commentators also point to attempts at depoliticisation of military affairs compared to the previous government, which was more inclined to exploit the armed forces for domestic political point-scoring.[65]

Critics, including within the military, suggest that purchases of front-line weaponry haven't been accompanied by the development of logistics and other enablers to ensure they are supported and remain functional. Urgent tank procurement has led to Poland operating a mixed fleet of German Leopard 2s, US M1A2s, Korean K2s, and indigenous PT-91s (a Polish upgrade to Soviet T-72s), leading to concern among allies and partners that the wide range of different components required for maintenance will pose additional logistics challenges. Disjointed planning has meant that there is not enough personnel to man the equipment purchased, and low rates of pay are hampering the armed forces from recruiting and retaining enough people to hit the manpower targets set by the government.[66] Some major infrastructure projects, like overhauling airbases, have not been publicly costed at all.[67] And the problem isn't limited to the armed forces: Poland's Supreme Audit Office has also pointed out major deficiencies in regulations, budgeting, planning and logistics in preparing civil defence infrastructure.[68]

But for the current government and many Polish citizens, challenges identified in managing Poland's enormously ambitious programme of rapid expansion do not cast any doubt on its urgent and absolute necessity. The clarity and immediacy of the threat has overridden fiscal concerns: as put by Marcin Przydacz, a senior official in Poland's presidential chancellery, "Can we afford it? We have no other choice."[69]

Poland has recognised the urgency of action, and is being guided by acceptance that defence of the nation in war – or, ideally, avoiding war altogether through strong deterrence – at times has to take primacy over other concerns. Criticism of the rearmament drive on financial grounds tends to focus on the need to spend more efficiently, rather than not spend at all. There's a recognition that while fiscal prudence is important, it shouldn't be prioritised over the survival of the nation.

One by-product of Warsaw's prioritisation of defence is that Poland has comprehensively moved from being a security consumer within NATO at the time of joining to a security provider for the alliance; and supporters of its military transformation programme say it sets an example for NATO allies of what can and must be done. Like the Baltic states, Poland has the moral authority that comes with having been right about Russia, and its long-standing warnings vindicated.

All these factors, together with Poland's leaders being less traditionally reluctant than those of Finland to step into the limelight, mean that Poland has an important role to play in setting the pace for European defence. Poland has built on its reconciliation with the EU to mount a diplomatic offensive. Prime Minister Tusk and Foreign Minister Radosław Sikorski have been touring European capitals as well as hosting inbound visits from European leaders, all highlighting Poland's willingness to take a leading role among its EU and NATO partners.[70] As this book goes to press, it remains to be seen how effective this campaign will be – and what the result will be in terms of European resolve and defence capacity overall.

For that resolve and capacity to improve requires countries west of Warsaw to accept the responsibility to protect their own citizens, as Finland, Poland and other front-line states have done. Not every country can be Finland. It takes decades, and a distinctive shared historical experience, to form the kind of society and social attitudes that will foster the nature of national resilience that is deeply embedded there. But more countries can be Poland – they can recognise the scale and nature of the threat, and what is necessary to meet it, and then have the political courage to state what needs to be done to protect the freedoms we for now still enjoy.[71]

For now, Poland's proactive diplomatic campaign and leadership in prioritising conventional defence is matched by the EU actively seeking lessons from Finland in how to build national resilience, as we saw in Chapter 6. That provides both countries with a route to leadership by example, and to setting the pace and the standard for other European states that wish to take an interest in ensuring their survival in the face of the Russian threat. The simple fact is that if the remainder of Europe treated their national security in the way its easternmost members do, the continent would be vastly safer.

8

WHAT COMES NEXT?

"The key mental transformation that we need in order to tackle Russia as a threat is to understand that competition is endless."

Russia researcher Oscar Jonsson,
Stockholm, May 2021

"Whatever plans you have, make sure you can survive a surprise. Because you will be surprised."

Michael Malm, Swedish Defence Staff
Department of Total Defence,
Vilnius, February 2024

It may not be too late to save the way of life generations of Europeans have come to take for granted. The repetitive cycle of Russian history is still trending towards totalitarianism at home and even greater aggression and expansionism abroad, but in 2025, it may still be possible for European states to neutralise the threat – by backing Ukraine, as the front line in the broader conflict between Russia and the West, to hold fast and eliminate as much Russian military capability as possible;

and by finally taking an interest in their own defence while there is still something to defend, so that future Russian aggression continues to be deterred. This will be a hard sell to European voters unaccustomed to having to fund their own protection: but the alternative is vastly greater human and economic cost as Europe sleepwalks into catastrophe.

Russia's war on Ukraine, Iran's war against Israel and the West via its proxies, and the growing threats from North Korea and China all stem from the loose coalition of rogue states that pose a global threat to the interests of the West founded on peace and stability. That means the West should be thinking globally about how to deter and defeat that coalition, both individually and as a bloc. That requires the kind of international strategic organisation, coordination, cooperation and focus that won the Second World War for the Allies. Above all it needs the West to realise that the global contest it is in is one it needs to win if it is to continue to exist as we know it today. The lessons of history show clearly how to deal with the global challenges facing it; Europe needs a strategy rather than an inexhaustible supply of excuses.

The former commander of the US Army in Europe, Lt-Gen Ben Hodges, compares today's European vacillation with the decisive leadership and political courage shown during the Second World War. He points to the Arcadia conference in January 1942, when in response to three years of disastrous defeats for first the UK and then the US, the two countries' leaders planned for victory, and made the decision to defeat Germany first, despite the remoteness of that prospect at the time. By the 1943 Casablanca Conference, there was still little reason for optimism, but the Allies agreed on fighting on till the unconditional surrender of the Axis powers – even though the Allies were nowhere near yet strong enough even to consider forcing Germany to negotiations. And all of this was communicated clearly to populations at home, with a clear explanation of the disaster that would inevitably result from failure. The US passed laws allowing a reorganising of its economy to fight a war, including directing industry to shift production to weapons rather than consumer goods, and the UK bankrupted itself to pay for the output.

Sadly, in the Western Europe of the twenty-first century, honesty about how much protecting a country's freedom against a determined invader actually costs doesn't win elections. And that will be a key determinant of whether Western European leaders possess the political courage required to act decisively in the face of the Russian threat. For the time being, most political leaders west of Warsaw have done an exceptionally poor job of explaining to their electorates what that entails – that huge reinvestment in defence and the industries supporting it is a matter of survival, and that people's lives will change as a result. As the US becomes increasingly focused on China, the defence of Europe will increasingly rely on those states that understand the threat and are willing to take it seriously. After decades when it could pretend to itself that military threats were a thing of the past, the rest of Europe needs urgently to realise that the cost of defence is not an optional luxury. Instead, it is the price that must be paid for sharing a continent with Russia.

As we saw in previous chapters, the task of European states in protecting themselves and their citizens remains the same with any plausible future Russia: it is to reduce to a minimum Russia's ability to cause harm. And that means adopting the whole-of-society defensive approach demonstrated by front-line states like Finland, including possessing credible military force and being visibly ready to use it. The clear understanding of that fact alone means that an eastward shift in the centre of gravity of leadership in Europe is overdue. That would help bring about a much deeper change of mindset on how to deal with Russia than is evident across the rest of the continent to date. And with the US increasingly out of the picture as the leader of a coalition of the unwilling, there is an opportunity for others to step up. Front-line states like Poland, acutely aware of the existential nature of the threat, can take a greater role in changing how the West as a whole approaches the conflict – not just in open combat in Ukraine, but in the wider war Russia is waging on the global system that has kept Europe safe for decades.

Above all it is vital that Russia does not once again convince itself that the time is right to attack. In late 2021 the combination of Russian confidence in its own capability and in the unwillingness of the West to oppose it set the context for the full-scale invasion of February 2022. In some ways there is a limit to what Western powers can do to influence that confidence. Sound decision-making in Moscow is hostage to the accuracy of information reaching Putin. Russian action in February 2022 was based on a fundamental misreading of the situation, and this could happen again. For instance, Russia tends to exaggerate its military power. If Russian military leaders do so in briefings to Vladimir Putin, including for example by concealing the scale of losses suffered by the Russian army and exaggerating the number of new recruits, that may lead Putin once again to an entirely wrong appraisal of the likely outcome of Russia's next aggressive move. (Ironically, meanwhile, in 2024 pro-Russian commentators in the West are now emphasising the opposite – they stress how much the Russian army has been weakened, in order to bolster their arguments that Russia does not present a threat.)[1] In short, what matters is not Russia's strength or weakness as objectively measured, but as it is described to Putin by those he listens to: so false confidence can drive actions that are damaging for Russia as well as devastating for its victims.

But there are elements of that decision that the countries of Europe *can* influence. Russia goes to war when it believes it is the most effective way of achieving its political objectives. The task for the rest of the world is to convince Moscow that that is not the case. And that depends entirely on the speed and seriousness with which European countries rebuild their military forces - as well as the credibility that they will be used when required.

Now that Russia has made its choice to go down the route of aggression, others have a simple choice in how to respond: they can either aim to win the fight, or surrender. Like so much else, there is no excuse for being surprised. It was clear before the February 2022 invasion that since the West had made the decision not to protect Ukraine from Russia, it would face the same decision again when Russia made its next demands on its next victim.[2] And as we saw in Chapter 2, there is no plausible outcome to the war that does not require both ongoing support to Ukraine and massive reinvestment in Western countries' own defences. For now, Ukraine continues to give Europe a breathing space for that reinvestment to be made, and so provides the opportunity for European powers to assure long-term peace by being sufficiently strong to deter Russia from further attacks.

There's a saying about deterrence that is usually (mis)quoted as "*si vis pacem, para bellum*" – if you want peace, prepare for war. It's an overused truism, but it comes from a text by the late Roman military writer Vegetius that contains advice on the basic principles of deterrence that is relevant for dealing with Russia today. The passage concludes "No-one dares to challenge, no one dares to offend someone who understands that he is superior, if he fights."[3] Russia won't start a fight it knows it can't win. It follows that the only way to prevent war with Russia is to prepare sufficiently well for it – and make it plain that the preparations are ready to be put into practice, in order to leave no doubt as to the "if" in "if he fights". And that defence has to be convincingly ready to cope with more than the first week of fighting. The experience of Ukraine shows not only that deep reserves are needed, to increase the size of the military in wartime not by a small increment as in the case of the UK but by multiples, but also that civil preparedness is essential, and comprehensive defence is key to survival.

At the beginning of this book I wrote about the parallels between today and the late 1930s. Almost a century ago, it was failure to confront the aggressors in Europe at the right time that meant conflicts there eventually formed part of a global war at an immensely greater cost. Failure to act today is a choice – and one that can have consequences at least as important as action. Every day of that failure comes at a price, as choosing to ignore the threat increases the costs of dealing with it when it finally becomes unavoidable. And the longer Western leaders hesitate to bolster their defences and establish credible deterrence, the greater the risk becomes for the continent as a whole. It's a risk that could lead to a catastrophic miscalculation by Russia, with immense human cost as other countries suffer the destruction of cities and communities, and the lost and broken lives that Ukraine has already experienced alone for years. I also suggested in the introduction that some countries had already awoken and belied the "sleeping continent" part of the book's title. But those front-line states can't continue to carry passengers who are not pulling their weight in collective defence. That was a luxury that the United States could, grudgingly, afford; but a new era where Europe has to be ready to do without US support demands a new seriousness about what must be available to replace it.

Being ready to deter Russia is a race against time. There is, as there always has been, a way to buy more time; and that is to assist Ukraine in bringing about the destruction of the Russian military machine to the point where it is incapable of posing a realistic threat to Ukraine or to any other of its Western neighbours. That would show not only Russia, but its coalition backers North Korea, Iran and China that aggression led eventually to failure because of Western determination to ensure that it would not pay. And that, in turn, would make the entire world safer.

In fact the fundamental condition for peace and security in Europe is Russia being neutralised as a threat. Since it is impossible to achieve this by diplomatic or political means, the only remaining option is through military ones. That means a commitment to deterrence, more and more of which Europe will inevitably have to manage on its own (since China will continue to divert resources and distract attention even if the US remains in principle fully committed to Europe). There's no doubt that Europe, collectively, is more than capable of dealing with Russia if it develops the collective will to do so. But pointing to the massive differential between the size of Russia's economy and that of collective Europe is not a substitute for actually doing something. War is not a contest of GDP if – as now – only one side is actually using its GDP.

And it is a long-term commitment, perhaps an indefinite one. Rather than being a temporary problem, containing Moscow's ambition should be thought of in similar timescales to the last time it was taken seriously in Europe. That was the Cold War, where the levels of investment necessary to deter the Kremlin were kept up for over forty years after the end of the Second World War. That commitment reflected a different world, and a different understanding of the price that must be paid for peace; but it's an understanding that is vital today, as there can be no going back to the Europe of the day before 24 February 2022.

If action comes too late to avoid disaster, it will have been because of criminal complacency among our decision-makers. And if it has not begun by the time you are reading this book, then it is dangerously late. There has been a crescendo of warnings, but in many countries insufficient evidence that the highest political level has understood the scale of the threat, or tried to explain it to voters and the public. In 2008, Russia fought a shorter, smaller war against another neighbour, Georgia. The nature of the renewed challenge that Europe would face from Moscow was already clear enough to those who paid attention, and there was no shortage of attempts to raise the alarm. In a study predicting Russia's trajectory written shortly after the war with Georgia, we concluded: "History demonstrates the enormous cost of failing to recognise, and invest in containing, the danger posed by a European power which is turbulent, truculent, confident, and heavily armed."[4] That recognition and containment did not happen, and now sixteen years later we see the result.

For the moment, the cost to European states of ensuring that Russia is deterred is economic and political. But while it's expensive to do what's necessary for deterrence, it would be vastly more expensive to fight a war if deterrence fails. And for some, the cost would be existential. Investment in defence and resilience is an insurance policy. But it is the kind that ensures you have extra protection, like immobilisers on your car or stronger locks and burglar alarms on your home. And, perhaps uniquely, the more you invest in this insurance, the less likely the insured event is to happen. That's because as consistent experience shows, making yourself difficult for Russia to attack is the best way of reducing the likelihood that it will try. And in today's Europe, just as with insurance, those countries that have not invested in it will be those that pay the highest price.

NOTES

INTRODUCTION

1. Keir Giles, "Putin's speech harked back to Russia's empire – the threat doesn't stop at Ukraine", *The Guardian*, 22 February 2022, https://www.theguardian.com/commentisfree/2022/feb/22/putin-speech-russia-empire-threat-ukraine-moscow

2. "War a real threat and Europe not ready, warns Poland's Tusk", BBC News, 30 March 2024, https://www.bbc.co.uk/news/world-europe-68692195

3. "Chatham House Rule", Chatham House, undated, https://www.chathamhouse.org/about-us/chatham-house-rule

4. Arne Delfs, "German Defense Chief Compares Putin to Hitler at Churchill Event", Bloomberg, 11 April 2024, https://www.bloomberg.com/news/articles/2024-04-11/german-defense-chief-compares-putin-to-hitler-at-churchill-event

5. Dan Sabbagh, "UK and its allies face 'deadly quartet' of nations, says defence expert", *The Guardian*, 16 July 2024, https://www.theguardian.com/politics/article/2024/jul/16/uk-and-its-allies-face-deadly-quartet-of-nations-says-defence-expert

6. Will Cain quoting David Sacks on Twitter, 23 April 2024, https://twitter.com/willcain/status/1782900445809131543

7. Poppy Koronka, "British public 'could be called up to fight in war against Russia'", *The Times*, 24 January 2024, https://www.thetimes.co.uk/article/british-public-could-be-called-to-fight-in-war-against-russia-wh75q6jj5

8. "Europe can no longer count on America's security umbrella", *Financial Times*, 12 February 2024, https://www.ft.com/content/171e136f-a5f2-47d8-8f3c-0eae3a8dbd74

9. Daniela Schwarzer, Opinion: "Will Europe ever get serious about defense?", *Kyiv Independent*, 21 February 2024, https://kyivindependent.com/opinion-will-europe-ever-get-serious-about-defense

10. Nicholas Vinocur, "Why The West Is Losing Ukraine", Politico, 21 February 2024, https://www.politico.eu/article/ukraine-war-russia-why-west-is-losing/

11. Anna Wieslander, "What I heard in Munich: Europe gets a brutal awakening", Atlantic Council, 21 February 2024, https://www.atlanticcouncil.org/blogs/new-atlanticist/what-i-heard-in-munich-europe-gets-a-brutal-awakening/

1. RUSSIA'S NEXT WAR

1. For one such minority view, see Keir Giles, "The west has a duty to help defend Ukraine – and to help Russia by ensuring its defeat", *The Guardian*, 25 February 2022, https://www.theguardian.com/commentisfree/2022/feb/25/ukraine-russia-defeat-military-putin

2. Taras Kuzio, "How Western Experts Got the Ukraine War So Wrong", *Geopolitical Monitor*, 14 November 2022, https://www.geopoliticalmonitor.com/how-western-experts-got-the-ukraine-war-so-wrong/

3. Richard Kemp, "A total Russian collapse is surprisingly close", *The Telegraph*, 28 February 2023, https://www.telegraph.co.uk/news/2023/02/28/total-russian-collapse-surprisingly-close/

4. Amy Mackinnon, "Russia's Military Is Already Preparing for Its Next War", *Foreign Policy*, 14 March 2024, https://foreignpolicy.com/2024/03/14/russia-military-war-nato-estonia-intelligence/

5. General Christopher G. Cavoli, "Statement of General Christopher G. Cavoli, United States Army, United States European Command", United States House Armed Services Committee, 10 April 2024, https://armedservices.house.gov/sites/evo-subsites/republicans-armedservices.house.gov/files/USEUCOM%20GEN%20Cavoli%20CPS_HASC_2024.pdf

6. Tweet by UK Ministry of Defence, 30 December 2023, https://x.com/defencehq/status/1741026561258573901

7. Matthew Loh, "Russia's military is 'almost completely reconstituted' as it goes into overdrive to shore up losses in Ukraine: US official", *Business Insider*, 4 April 2024, https://www.businessinsider.com/russia-military-almost-completely-reconstituted-after-ukraine-losses-us-official-2024-4

8. Murray Brewster, "Ravaged by war, Russia's army is rebuilding with surprising speed", CBC News, 23 February 2024, https://www.cbc.ca/news/politics/russia-army-ukraine-war-1.7122808

9. Dara Massicot, "Russian Military Wartime Personnel Recruiting and Retention 2022–2023", RAND, 16 July 2024, https://www.rand.org/pubs/research_reports/RRA2061-4.html

10. Maria Snegovaya et al., "Back in Stock? The State of Russia's Defense Industry after Two Years of the War", CSIS, 22 April 2024, https://www.csis. org/analysis/back-stock-state-russias-defense-industry-after-two-years-war

11. Jahara Matisek et al., "What Does European Union Advising of Ukrainian Troops Mean for the Bloc's Security Policies? An Inside Look at the Training Mission", Modern War Institute, 11 June 2024, https://mwi.westpoint.edu/ what-does-european-union-advising-of-ukrainian-troops-mean-for-the-blocs-security-policies-an-inside-look-at-the-training-mission/

12. Andrew Kramer et al., "Motorcycles and Mayhem in Ukraine's East", *The New York Times*, 29 June 2024, https://www.nytimes.com/2024/06/29/ world/europe/ukraine-russia-war-donbas.html

13. Isabelle Khurshudyan and Alex Horton, "Russian jamming leaves some high-tech U.S. weapons ineffective in Ukraine", *The Washington Post*, 24 May 2024, https://www.washingtonpost.com/world/2024/05/24/russia-jamming-us-weapons-ukraine/

14. Mathieu Boulegue et al., "Assessing Russian plans for military regeneration: Modernization and reconstitution challenges for Moscow's war machine", Chatham House, 9 July 2024, https://www.chathamhouse.org/2024/07/ assessing-russian-plans-military-regeneration

15. General Christopher G. Cavoli, "Statement of General Christopher G. Cavoli, United States Army, United States European Command", United States House Armed Services Committee, 10 April 2024, https://armedservices. house.gov/sites/evo-subsites/republicans-armedservices.house.gov/files/ USEUCOM%20GEN%20Cavoli%20CPS_HASC_2024.pdf

16. "Foreign Intelligence Service: Russia's offensive capabilities near Estonia to increase", ERR, 13 February 2024, https://news.err.ee/1609251780/foreign-intelligence-service-russia-s-offensive-capabilities-near-estonia-to-increase "Annual Threat Assessment Of The U.S. Intelligence Community", Office of the Director of National Intelligence, 5 February 2024, https://www.dni.gov/ files/ODNI/documents/assessments/ATA-2024-Unclassified-Report.pdf

17. Noah Robertson, "'They've grown back': How Russia surprised the West and rebuilt its force", DefenseNews, 21 May 2024, https://www.defensenews. com/global/europe/2024/05/21/theyve-grown-back-how-russia-surprised-the-west-and-rebuilt-its-force/

18. Dmitriy Nekrasov, "Сколько российская экономика сможет выдерживать войну" (How long can the Russian economy survive the war), iStories, 5 June 2024, https://istories.media/opinions/2024/06/05/skolko-rossiiskaya-ekonomika-smozhet-viderzhivat-voinu/

19. Denis Kasyanchuk, "«Никакой успешной экономики без успешной армии не бывает». О чем говорили участники главной экономической сессии на

ПМЭФ" ("There can be no successful economy without a successful army." What the participants of the main economic session at SPIEF talked about), The Bell, 6 June 2024, https://thebell.io/nikakoy-uspeshnoy-ekonomiki-bez-uspeshnoy-armii-ne-byvaet-o-chem-govorili-uchastniki-glavnoy-ekonomicheskoy-sessii-na-pmef

20. Roland Oliphant et al., "From scones to drones: inside Putin's arms race that is leaving the West behind", The Telegraph, 26 January 2024, https://www.telegraph.co.uk/world-news/2024/01/26/russia-arming-itself-faster-than-nato/

21. Georgi Kantchev, "Russia's Economy Goes All In on War", The Wall Street Journal, 6 October 2023, https://www.wsj.com/world/russia/putin-redirects-russias-economy-to-war-production-1e14265f

22. Jack Watling and Nick Reynolds, "Russian Military Objectives and Capacity in Ukraine Through 2024", RUSI, 13 February 2024, https://www.rusi.org/explore-our-research/publications/commentary/russian-military-objectives-and-capacity-ukraine-through-2024

23. Oleg Itskhoki, "США могли бы задушить Россию. Почему они этого не делают?" (The US could throttle Russia. Why doesn't it?), iStories, 16 January 2024, https://istories.media/opinions/2024/01/16/ssha-mogli-bi-zadushit-rossiyu-pochemu-oni-etogo-ne-delayut/
Anders Åslund, "How to Kill Russia's Oil Economy", The National Interest, 29 January 2024, https://nationalinterest.org/feature/how-kill-russia%E2%80%99s-oil-economy-208937

24. Jim Tankersley and Alan Rappeport, "New Plan to Target Russia's Oil Revenue Brings Debate in White House", The New York Times, 7 July 2024, https://www.nytimes.com/2024/07/07/us/politics/russia-oil-ukraine-shadow-fleet.html

25. Andrew Rettman, "EU billions still flowing to Russia, diplomatic notes detail", EUobserver, 22 May 2024, https://euobserver.com/EU%20&%20the%20World/ar8a2a0b61
Wester van Gaal, "EU paid Russia €420-per-capita for fossil fuels since war began", EUobserver, 23 February 2024, https://euobserver.com./world/158128

26. Nigel Gould-Davies, "Ukraine: the balance of resources and the balance of resolve", IISS, 26 February 2024, https://www.iiss.org/online-analysis/online-analysis/2024/02/ukraine-the-balance-of-resources-and-the-balance-of-resolve/

27. Michael Race, "Russian oil getting into UK via refinery loophole, reports claim", BBC News, 5 February 2024, https://www.bbc.co.uk/news/business-68018660

28. Will Dunn, "Revealed: how the City of London keeps Putin's oil flowing", *New Statesman*, 20 January 2024, https://www.newstatesman.com/the-weekend-report/2024/01/revealed-city-of-london-vladimir-putin-oil

29. Ian Talley and Brett Forrest, "Russia Doubled Imports of an Explosives Ingredient—With Western Help", *Wall Street Journal*, 29 March 2024, https://www.wsj.com/world/russia-doubled-imports-of-an-explosives-ingredientwith-western-help-fd8d18bc

30. Andrei Kolesnikov, "How Russians Learned to Stop Worrying and Love the War", Foreign Affairs, 1 February 2023, https://www.foreignaffairs.com/ukraine/how-russians-learned-stop-worrying-and-love-war

31. Jack Watling, "Russia Through the Kremlin's Eyes", RUSI, 27 January 2023, https://rusi.org/explore-our-research/publications/commentary/russia-through-kremlins-eyes

32. Michael Kimmage and Maria Lipman, "Will Russia's Break With the West Be Permanent?", *Foreign Affairs*, 19 June 2023, https://www.foreignaffairs.com/united-states/putin-will-russia-break-west-be-permanent-kimmage

33. Tatiana Stanovaya, "Russia's Pro-Putin Elites: How the Dictator Recruited Them to His Anti-Western Agenda", *Foreign Affairs*, 9 May 2024, https://www.foreignaffairs.com/russia/russias-pro-putin-elites

34. Astolphe de Custine, *Lettres de Russie: La Russie en 1839*, edited by Pierre Nora, Gallimard, Paris, 1975, p. 57.

35. Anastasia Edel, "Why Russia Is Happy at War", *The Atlantic*, 9 June 2024, https://www.theatlantic.com/international/archive/2024/06/russia-vladimir-putin-war-imperialism/678625/

36. Sergio Miller, "It's official – Russia is a dictatorship", Wavell Room, 25 January 2023, https://wavellroom.com/2023/01/25/its-official-russia-is-a-dictatorship/

37. Liana Fix and Maria Snegovaya, "Leadership Change in Russia", Council on Foreign Relations, 15 February 2024, https://www.cfr.org/report/leadership-change-russia

38. "Opening Remarks by Secretary of Defense Lloyd J. Austin III at the 20th Ukraine Defense Contact Group", Ramstein Air Base, Germany, 19 March 2024, available at https://www.defense.gov/News/Speeches/Speech/Article/3710899/opening-remarks-by-secretary-of-defense-lloyd-j-austin-iii-at-the-20th-ukraine/

39. Steen A. Jørgenssen, "Ny trusselsvurdering fra FE: »Meget sandsynligt«, at Rusland vil bruge militære midler til at udfordre Nato" (New threat assessment from FE: "Very likely" that Russia will use military means to challenge NATO), *Jyllands-Posten*, 4 February 2024, https://jyllands-posten.

dk/indland/ECE16816399/ny-trusselsvurdering-fra-fe-meget-sandsynligt-at-rusland-vil-bruge-militaere-midler-til-at-udfordre-nato/

40. Steven Erlanger and David E. Sanger, "Germany Braces for Decades of Confrontation With Russia", *The New York Times*, 3 February 2024, https://www.nytimes.com/2024/02/03/world/europe/germany-russia.html

41. Nikolaj Nielsen, "Russia may attack Baltic nations after Ukraine, says Lithuania", *EUobserver*, 22 January 2024, https://euobserver.com/ukraine/157958

42. Sky News, 26 January 2024, available at https://www.facebook.com/watch/?v=1451047159155128

43. Lisa Aronsson and John Deni, "Agile and Adaptable: U.S. and NATO Approaches to Russia's Short-Term Military Potential", CSIS, September 2023, https://www.csis.org/analysis/agile-and-adaptable-us-and-nato-approaches-russias-short-term-military-potential

44. Joe Barnes, Matt Oliver and Henry Samuel, "Nato warns of all-out war with Russia in next 20 years", *The Telegraph*, 18 January 2024, https://www.telegraph.co.uk/world-news/2024/01/18/nato-warns-of-war-with-russia-putin-next-20-years-ukraine/

45. "Germany's highest officer demands 'In five years we have to be ready for war'", *Bild*, 10 February 2024, https://www.bild.de/politik/inland/news-ausland/bundeswehr-in-fuenf-jahren-muessen-wir-kriegstuechtig-sein-87105600.bild.html

46. Jerome Starkey and Ellie Doughty, "STARK WARNING Britain facing wars in Russia, China, Iran & North Korea in five years – as world in 'pre-war' phase, warns Grant Shapps", *The Sun*, 15 January 2024, https://www.thesun.co.uk/news/25372068/grant-shapps-grow-army-ww3-threat/

47. "Polish security chief: NATO Eastern Flank states have 3 years to prepare for Russia attack", ERR, 3 December 2023, https://news.err.ee/1609183456/polish-security-chief-nato-eastern-flank-states-have-3-years-to-prepare-for-russia-attack

48. "Eirik Kristoffersen: - Vi har dårlig tid", *Dagbladet*, 21 January 2024, https://www.dagbladet.no/nyheter/vi-har-darlig-tid/80855200

49. Viljar Lubi, Ivita Burmistre and Lina Zigmantaite, "Our Baltic states are on Europe's new frontline. Nato and Britain must step up", *The Telegraph*, 30 March 2024, https://www.telegraph.co.uk/news/2024/03/30/baltic-states-on-europes-new-frontline-nato-britain

50. Jette Elbæk Maressa, "Ny viden får forsvarsministeren til at advare om, at Nato risikerer russisk angreb", *Jyllands-Posten*, 9 February 2024, https://jyllands-posten.dk/politik/ECE16831303/ny-viden-faar-forsvarsministeren-til-at-advare-om-at-nato-risikerer-russisk-angreb/

51. Ott Tammik, "Russian Ability to Sustain War Was Underestimated, Says

Estonia General", Bloomberg, 24 January 2024, https://www.bloomberg.com/news/articles/2024-01-24/russian-ability-to-sustain-war-was-underestimated-says-general

52. "France boosts military spending amid war in Ukraine", AP, 4 April 2023, https://apnews.com/article/france-boosts-military-spending-amid-ukraine-war-db213e964b2ff26f3d87e7a4a3ba0cdc

53. "Address by the President of the Russian Federation", Russian presidential website, 21 February 2022, http://kremlin.ru/events/president/news/67828

54. Paul Goble, "Putin teaches geography: 'All the former USSR is Russia'", *EuroMaidan Press*, 28 April 2015, https://euromaidanpress.com/2015/04/28/putin-gives-the-world-his-geography-lesson-all-the-former-ussr-is-russia/

55. "ANALYSIS: Russian Orthodox Church Hails Moscow's Imperialist Expansionism as a 'Holy War'", *Kyiv Post*, 30 March 2024, https://www.kyivpost.com/analysis/30315

56. James Sherr, "The Dangers of an Undefeated Russia", National Institute for Strategic Studies, 17 August 2022, https://niss.gov.ua/en/news/articles/dangers-undefeated-russia

57. David Albright et al., "Alabuga's Greatly Expanded Production Rate of Shahed 136 Drones", Institute for Science and International Security, 10 May 2024, https://isis-online.org/isis-reports/detail/alabugas-greatly-expanded-production-rate-of-shahed-136-drones/

58. Joe Saballa, "US Monitoring Potential Deployment of N. Korean Troops in Ukraine", The Defense Post, 27 June 2024, https://www.thedefensepost.com/2024/06/27/us-korean-troops-ukraine/

59. "Russia's vast stocks of Soviet-era weaponry are running out", *The Economist*, 16 July 2024, https://www.economist.com/europe/2024/07/16/russias-vast-stocks-of-soviet-era-weaponry-are-running-out

60. Andrew Monaghan, "The Future of Russian Military Power", RUSI, 21 July 2023, https://www.rusi.org/explore-our-research/publications/rusi-newsbrief/future-russian-military-power

61. Eugene Rumer and Andrew S. Weiss, "It's Time to End Magical Thinking About Russia's Defeat", *The Wall Street Journal*, 16 November 2023, https://www.wsj.com/world/russia/its-time-to-end-magical-thinking-about-russias-defeat-f6d0b8de

62. Nate Ostiller, "Stoltenberg: West must be prepared for 'decades-long confrontation' with Russia", *The Kyiv Independent*, 10 February 2024, https://kyivindependent.com/stoltenberg-west-must-be-prepared-for-decades-long-confrontation-with-russia/

63. As detailed in Keir Giles, "What Deters Russia", Chatham House, September 2021, https://www.chathamhouse.org/2021/09/what-deters-russia

64. Abbey Fenbert, "Estonian PM: Russia provoked by weakness, not strength", Kyiv Independent, 12 February 2024, https://kyivindependent.com/estonian-pm-russia-provoked-by-weakness-not-strength/
65. Keir Giles, "What Deters Russia", Chatham House, September 2021, https://www.chathamhouse.org/2021/09/what-deters-russia

2. THE FUTURE OF UKRAINE AND THE FUTURE OF EUROPE

1. Keir Giles, "What Deters Russia", Chatham House, September 2021, https://www.chathamhouse.org/2021/09/what-deters-russia
2. Jack Watling, "The War in Ukraine Is Not a Stalemate", *Foreign Affairs*, 3 January 2024, https://www.foreignaffairs.com/ukraine/war-ukraine-not-stalemate
3. Henry Foy, Felicia Schwartz and Christopher Miller, "Ukraine faces 'gap in the hose' as western ammunition dries up", *Financial Times*, 9 February 2024, https://www.ft.com/content/6594e548-8b2e-4c95-a589-7d9e358062d2
Jack Watling, "The Peril of Ukraine's Ammo Shortage", *Time*, 19 February 2024, https://time.com/6694885/ukraine-russia-ammunition/
4. Olaf Scholz, Mette Frederiksen, Petr Fiala, Kaja Kallas and Mark Rutte, "Letter: Call for a collective effort to arm Ukraine for the long term", *Financial Times*, 31 January 2024, https://www.ft.com/content/0d24aade-7701-4298-89ff-2843a47466c5
5. Tom Nicholson, "Slovakia enables arms exports to Ukraine as Fico completes backflip". Politico, 16 January 2024, https://www.politico.eu/article/in-post-election-reversal-slovakia-enables-weapons-exports-to-ukrainef-fico/
6. Emily Rauhala and Mary Ilyushina, "Hungarian leader Viktor Orban visits Moscow, angering E.U. allies", *The Washington Post*, 5 July 2024, https://www.washingtonpost.com/world/2024/07/05/viktor-orban-russia-putin-eu/
7. Andrew E. Kramer, "Ukraine Strained by Stalled Aid in War Against Russia", *The New York Times*, 31 January 2024, https://www.nytimes.com/2024/01/31/world/europe/ukraine-economy-war.html
8. Jason Beaubien, "Screams from Russia's alleged torture basements still haunt Ukraine's Kherson", NPR, 18 November 2022, https://www.npr.org/2022/11/18/1137473863/ukraine-kherson-alleged-torture-russia
9. Julian Barnes et al., "Russian Casualties in Ukraine Mount, in a Brutal Style of Fighting", *The New York Times*, 27 June 2024, https://www.nytimes.com/2024/06/27/us/politics/russia-casualties-ukraine-war.html
10. "What Is Zelenskyy's 10-Point Peace Plan?", Ukrainian state website, 11 August 2023, https://war.ukraine.ua/faq/zelenskyys-10-point-peace-plan/
11. "Estonian PM urges Nato to bolster support for Ukraine", BBC News, 24 February 2024, https://www.bbc.co.uk/news/uk-68391780

12. Patrick Tucker, "Europe is already planning for what happens if Ukraine loses. It's ugly", Defense One, 12 April 2024, https://www.defenseone.com/threats/2024/04/europe-already-planning-what-happens-if-ukraine-loses-its-ugly/395715/

13. Elena Sánchez Nicolás, "Kallas: Russia's defeat crucial to avoid Third World War", EUObserver, 21 March 2024, https://euobserver.com/world/158259

14. Timothy Garton Ash, "Ukraine's fate, Europe's choice", *Prospect*, 24 January 2024, https://www.prospectmagazine.co.uk/world/europe/ukraine/64563/ukraines-fate-europes-choice

15. "H.R. McMaster Statement on Ukraine", Hudson Institute, 5 February 2024, https://www.hudson.org/foreign-policy/hr-mcmaster-statement-ukraine-aid-russia

16. "What happens if Ukraine loses?", *The Economist*, 11 April 2024, https://www.economist.com/europe/2024/04/11/what-happens-if-ukraine-loses

17. Sam Greene, "US Capitulation on Ukraine Will Bring Another War", CEPA, 14 February 2024, https://cepa.org/article/us-capitulation-on-ukraine-will-bring-another-war/

18. Sam Greene and Alina Polyakova, "Russia Wants a Long War", Foreign Affairs, 16 March 2023, https://www.foreignaffairs.com/united-states/russia-wants-long-war

19. "Full text of Japanese Prime Minister Kishida's speech to U.S. Congress", *Nikkei Asia*, 12 April 2024, https://asia.nikkei.com/Politics/International-relations/Full-text-of-Japanese-Prime-Minister-Kishida-s-speech-to-U.S.-Congress

20. Phillips P. O'Brien, "What Happens to Europe If America Withdraws?", *The Bulwark*, 24 January 2024, https://plus.thebulwark.com/p/what-happens-europe-after-america-ukraine

21. Keir Giles, "Russian nuclear intimidation: How Russia uses nuclear threats to shape Western responses to aggression", Chatham House, 29 March 2023, https://www.chathamhouse.org/2023/03/russian-nuclear-intimidation

22. Nataliya Bugayova et al., "Denying Russia's Only Strategy for Success", Institute for the Study of War, 27 March 2024, https://www.understandingwar.org/backgrounder/denying-russia%E2%80%99s-only-strategy-success

23. Bethan McKernan, "With bloodied gloves, forensic teams uncover gruesome secrets of Bucha in Ukraine", *The Guardian*, 9 April 2022, https://www.theguardian.com/world/2022/apr/09/with-bloodied-gloves-forensic-teams-uncover-gruesome-secrets-of-bucha-in-ukraine

24. Alexey Kovalev, "Russia's Ukraine Propaganda Has Turned Fully Genocidal", *Foreign Policy*, 9 April 2022, https://foreignpolicy.com/2022/04/09/russia-putin-propaganda-ukraine-war-crimes-atrocities/

25. "What happens if Ukraine loses?", *The Economist*, 11 April 2024.
26. Mark Galeotti, "The Minsk Accords: Should Britain declare them dead?", Council on Geostrategy, 24 May 2021, https://www.geostrategy.org.uk/britains-world/the-minsk-accords-should-britain-declare-them-dead/
27. Robbie Gramer and Jack Detsch, "Ukraine's Push to Join NATO Faces Roadblocks", *Foreign Policy*, 30 January 2024, https://foreignpolicy.com/2024/01/30/ukraine-nato-membership-delay-war-russia-alliance/
28. James Landale, "Sunak vows that Ukraine will never be alone as he pledges £2.5bn package", BBC News, 12 January 2024, https://www.bbc.co.uk/news/uk-67954152
29. Euheniia Martyniuk, "UK security deal with Ukraine: Budapest Memorandum 2.0 or road to NATO?", Euromaidan, 18 January 2024, https://euromaidanpress.com/2024/01/18/uk-security-deal-with-ukraine-budapest-memorandum-2-0-or-road-to-nato/
30. Michael Kofman, Rob Lee and Dara Massicot, "Hold, Build, and Strike: A Vision For Rebuilding Ukraine's Advantage in 2024", War On The Rocks, 26 January 2024, https://warontherocks.com/2024/01/hold-build-and-strike-a-vision-for-rebuilding-ukraines-advantage-in-2024/
    Franz-Stefan Gady and Michael Kofman, "Making Attrition Work: A Viable Theory of Victory for Ukraine", International Institute for Strategic Studies, *Survival Online*, 9 February 2024, https://www.iiss.org/online-analysis/survival-online/2024/01/making-attrition-work-a-viable-theory-of-victory-for-ukraine/
31. Keir Giles, "Russian cyber and information warfare in practice: Lessons observed from the war on Ukraine", Chatham House, 14 December 2023, https://www.chathamhouse.org/2023/12/russian-cyber-and-information-warfare-practice
32. Timothy Ash, "The Sky-High Costs of Abandoning Ukraine", CEPA, 23 October 2023, https://cepa.org/article/the-sky-high-costs-of-abandoning-ukraine/

3. AMERICA, DISTRACTED AND DIVIDED

1. Seth G. Jones et al., "Forward Defense: Strengthening U.S. Force Posture in Europe", CSIS, 11 March 2024, https://www.csis.org/analysis/forward-defense-strengthening-us-force-posture-europe
2. See for example Samuel Charap and Miranda Priebe, "Planning for the Aftermath: Assessing Options for U.S. Strategy Toward Russia After the Ukraine War", RAND, 9 February 2024, https://www.rand.org/pubs/research_reports/RRA2510-2.html
3. Max Colchester and Isabel Coles, "U.K. Boosts Military Aid to Ukraine

Amid U.S. Deadlock", *The Wall Street Journal*, 12 January 2024, https://www.wsj.com/world/europe/u-k-boosts-military-aid-to-ukraine-amid-u-s-deadlock-0523f356

4. Anthony Cordesman, "NATO and the Claim the U.S. Bears 70% of the Burden: A False and Dysfunctional Approach to Burdensharing", CSIS, 25 July 2018, https://www.csis.org/analysis/nato-and-claim-us-bears-70-burden-false-and-dysfunctional-approach-burdensharing "Assessing The Value Of The NATO Alliance", Hearing Before The Committee On Foreign Relations, United States Senate, 5 September 2018, https://www.govinfo.gov/content/pkg/CHRG-115shrg40165/html/CHRG-115shrg40165.htm

5. Richard Hooker, "Why NATO matters", Atlantic Council, 28 May 2024, https://www.atlanticcouncil.org/blogs/new-atlanticist/nato-us-interest-washington-summit/

6. Kathryn Levantovscaia, "Overstretched and undersupplied: Can the US afford its global security blanket?" Atlantic Council, 5 January 2024, https://www.atlanticcouncil.org/blogs/new-atlanticist/overstretched-and-undersupplied-can-the-us-afford-its-global-security-blanket/

7. Gregg Weaver and Andrea Kendall-Taylor, "What NATO allies must do to prepare for Russian aggression", Politico, 5 March 2024, https://www.politico.eu/article/nato-allies-prepare-russia-aggression-defense-military

8. Tod D. Wolters and Ann Marie Dailey, "Help Ukraine win—or risk kicking off a US losing streak", Atlantic Council, 15 March 2024, https://www.atlanticcouncil.org/blogs/new-atlanticist/help-ukraine-win-or-risk-kicking-off-a-us-losing-streak/

9. John Kampfner, "In Finland, the 'existential threat' of Russia looms - and US rescue is far from certain", *The Guardian*, 2 February 2024, https://www.theguardian.com/commentisfree/2024/feb/02/finland-russia-us-election-president-vladimir-putin-donald-trump

10. Stanley Sloan, "De-Trumping U.S. Foreign Policy: Can Biden Bring America Back?" (De Gruyter, 2021)

11. Speaking on CNN, 14 February 2024.

12. "Kaine & Rubio Applaud Senate Passage of Their Bipartisan Bill to Prevent Any U.S. President from Leaving NATO", Press Office for Senator Tim Kaine, 13 December 2023, https://www.kaine.senate.gov/press-releases/kaine-and-rubio-applaud-senate-passage-of-their-bipartisan-bill-to-prevent-any-us-president-from-leaving-nato

13. Michael Peck, "A wargame simulated a 2nd Trump presidency. It concluded NATO would collapse", *Business Insider*, 12 May 2024, https://www.businessinsider.com/a-wargame-simulated-a-2nd-trump-presidency-it-found-nato-would-collapse-2024-5

14. Hans Binnendijk et al., "NATO Cannot Survive Without America", Foreign Affairs, 13 May 2024, https://www.foreignaffairs.com/nato-cannot-survive-without-america

15. Ivo Daalder, "What another Trump presidency would mean for NATO", Politico, 25 January 2024, https://www.politico.eu/article/what-another-trump-presidency-would-mean-for-nato/

16. Marianne LeVine, "Trump says he'd disregard NATO treaty, urge Russian attacks on U.S. allies", *The Washington Post*, 10 February 2024, https://www.washingtonpost.com/politics/2024/02/10/trump-nato-allies-russia/

17. Ian Bond, "Europe and the US election: Hope for the best, prepare for the worst", Centre for European Reform, 22 January 2024, https://www.cer.eu/node/10724/view-email

18. Anne Applebaum, "Trump Will Abandon NATO", *The Atlantic*, 4 December 2023, https://www.theatlantic.com/magazine/archive/2024/01/trump-2024-reelection-pull-out-of-nato-membership/676120/

19. Moritz Koch, Martin Greive and Annett Meiritz, "Nato will Waffenhilfen an die Ukraine koordinieren", *Handelsblatt*, 9 February 2024, https://www.handelsblatt.com/politik/international/sicherheitspolitik-nato-will-waffenhilfen-an-die-ukraine-koordinieren/100013953.html

20. Stuart Lau, "NATO's Stoltenberg floats $100B, five-year fund for Ukraine", Politico, 2 April 2024, https://www.politico.eu/article/natos-stoltenberg-floats-100b-five-year-fund-for-ukraine/

21. Jonathan Karl, "'You're Telling Me That Thing Is Forged?': The Inside Story of How Trump's 'Body Guy' Tried and Failed to Order a Massive Military Withdrawal", *Vanity Fair*, 10 November 2023, https://www.vanityfair.com/news/2023/11/the-inside-story-of-how-trumps-body-guy-tried-to-order-a-massive-military-withdrawal

22. Isaac Arnsdorf, Nick Miroff and Josh Dawsey, "Trump and allies planning militarized mass deportations, detention camps", *The Washington Post*, https://www.washingtonpost.com/politics/2024/02/20/trump-mass-deportations-immigration/

23. Ann Marrimow, "Tossing Trump's case was risky for Judge Cannon — at least for now", *The Washington Post*, 20 July 2024, https://www.washingtonpost.com/politics/2024/07/20/cannon-trump-florida-appeal-special-counsel/

24. Meredith Deliso, "Hypothetical SEAL Team 6 political assassination resurfaces in Supreme Court presidential immunity dissent", ABC News, 1 July 2024, https://abcnews.go.com/Politics/seal-team-6-assassination-hypothetical-scotus-presidential-immunity/story?id=111583216

25. See for example tweet by Elbridge Colby, 18 April 2024, https://twitter.com/ElbridgeColby/status/1781056128840868202

26. Jaushieh Joseph Wu, "Defending Taiwan by Defending Ukraine: The Interconnected Fates of the World's Democracies", *Foreign Affairs*, 9 May 2024, https://www.foreignaffairs.com/china/defending-taiwan-ukraine-jaushieh-joseph-wu

27. Tweet by Elbridge Colby, 11 May 2024, https://twitter.com/elbridgecolby/status/1789298751359607235

28. Tweet by Elbridge Colby, 17 April 2024, https://twitter.com/elbridgecolby/status/1780411386532594167

29. Jacob Heilbrunn, "Elbridge Colby Wants to Finish What Donald Trump Started", Politico, 11 April 2023, https://www.politico.com/news/magazine/2023/04/11/tucker-carlson-eldridge-colby-00090211

30. Isabel van Brugen, "Russian TV Celebrates Trump's Project 2025 Ally: 'Don't Need Ukraine'", *Newsweek*, 5 July 2024, https://www.newsweek.com/russia-state-tv-trump-project-2025-elbridge-colby-1921462

31. Thomas Kika, "Donald Trump's Taiwan Remarks Spark Fury and Concern", *Newsweek,* 22 January 2024, https://www.newsweek.com/donald-trumps-taiwan-remarks-spark-fury-concern-1862602

32. Phil Stewart, "Trump asked China to help him win in 2020, offered 'favors to dictators,' Bolton says", Reuters, 18 June 2020, https://www.reuters.com/article/idUSKBN23P054/

33. A collection of previous Vance commentary arguing against supporting Ukraine against Russia is available in a Twitter thread by Ostap Yarysh, 16 July 2024, https://x.com/ostapyarysh/status/1813071501710467325

34. "Russian state TV is giddy about JD Vance as the VP", Russian Media Monitor, 17 July 2024, https://www.youtube.com/watch?v=jty49i_ZglY
"Russia's Lavrov welcomes Vance stance on Ukraine amid European concern", Reuters, 17 July 2024. https://www.reuters.com/world/russia-ready-work-with-any-us-leader-says-lavrov-2024-07-17/

35. Jada Yuan, "Inside the battle to release controversial Trump movie 'The Apprentice'", *The Washington Post*, 25 June 2024, https://www.washingtonpost.com/entertainment/movies/2024/06/25/donald-trump-movie-the-apprentice-release/

36. Michael Sisak et al., "Guilty: Trump becomes first former US president convicted of felony crimes", AP, 31 May 2024, https://apnews.com/article/trump-trial-deliberations-jury-testimony-verdict-85558c6d08efb434d05b694364470aa0

37. Jonathan V. Last, "The New York Times Is Part of the Effing Problem", *The Bulwark*, 18 December 2023, https://plus.thebulwark.com/p/the-new-york-times-is-part-of-the

38. Ishan Tharoor, "Ukraine's hopes for victory over Russia are slipping away",

The Washington Post, 29 January 2024, https://www.washingtonpost.com/world/2024/01/29/ukraine-victory-russia-defeat-hopes/

39. "David Cameron seemingly fails in bid to persuade Trump on Ukraine aid", *The Guardian*, 9 April 2024, https://www.theguardian.com/politics/2024/apr/09/david-cameron-trump-ukraine-aid

40. Dan Mangan and Kevin Breuninger, "Trump administration broke law in withholding Ukraine aid, watchdog says as Senate prepares for impeachment trial", CNBC, 16 January 2020, https://www.cnbc.com/2020/01/16/trump-administration-broke-law-in-withholding-ukraine-aid.html

41. Speaking in Vilnius, Lithuania, February 2024.

42. As partially detailed in Alberto Nardelli and Julia Ioffe, "Trump Told G7 Leaders That Crimea Is Russian Because Everyone Speaks Russian In Crimea", Buzzfeed News, 14 June 2018, https://www.buzzfeednews.com/article/albertonardelli/trump-russia-crimea

43. Laura Barrón-López and Shrai Popat, "Informant in GOP's Biden investigation accused of lying and having ties to Russia", PBS News, 21 February 2024, https://www.pbs.org/newshour/show/informant-in-gops-biden-investigation-accused-of-lying-and-having-ties-to-russia

44. John Haltiwanger, "Trump is applauding Russia's victory in Syria after handing it to them on a platter", *Business Insider*, 15 October 2019, https://www.businessinsider.com/trump-applauds-russia-victory-syria-handing-platter-2019-10

45. Nina Jankowicz, "The Coming Flood of Disinformation", *Foreign Affairs*, 7 February 2024, https://www.foreignaffairs.com/united-states/coming-flood-disinformation

46. As detailed at length in, for example, Timothy Snyder's *The Road to Unfreedom* (Bodley Head, 2018). For a summary, see Timothy Snyder on Twitter, 14 April 2019, https://twitter.com/timothydsnyder/status/1117433512863371267

47. "G.O.P.-Led Senate Panel Details Ties Between 2016 Trump Campaign and Russia", *The New York Times*, 18 August 2020, https://www.nytimes.com/2020/08/18/us/politics/senate-intelligence-russian-interference-report.html

48. Olivia Gazis and Robert Costa, "Documents from binder with intelligence on Russian election interference went missing at end of Trump's term", CBS News, 15 December 2023, https://www.cbsnews.com/news/documents-intelligence-russian-election-trump-missing-sources-say/

49. Anne Applebaum, "Why Is Trump Trying to Make Ukraine Lose?", *The Atlantic*, 29 February 2024, https://www.theatlantic.com/ideas/archive/2024/02/one-global-issue-trump-cares-about/677592/

50. Adam Taylor, "Trump's vague peace plan casts a shadow over Ukraine",

The Washington Post, 21 March 2024, https://www.washingtonpost.com/world/2024/03/21/trump-ukraine-russia-funding-peace-plan-aid-republican-future/

51. Peter Stone, "Putin bromance has US intelligence officials fearing second Trump term", *The Guardian*, 18 March 2024, https://www.theguardian.com/us-news/2024/mar/18/us-intelligence-trump-putin-threat

52. Anne Applebaum, "Is Congress Really Going to Abandon Ukraine Now?", *The Atlantic*, 27 January 2024, https://www.theatlantic.com/ideas/archive/2024/01/us-congress-support-ukraine-war/677256/

53. Doug Klain, "U.S. Funding Delay Is Hurting Ukraine", *Foreign Policy*, 15 March 2024, https://foreignpolicy.com/2024/03/15/russia-ukraine-war-offensive-ammunition-military-aid/

54. Colin Freeman, "Should this Ukrainian city fall to Russia, 'it will be America's fault'", *The Times*, 9 February 2024, https://www.telegraph.co.uk/world-news/2024/02/09/russia-closes-in-ukraine-city-west-supplies-falter/

55. Leo Chiu, "Washington Has Run Out of Money for Ukraine - US Defense Secretary", *Kyiv Post*, 25 January 2024, https://www.kyivpost.com/post/27170

56. Connor O'Brien and Joe Gould, "Critics say border bill would send $60B to Ukraine. Here's where it's really going", Politico, 6 February 2024, https://www.politico.com/news/2024/02/06/border-bill-ukraine-aid-military-00139870

57. "David Cameron: Pass Ukraine funding for the sake of global security", *The Hill*, 14 February 2024, https://thehill.com/opinion/international/4465907-david-cameron-pass-ukraine-funding-for-the-sake-of-global-security/

58. Anthony Salvanto et al., "How Ukraine aid views are shaped by Cold War memories, partisanship... and Donald Trump — CBS News poll", CBS News, 14 April 2024, https://www.cbsnews.com/news/ukraine-aid-cold-war-donald-trump-opinion-poll/

59. Ian Bond, "Europe and the US election: Hope for the best, prepare for the worst", Centre for European Reform, 22 January 2024, https://www.cer.eu/node/10724/view-email

60. Alexander Ward and Lara Seligman, "The US secretly sent long-range missiles to Ukraine — and Kyiv used them", Politico, 24 April 2024, https://www.politico.com/news/2024/04/24/us-long-range-missiles-ukraine-00154110

61. Siobhán O'Grady et al., "Ukraine, pumped up by Western weapons, is held back by slow deliveries", *The Washington Post*, 22 March 2023, https://www.washingtonpost.com/world/2023/03/22/ukraine-pumped-up-by-western-weapons-is-held-back-by-slow-deliveries/

62. Walter Landgraf, "'For as Long as it Takes': Putting US Aid to Ukraine into

Perspective", Foreign Policy Research Institute, 25 October 2023, https://www.fpri.org/article/2023/10/for-as-long-as-it-takes-putting-us-aid-to-ukraine-into-perspective/

63. "Military assistance to Ukraine since the Russian invasion", Research Briefing, House of Commons Library, 2 May 2024, https://commonslibrary.parliament.uk/research-briefings/cbp-9477/

64. See for example list of US statements compiled by Twitter user @Shchizointel, 11 April 2024, https://x.com/Schizointel/status/1778246108788977892

65. Michael Liebreich et al., "Why Ukraine Should Keep Striking Russian Oil Refineries", *Foreign Affairs*, 8 May 2024, https://www.foreignaffairs.com/ukraine/why-ukraine-should-keep-striking-russian-oil-refineries

66. Michael Weiss and James Rushton, "Ukraine Has Every Right To Hit Russians in Russia With US Weapons", *New Lines*, 24 May 2024, https://newlinesmag.com/argument/ukraine-has-every-right-to-hit-russians-in-russia-with-us-weapons/

67. Keir Giles, "Opinion: What would happen if the West stopped playing by Russia's rules?", CNN, 5 January 2024, https://edition.cnn.com/2024/01/05/opinions/rethink-west-response-putin-giles/index.html

68. Jack Detsch, "Russia Kharkiv Offensive Puts Ukrainian Troops in Retreat", *Foreign Policy*, 15 May 2024, https://foreignpolicy.com/2024/05/15/russia-kharkiv-offensive-ukraine-vovchansk-weapons-biden/

69. Dominic Lawson, "In spiking Kyiv's guns, Biden has given a gift to Putin", *The Times*, 26 May 2024, https://www.thetimes.co.uk/article/df863dab-b306-45ec-8255-2dbbd7046b20

70. Michael Birnbaum et al., "Ukraine can use U.S. weapons for limited strikes in Russia, Biden says", *The Washington Post*, 30 May 2024, https://www.washingtonpost.com/world/2024/05/30/nato-europe-us-weapons-ukraine-russia/

71. "Finland's President on refineries strikes: Russia only understands this language", RBC-Ukraine, 3 April 2024, https://newsukraine.rbc.ua/news/finland-s-president-on-refineries-strikes-1712147328.html

72. "Secretary Antony J. Blinken and French Foreign Minister Stéphane Séjourné at a Joint Press Availability", US Department of State, 2 April 2024, https://www.state.gov/secretary-antony-j-blinken-and-french-foreign-minister-stephane-sejourne-at-a-joint-press-availability/

73. John Paul Rathbone, "Ukraine to increase long-range strikes in Russia, says UK defence chief", *Financial Times*, 25 April 2024, https://www.ft.com/content/06a48bab-2eb6-4cc4-9d9f-e72a22ba5d7e

74. "Belgium Pledges $1 Billion In Military Aid, 30 F-16s For Ukraine", RFE/RL, 28 May 2024, https://www.rferl.org/a/32966513.html

75. Erin Banco et al., "How Biden got to a 'yes' on letting Ukraine hit inside Russia", Politico, 31 May 2024, https://www.politico.com/news/2024/05/31/biden-ukraine-kyiv-zelenskyy-00161082

76. Siobhán O'Grady et al., "U.S. restrictions put key Russian air bases out of firing range, officials say", *The Washington Post*, 21 June 2024, https://www.washingtonpost.com/world/2024/06/21/ukraine-firing-range-us-weapons-russia/

77. Rob Corp and Kyla Herrmannsen, "Children's hospital hit as Russian strikes kill dozens in Ukraine", BBC News, 8 July 2024, https://www.bbc.co.uk/news/articles/cl4y1pjk2dzo

78. "On-the-Record Press Gaggle by APNSA Jake Sullivan", The White House, 11 July 2024, https://www.whitehouse.gov/briefing-room/press-briefings/2024/07/11/on-the-record-press-gaggle-by-apnsa-jake-sullivan/

79. John Hudson, "U.S. floods arms into Israel despite mounting alarm over war's conduct", *The Washington Post*, 6 March 2024, https://www.washingtonpost.com/national-security/2024/03/06/us-weapons-israel-gaza/

80. John Hudson, "U.S. signs off on more bombs, warplanes for Israel", *The Washington Post*, 29 March 2024, https://www.washingtonpost.com/national-security/2024/03/29/us-weapons-israel-gaza-war/

81. "Statement from President Joe Biden on Coalition Strikes in Houthi-Controlled Areas in Yemen", The White House, 11 January 2024, https://www.whitehouse.gov/briefing-room/statements-releases/2024/01/11/statement-from-president-joe-biden-on-coalition-strikes-in-houthi-controlled-areas-in-yemen/

82. Eric Schmitt, "U.S. Expands Attacks on Houthis With New Strikes in Yemen", *The New York Times*, 22 January 2024, https://www.nytimes.com/2024/01/22/us/politics/houthi-yemen-strikes.html

83. Jeff Stein, "U.S. sanctions target Iran's drone production after attack on Israel", *The Washington Post*, 18 April 2024, https://www.washingtonpost.com/business/2024/04/18/iran-treasury-drone-sanctions/

84. Ishaan Tharoor, "Russia's deadly attacks see Ukraine call out a Western double standard", *The Washington Post*, 18 April 2024, https://www.washingtonpost.com//world/2024/04/18/ukraine-israel-defense-support-double-standard-west/

85. Dominic Lawson, "Does Biden actually want Ukraine to win?", *The Times*, 14 January 2024, https://www.thetimes.co.uk/article/nc14lawson-0f2ptrcc0

86. Martha McHardy, "'Putin will not break our resolve,' Joe Biden tells G7", *The Independent*, 21 May 2023, https://www.independent.co.uk/news/long_reads/world/g7-putin-biden-sunak-russia-ukraine-war-b2342922.html

87. Sam Greene and Alina Polyakova, "Russia Wants a Long War", *Foreign Affairs*,

16 March 2023, https://www.foreignaffairs.com/united-states/russia-wants-long-war

88. Oleksandr V Danylyuk, "What Ukraine's Defeat Would Mean for the US, Europe and the World", RUSI, 24 January 2024, https://www.rusi.org/explore-our-research/publications/commentary/what-ukraines-defeat-would-mean-us-europe-and-world

89. Catherine Belton, "Secret Russian foreign policy document urges action to weaken the U.S.", *The Washington Post*, 17 April 2024, https://www.washingtonpost.com/world/2024/04/17/russia-foreign-policy-us-weaken/

90. Catherine Belton and Joseph Menn, "Russian trolls target U.S. support for Ukraine, Kremlin documents show", *The Washington Post*, 8 April 2024, https://www.washingtonpost.com/world/2024/04/08/russia-propaganda-us-ukraine/

91. Alex Finley, "Russia Is Buying Politicians in Europe. Is It Happening Here Too?", *The New Republic*, 12 April 2024, https://newrepublic.com/article/180630/russia-corruption-network-europe-buying-politicians-america

92. For example "Amendment to Ukraine Security Supplemental Appropriations Act, 2024 Offered by Mrs. Greene of Georgia", US House of Representatives, 17 April 2024, https://amendments-rules.house.gov/amendments/GREENE_218_xml240417151911517.pdf
For a full list, see "H.R. 8035 - Ukraine Security Supplemental Appropriations Act, 2024", House Committee on Rules, undated, https://rules.house.gov/bill/118/hr-8035

93. Text of amendment available at https://amendments-rules.house.gov/amendments/ethnic%20minorities%20amendment240418131602176.pdf

94. Jason Jay Smart and Hether Beck, "Is a Leading Ukraine Skeptic Influencing White House Policy?", *Kyiv Post*, 10 January 2024, https://www.kyivpost.com/post/26556

95. For one example of many, see Isabelle Khurshudyan, "With no way out of a worsening war, Zelensky's options look bad or worse", *The Washington Post*, 8 April 2024, https://www.washingtonpost.com/world/2024/04/06/ukraine-war-zelensky-options/

96. Dominic Lawson, "Does Biden actually want Ukraine to win?", *The Times*, 14 January 2024, https://www.thetimes.co.uk/article/nc14lawson-0f2ptrcc0

97. Garry Kasparov, "A History of Betrayal: Biden's Team Keeps Negotiating About Ukraine Without Ukraine", Kasparov.com, 13 August 2023, https://www.kasparov.com/a-history-of-betrayal-biden-keeps-negotiating-about-ukraine-without-ukraine-august-13-2023/

98. William M Arkin, "Exclusive: The CIA's Blind Spot about the Ukraine War",

Newsweek, 5 July 2023, https://www.newsweek.com/2023/07/21/exclusive-cias-blind-spot-about-ukraine-war-1810355.html

99. «ЗЕЛЕНСЬКИЙ в інтерв'ю The New York Times» (Zelenskyy in *New York Times* interview), YouTube, 27 May 2024, https://www.youtube.com/shorts/XJeeY8cWsGA

100. Speaking at Chatham House, London, 11 December 2023.

101. James Politi, "Joe Biden says US will back Ukraine 'as long as we can'", *Financial Times*, 13 December 2023, https://www.ft.com/content/c5b8a94f-4bf9-422f-b4de-db5dcfc7ca0a

102. Keir Giles, "Russian nuclear intimidation: How Russia uses nuclear threats to shape Western responses to aggression", Chatham House, 29 March 2023, https://www.chathamhouse.org/2023/03/russian-nuclear-intimidation

103. James Sherr, "The Moment of Truth", ICDS, 10 January 2024, https://icds.ee/en/the-moment-of-truth/

104. Peter Dickinson, "Ukraine's Black Sea success exposes folly of West's "don't escalate" mantra", Atlantic Council, 22 January 2024, https://www.atlanticcouncil.org/blogs/ukrainealert/ukraines-black-sea-success-provides-a-blueprint-for-victory-over-putin/

105. "Remarks of President Joe Biden -- State of the Union Address As Prepared for Delivery", The White House, 7 March 2024, https://www.whitehouse.gov/briefing-room/speeches-remarks/2024/03/07/remarks-of-president-joe-biden-state-of-the-union-address-as-prepared-for-delivery-2/

106. Keith Johnson, "The U.S. Still Has a Lend-Leash Act for Ukraine", *Foreign Policy*, 22 May 2024, https://foreignpolicy.com/2024/05/22/us-russian-frozen-assets-ukraine-war/

107. "Miscalculations, divisions marked offensive planning by U.S., Ukraine", *The Washington Post*, 4 December 2023, https://www.washingtonpost.com/world/2023/12/04/ukraine-counteroffensive-us-planning-russia-war/

108. Phillips O'Brien, "Does Biden Want Ukraine to Win?", *The Wall Street Journal*, 1 January 2024, https://www.wsj.com/articles/does-biden-want-ukraine-to-win-deal-russia-war-crimea-military-aid-630dbe60

109. Andrew Michta, "The West needs to get real about security", Politico, 15 January 2024, https://www.politico.eu/article/west-us-needs-get-real-about-security-nato-ukraine-war-russia/

110. Nataliya Bugayova, "The High Price of Losing Ukraine: Part 2 — The Military Threat and Beyond", Institute for the Study of War, 22 December 2023, https://www.understandingwar.org/backgrounder/high-price-losing-ukraine-part-2-%E2%80%94-military-threat-and-beyond

111. Nick Schifrin, Dan Sagalyn, Sonia Kopelev, "Poland's foreign minister on concerns the U.S. will abandon Ukraine, Europe", PBS, 19 February 2024,

https://www.pbs.org/newshour/show/polands-foreign-minister-discusses-the-war-in-ukraine

112. Ian Bond, "Europe And The Us Election: Hope For The Best, Prepare For The Worst", Centre for European Reform, 22 January 2024, https://www.cer.eu/insights/europe-and-us-election-hope-best-prepare-worst

4. A FADING ROLE FOR A FADING BRITAIN

1. Tim Shipman, "How Ben Wallace fought 'securocrats' to donate UK's tank-busting weapons to Ukraine", *The Times*, 13 March 2022, https://www.thetimes.co.uk/article/how-ben-wallace-fought-securocrats-to-donate-uks-tank-busting-weapons-to-ukraine-zz05m28g2

2. Ellie Cook, "What Are Martlet Missiles? Ukraine's NATO-Made Laser-Guided Drone Busters", *Newsweek*, 5 December 2023, https://www.newsweek.com/martlet-missile-ukraine-lightweight-multirole-missiles-russia-shahed-drones-1849617

3. "Ukraine and Britain sign security agreement in Kyiv", Reuters, 12 January 2024, https://www.reuters.com/world/europe/ukraine-britain-sign-security-agreement-kyiv-2024-01-12/

4. Tim Shipman, "How Ben Wallace fought 'securocrats' to donate UK's tank-busting weapons to Ukraine", *The Times*, 13 March 2022, https://www.thetimes.co.uk/article/how-ben-wallace-fought-securocrats-to-donate-uks-tank-busting-weapons-to-ukraine-zz05m28g2

5. Will Hazell and Edward Malnick, "Defence firms seeking to arm Ukraine hamstrung by 'nightmare' MoD", *The Telegraph*, 2 March 2024, https://www.telegraph.co.uk/politics/2024/03/02/british-weapons-firms-ukraine-mod-failures/

6. Volodymyr Zelensky, "With British help we can ensure freedom defeats aggression", *The Times*, 14 January 2024, https://www.thetimes.co.uk/article/with-british-help-we-can-ensure-that-freedom-defeats-aggression-wzpl9g9j5

7. Tweet by Grant Shapps, 30 December 2023, https://twitter.com/grantshapps/status/1741069522398839139

8. Viljar Lubi, Ivita Burmistre and Lina Zigmantaite, "Our Baltic states are on Europe's new frontline. Nato and Britain must step up", *The Telegraph*, 30 March 2024, https://www.telegraph.co.uk/news/2024/03/30/baltic-states-on-europes-new-frontline-nato-britain

9. Tom Calver, "Docked ships and shrinking fleets: just how strong is our Royal Navy?", *Sunday Times*, 21 January 2024, https://www.thetimes.co.uk/article/how-strong-royal-navy-uk-fleet-british-ships-red-sea-mpn8kmhk6

10. "London's £36bn benefits bill is bigger than the UK's whole defence budget",

London Evening Standard, 20 May 2013, https://www.standard.co.uk/news/london/londons-ps36bn-benefits-bill-is-bigger-than-the-uks-whole-defence-budget-8623674.html

11. George Grylls and Chris Smyth, "UK strikes in Yemen: Britain 'should prepare for further wars'", *The Times*, 15 January 2024, https://www.thetimes.co.uk/article/uk-strikes-yemen-houthis-rishi-sunak-mps-address-red-sea-b2zwdrl2m

12. Will Hazell, "UK has failed to prepare itself for war, warn former defence ministers", *The Telegraph*, 6 April 2024, https://www.telegraph.co.uk/politics/2024/04/06/uk-failed-prepare-war-former-defence-ministers/

13. Larisa Brown, "Army numbers to drop below 70,000 'in two years'", *The Times*, 20 January 2024, https://www.thetimes.co.uk/article/uk-military-is-too-small-to-fight-key-allies-warn-f6lv9gtxw

14. Deborah Haynes, "US general warns British Army no longer top-level fighting force, defence sources reveal", Sky News, 30 January 2023, https://news.sky.com/story/us-general-warns-british-army-no-longer-top-level-fighting-force-defence-sources-reveal-12798365

15. Deborah Haynes, "Budget's lack of new defence spending dismays insiders and Tory MPs", Sky News, 7 March 2024, https://news.sky.com/story/budgets-lack-of-new-defence-spending-dismays-insiders-and-tory-mps-13088941

16. Dylan Malyasov, "Ukraine to get additional artillery systems from UK", Defence Blog, 9 July 2024, https://defence-blog.com/ukraine-to-get-additional-artillery-systems-from-uk/

17. "Defence Secretary address to staff", UK MOD, 6 July 2024, https://www.gov.uk/government/speeches/defence-secretary-address-to-staff

18. "Exclusive: NATO will need 35-50 extra brigades under new defence plans", Reuters, 8 July 2024, https://www.reuters.com/world/nato-will-need-35-50-extra-brigades-under-new-defence-plans-source-says-2024-07-08/

19. Chas Geiger, "UK armed forces not ready for high-intensity war, MPs warn", BBC News, 4 February 2024, https://www.bbc.co.uk/news/uk-politics-68181275

20. "UK defence: No credible Government plan to deliver desired military capabilities", Public Accounts Committee, 8 March 2024, https://committees.parliament.uk/committee/127/public-accounts-committee/news/200289/uk-defence-no-credible-government-plan-to-deliver-desired-military-capabilities/

21. Paul Mason, "Lessons from the 1930s: Rearm according to the threat, not the fiscal rules", Council on Geostrategy, 8 May 2024, https://www.geostrategy.org.uk/britains-world/lessons-from-the-1930s-rearm-according-to-the-threat-not-the-fiscal-rules/

22. George Allison, "Britain appears to cut defence budget during war in Europe", UK Defence Journal, 8 March 2024, https://ukdefencejournal.org. uk/britain-appears-to-cut-defence-budget-during-war-in-europe
'Sir Humphrey', "Is The MOD Budget Really Growing? Arguably No.", The Pinstriped Line, 8 March 2024, https://thinpinstripedline.blogspot. com/2024/03/is-mod-budget-really-growing-arguably-no.html

23. Joe Hill on Twitter, 8 March 2024, https://twitter.com/jo3hill/status/ 1766107145534152781

24. Larisa Brown, "Failure to fund military puts Britain in 'alarming place', MPs say", The Times, 8 March 2024, https://www.thetimes.co.uk/article/failure-to-fund-military-puts-britain-in-alarming-place-mps-say-6nz6sbls8

25. Deborah Haynes, "Ministers urge government to increase defence spending in highly unusual intervention", Sky News, 9 March 2024, https://news.sky. com/story/ministers-urge-government-to-increase-defence-spending-in-highly-unusual-intervention-13090562

26. "Armed Forces Minister James Heappey to quit role and stand down as MP at next election", Forces.net, 15 March 2024, https://www.forces.net/services/ army/armed-forces-minister-quit-role-and-stand-down-mp-next-election

27. James Heappey, "Britain is not ready for war – ministers couldn't even turn up to the bunker", The Telegraph, 6 April 2024, https://www.telegraph.co.uk/ news/2024/04/06/britain-is-not-ready-for-war-ministers-defence-mod/

28. Nick Gutteridge and Daniel Martin, "Sunak unveils biggest military spending increase in a generation", The Telegraph, 23 April 2024, https:// www.telegraph.co.uk/politics/2024/04/23/britain-boost-defence-spending-2030-rishi-sunak/

29. Malcolm Chalmers, "Committing to 2.5%: Is Help at Hand for the UK's Defences?", RUSI, 24 April 2024, https://rusi.org/explore-our-research/ publications/commentary/committing-25-help-hand-uks-defences

30. Samir Puri and Olivia O'Sullivan, "The UK defence budget increase is welcome but defers tough choices", Chatham House, 29 April 2024, https:// www.chathamhouse.org/2024/04/uk-defence-budget-increase-welcome-defers-tough-choices

31. "Jeremy Hunt defends civil service job cuts to increase defence spending", BBC News, 25 April 2024, https://www.bbc.co.uk/news/uk-politics-68893859

32. "Ready for War?" House of Commons Defence Committee, 4 February 2024, https://committees.parliament.uk/publications/43178/documents/214880/ default/

33. "Is The MOD Budget Really Growing? Arguably No", Thin Pinstriped Line blog, 8 March 2024, https://thinpinstripedline.blogspot.com/2024/03/is-mod-budget-really-growing-arguably-no.html

34. "New Golden Age of shipbuilding as new UK-built warships boost Navy building programme to up to 28 ships and submarines", UK Government, 14 May 2024, https://www.gov.uk/government/news/new-golden-age-of-shipbuilding-as-new-uk-built-warships-boost-navy-building-programme-to-up-to-28-ships-and-submarines

35. Tweet by Grant Shapps, 6 May 2024, https://twitter.com/grantshapps/status/1787432158325297392

36. For example, Statement in Parliament by The Earl of Minto, Minister of State, Ministry of Defence, 12 March 2024, https://hansard.parliament.uk/Lords/2024-03-12/debates/6B21626B-5DB4-497F-B8E7-7F0DBE3D92CE/UKArmedForces

37. Tweet by Ben Wallace, 16 April 2024, https://x.com/bwallacemp/status/1780171034143896051

38. "Committee reports: 2% defence target achieved only through creative accounting", House of Commons Defence Committee, 21 April 2016, https://committees.parliament.uk/committee/24/defence-committee/news/185571/committee-reports-2-defence-target-achieved-only-through-creative-accounting/

39. Deborah Haynes, "UK 'increasingly vulnerable' to threat of missile and drone attacks after decades of cuts", Sky News, 2 May 2024, https://news.sky.com/story/uk-increasingly-vulnerable-to-threat-of-missile-and-drone-attacks-after-decades-of-cuts-experts-warn-13127263

40. "Ready for War?" House of Commons Defence Committee, 4 February 2024, https://committees.parliament.uk/publications/43178/documents/214880/default/

41. Jack Watling and Sidharth Kaushal, "Requirements for the Command and Control of the UK's Ground-Based Air Defence", RUSI, 17 April 2024, https://www.rusi.org/explore-our-research/publications/occasional-papers/requirements-command-and-control-uks-ground-based-air-defence

42. "First Impressions - Impact for UK of Iranian Strikes on Israel", Thin Pinstriped Line blog, 14 April 2024, https://thinpinstripedline.blogspot.com/2024/04/first-impressions-impact-for-uk-of.html

43. "Written questions", UK Parliament website, 18 January 2024, https://members.parliament.uk/member/4470/writtenquestions?page=2#expand-1683324

44. Deborah Haynes, "Size of UK armed forces shrinks by more than 7,000 personnel in a year", Sky News, 8 March 2024, https://news.sky.com/story/size-of-uk-armed-forces-shrinks-by-more-than-7-000-personnel-in-a-year-13089861

45. Rick Haythornthwaite, "Agency and Agility: Incentivising people in a new era", UK Ministry of Defence, June 2023, https://assets.publishing.service.

gov.uk/media/648ad6b8b32b9e000ca967c9/Incentivising_people_in_a_new_era_-_a_review_of_UK_Armed_Forces.pdf

46. Lucy Denyer, "'No longer a top-level fighting force': How the British Army lost its way", *The Telegraph*, 3 February 2024, https://www.telegraph.co.uk/news/2024/02/03/how-the-british-army-lost-its-way/

47. Try searching for Capita on the Army Rumour Service for a rich selection of tales of woe from current and former recruits: https://www.arrse.co.uk/community/search/1858883/?q=capita&c[title_only]=1&o=relevance

48. Larisa Brown, "Army numbers to drop below 70,000 'in two years'", *The Times*, 20 January 2024, https://www.thetimes.co.uk/article/uk-military-is-too-small-to-fight-key-allies-warn-f6lv9gtxw

49. "'Our finest asset' What it means to serve in the 21st century", UK MOD, 2021, https://assets.publishing.service.gov.uk/media/608139708fa8f51b91f3d7b2/MOD_MinDPV_IR_Report_Brochure_A4_Digital_version_single_page_4_QR.pdf

50. "SO2portaloos" on Twitter, 25 February 2024, https://twitter.com/so2portaloos/status/1761663675503382752

51. Steven Edginton, "Army to relax security checks for recruits in diversity drive", *The Telegraph*, 10 February 2024, https://www.telegraph.co.uk/news/2024/02/10/army-challenge-overseas-recruits-security-checks/

52. Stuart Crawford, "Beards in the Army", *UK Defence Journal*, 3 April 2024, https://ukdefencejournal.org.uk/beards-in-the-army/

53. George Bowden, "New UK Army chief issues Russia rallying cry", BBC News, 19 June 2022, https://www.bbc.co.uk/news/uk-61858476

54. "The Infantry", British Army, undated, https://www.army.mod.uk/who-we-are/corps-regiments-and-units/infantry/

55. Stuart Crawford, "Challenger 3 – The new tank for The British Army", *UK Defence Journal*, https://ukdefencejournal.org.uk/challenger-3-the-new-tank-for-the-british-army/

56. Richard Thomas, "How many RCH 155 artillery systems will the British Army acquire?", Army Technology, 16 May 2024, https://www.army-technology.com/features/how-many-rch-155-artillery-systems-will-the-british-army-acquire/

57. "Boxer for the British Army", British Army, undated, https://www.army.mod.uk/equipment/boxer/

58. Jahara Matisek et al., "What Does European Union Advising of Ukrainian Troops Mean for the Bloc's Security Policies? An Inside Look at the Training Mission", Modern War Institute, 11 June 2024, https://mwi.westpoint.edu/what-does-european-union-advising-of-ukrainian-troops-mean-for-the-blocs-security-policies-an-inside-look-at-the-training-mission/

59. "Royal Air Force jets moved from Romania to help shore up defence of Israel", Forces.net, 15 April 2024, https://www.forces.net/services/raf/raf-jets-moved-romania-help-shore-defence-israel

60. "The Thin Crabfat Blue Line - D-Day & Defence Cuts", The Thin Pinstriped Line, 19 May 2024, https://thinpinstripedline.blogspot.com/2024/05/the-thin-crabfat-blue-line-d-day.html

61. Alex Candlin, "British and American paras make combined drop into Estonia on Ex Swift Response", Forces.net, 12 May 2024, https://www.forces.net/operations/exercises/uk-and-us-paratroopers-drop-estonia-under-steadfast-defender
     Marco Giannangeli, "Spectacular D-Day display under threat as Army grapples with major RAF shortages", Daily Express, 19 May 2024, https://www.express.co.uk/news/uk/1900911/RAF-shortages-hit-D-Day-ceremony

62. "Urgent review as D-Day parachute jump scaled back due to lack of RAF aircraft", Sky News, 19 May 2024, https://news.sky.com/story/urgent-review-as-d-day-parachute-jump-scaled-back-due-to-lack-of-raf-aircraft-13139179

63. Tom Dunlop, "Serious capability gaps facing Royal Navy says report", *UK Defence Journal*, 5 February 2024, https://ukdefencejournal.org.uk/serious-capability-gaps-facing-royal-navy-says-report/

64. Deborah Haynes, "Royal Navy support sailors vote to strike - and it 'could put security at risk'", Sky News, 5 April 2024, https://news.sky.com/story/royal-navy-support-sailors-vote-to-strike-and-it-could-put-security-at-risk-13108738

65. James Knuckey, "HMS Vengeance: Vanguard-class submarine's secret monster deployment beneath the waves", Forces.net, 21 March 2024, https://www.forces.net/services/navy/hms-vengeance-vanguard-class-submarines-secret-monster-deployment-beneath-waves

66. Tom Calver, "Docked ships and shrinking fleets: just how strong is our Royal Navy?", *Sunday Times*, 21 January 2024, https://www.thetimes.co.uk/article/how-strong-royal-navy-uk-fleet-british-ships-red-sea-mpn8kmhk6

67. Larisa Brown, "Army numbers to drop below 70,000 'in two years'", *The Times*, 20 January 2024, https://www.thetimes.co.uk/article/uk-military-is-too-small-to-fight-key-allies-warn-f6lv9gtxw

68. Andrew Dorman, "Are we heading for World War Three – and is Britain's military ready?", Chatham House, 24 January 2024, https://www.chathamhouse.org/2024/01/are-we-heading-world-war-three-and-britains-military-ready

69. "Diminishing strength of the Royal Fleet Auxiliary undermines the Royal Navy's global reach", Navy Lookout, 10 May 2024, https://www.navylookout.

com/diminishing-strength-of-the-royal-fleet-auxiliary-undermines-the-royal-navys-global-reach/

70. Chris Broom, "Government defence ministers are invited to see 'truly awful' state of HMS *Collingwood* accommodation for themselves", The News, 6 February 2023, https://www.portsmouth.co.uk/news/defence/government-defence-ministers-are-invited-to-see-truly-awful-state-of-hms-collingwood-accommodation-for-themselves-4014930

71. Larisa Brown, "Army numbers to drop below 70,000 'in two years'", *The Times*, 20 January 2024, https://www.thetimes.co.uk/article/uk-military-is-too-small-to-fight-key-allies-warn-f6lv9gtxw

72. Eliot Wilson, "The Tip of the American Spear, How the United Kingdom Could Pursue Military Specialization", War On The Rocks, 2 February 2024, https://warontherocks.com/2024/02/the-tip-of-the-american-spear-how-the-united-kingdom-could-pursue-military-specialization/

73. Gavin Wilde, "Technology Alone Won't Break the Stalemate in Ukraine", *Foreign Policy*, 19 March 2024, https://foreignpolicy.com/2024/03/19/technology-ai-drones-stalemate-ukraine-russia-manpower/

74. Andrew Dorman, "Are we heading for World War Three – and is Britain's military ready?", Chatham House, 24 January 2024, https://www.chathamhouse.org/2024/01/are-we-heading-world-war-three-and-britains-military-ready

75. Poppy Koronka, "British public 'could be called up to fight in war against Russia'", *The Times*, 24 January 2024, https://www.thetimes.co.uk/article/british-public-could-be-called-to-fight-in-war-against-russia-wh75q6jj5

76. "Britain's armed forces are stretched perilously thin", *The Economist*, 29 January 2024, https://www.economist.com/britain/2024/01/29/britains-armed-forces-are-stretched-perilously-thin

77. This section is based on personal conversations with senior military officers combined with an explanation on Twitter by Greg Bagwell, to whom many thanks.
See tweet by @gregbagwell, 20 April 2024, https://twitter.com/gregbagwell/status/1781643558287560787

78. Deborah Haynes, "US general warns British Army no longer top-level fighting force, defence sources reveal", Sky News, 30 January 2023, https://news.sky.com/story/us-general-warns-british-army-no-longer-top-level-fighting-force-defence-sources-reveal-12798365

79. Deborah Haynes, "Is the UK preparing for war amid threats of conflict? Here is what Sky News has found", Sky News, 3 April 2024, https://news.sky.com/story/is-the-uk-preparing-for-war-amid-threats-of-conflict-here-is-what-sky-news-has-found-13106616

80. Edward Malnick, "Britain's 'hollowed out' Armed Forces not ready to fight Russia", *The Telegraph*, 4 February 2024, https://www.telegraph.co.uk/politics/2024/02/04/britains-hollowed-out-armed-forces-not-ready-fight-russia/

81. "Ready for War?" House of Commons Defence Committee, 4 February 2024, https://committees.parliament.uk/publications/43178/documents/214880/default/

82. Daniel Boffey, "MoD accused of 'go-slow' with half of £900m Ukraine fund unused", *The Guardian*, 19 April 2024, https://www.theguardian.com/politics/2024/apr/19/ministry-of-defence-accused-of-go-slow-ukraine-fund-unused

83. George Allison, "Britain to boost Ukraine's artillery munitions", UK Defence Journal, 24 February 2024, https://ukdefencejournal.org.uk/britain-to-boost-ukraines-artillery-munitions/

84. Colin Freeman, "What war could mean for life in modern Britain", *The Telegraph*, 27 January 2024, https://www.telegraph.co.uk/news/2024/01/27/what-would-happen-britain-at-war/

85. Stephen Grey et al., "Years of U.S., NATO miscalculations left Ukraine massively outgunned", Reuters, 19 July 2024, https://www.reuters.com/investigates/special-report/ukraine-crisis-artillery/

86. "UK Government and defence industry stepping up support for Ukraine", UK Ministry of Defence, 19 July 2024, https://www.gov.uk/government/news/uk-government-and-defence-industry-stepping-up-support-for-ukraine

87. Zac Sherratt, "Brighton weapons factory application rejected by council", BBC News, 5 June 2024, https://www.bbc.co.uk/news/articles/ceqq5z1nwwvo

88. "Ready for War?" House of Commons Defence Committee, 4 February 2024, https://committees.parliament.uk/publications/43178/documents/214880/default/

89. Deborah Haynes, "Army must 'prepare genuinely for war', ex-defence and security chiefs warn", Sky News, 20 March 2024, https://news.sky.com/story/army-must-prepare-genuinely-for-war-ex-defence-and-security-chiefs-warn-13098365

90. Larisa Brown, "Army numbers to drop below 70,000 'in two years'", *The Times*, 20 January 2024, https://www.thetimes.co.uk/article/uk-military-is-too-small-to-fight-key-allies-warn-f6lv9gtxw

91. Albin Aronsson et al., "Western Military Capability in Northern Europe 2023", FOI (Swedish Defence Research Agency), March 2024, https://www.foi.se/rest-api/report/FOI-R--5527--SE

92. Deborah Haynes, "US general warns British Army no longer top-level fighting force, defence sources reveal", Sky News, 30 January 2023, https://

news.sky.com/story/us-general-warns-british-army-no-longer-top-level-fighting-force-defence-sources-reveal-12798365

93. Larisa Brown, "Army numbers to drop below 70,000 'in two years'", *The Times*, 20 January 2024, https://www.thetimes.co.uk/article/uk-military-is-too-small-to-fight-key-allies-warn-f6lv9gtxw

94. Larisa Brown, "Reconsider size of your forces, head of US navy tells Britain", *The Times*, 25 January 2024, https://www.thetimes.co.uk/article/reconsider-size-of-your-forces-head-of-us-navy-tells-britain-06pwpkk37

95. Former RAF Air Marshal Edward Stringer, on Twitter, 9 April 2024, https://twitter.com/edwardstrngr/status/1777603926189035581

96. Sergio Miller, "2026: British Army brigade destroyed in Suravia", Wavell Room, 9 April 2024, https://wavellroom.com/2024/04/09/2026-british-army-brigade-destroyed-in-suravia/

97. Sam Skove, "How Estonia is becoming a hotbed for drone warfare", Defense One, 11 June 2024, https://www.defenseone.com/defense-systems/2024/06/how-estonia-becoming-hotbed-drone-warfare/397280/

98. Nate Ostiller, "Baltics, Poland, other countries agree to create 'drone wall'", *Kyiv Independent*, 26 May 2024, https://kyivindependent.com/lithuanias-interior-minister-says-group-of-countries-including-baltic-states-poland-have-agreed-to-create-drone-wall/

99. Luke Mogelson, "Battling Under a Canopy of Russian and Ukrainian Drones", *The New Yorker*, 8 April 2024, https://www.newyorker.com/magazine/2024/04/15/battling-under-a-canopy-of-drones

100. Mykhaylo Zabrodskyi et al., "Preliminary Lessons in Conventional Warfighting from Russia's Invasion of Ukraine: February–July 2022", RUSI Special Report, 30 November 2022, https://www.rusi.org/explore-our-research/publications/special-resources/preliminary-lessons-conventional-warfighting-russias-invasion-ukraine-february-july-2022

101. Josh Glancy, "National service in the happiest country: how Finland faces down Putin", *The Times*, 1 June 2024, https://www.thetimes.com/world/russia-ukraine-war/article/finland-front-line-russia-nato-zwdj28rnq

102. "If a new world war broke out and the UK was under imminent threat of invasion, which of the following would you do?", YouGov, 26 January 2024, https://yougov.co.uk/topics/politics/survey-results/daily/2024/01/26/2b544/2

103. Frank Gardner and André Rhoden-Paul, "Government launches 'root and branch' defence review", BBC News, 16 July 2024, https://www.bbc.co.uk/news/articles/crgmxw7g0veo
Jill Lawless, "Ex-NATO chief George Robertson to lead a UK defense review, says China among 'deadly' challenges", AP, 16 July 2024, https://apnews.

com/article/uk-defense-review-china-russia-iran-9e714857b27167557395bb
57fe0a1b20

104. Edward Stringer, "British defence needs root and branch reform", *The Telegraph*, 11 July 2024, https://www.telegraph.co.uk/news/2024/07/11/britains-defence-capability-is-in-a-worse-state/

105. Paul Mason, "UK defence spending debate gets real", Medium, 25 March 2024, https://paulmasonnews.medium.com/uk-defence-spending-debate-gets-real-581e61403215

5.   NATO AND EUROPE: HALF-PROMISES AND BROKEN PLEDGES

1.   "The North Atlantic Treaty", NATO website, https://www.nato.int/cps/en/natolive/official_texts_17120.htm

2.   Chief of the Defence Staff Admiral Sir Tony Radakin, speaking on 27 February 2024, https://www.gov.uk/government/speeches/chief-of-the-defence-chatham-house-security-and-defence-conference-2024-keynote-speech

3.   Eric S. Edelman, David Manning, and Franklin C. Miller, "NATO's decision process has an Achilles' heel", Atlantic Council, 12 March 2024, https://www.atlanticcouncil.org/blogs/new-atlanticist/natos-decision-process-has-an-achilles-heel/

4.   Kalev Stoicescu, "Myth 3: 'Russia wouldn't attack a NATO member state'", in "Myths and misconceptions around Russian military intent: How they affect Western policy, and what can be done", Chatham House, 14 July 2022, https://www.chathamhouse.org/2022/06/myths-and-misconceptions-around-russian-military-intent/myth-3-russia-wouldnt-attack-nato

5.   Phillips O'Brien, "Europe Needs to Look to Its Own Nuclear Deterrent: Part 1", Phillips's Newsletter, 16 April 2024, https://phillipspobrien.substack.com/p/europe-needs-to-look-to-its-own-nuclear

6.   Jack Detsch, "NATO's Military Has a New Nerve Center", *Foreign Policy*, 28 February 2024, https://foreignpolicy.com/2024/02/28/nato-russia-ukraine-war-shape-command-center-headquarters-military-reforms/

7.   Patrick Turner, "Ukraine: We Can Choose Victory", CEPA, 21 February 2024, https://cepa.org/article/ukraine-we-can-choose-victory/

8.   "Defence expenditures and NATO's 2% guideline", NATO, 14 March 2024, https://www.nato.int/cps/en/natohq/topics_49198.htm

9.   "Defence Expenditure of NATO Countries (2014-2024)", NATO, 17 June 2024, https://www.nato.int/cps/en/natohq/news_226465.htm

10. Jack Detsch and Robbie Gramer, "State Department Beefs Up U.S. Diplomatic Presence in Kyiv", *Foreign Policy*, 8 March 2024, https://

foreignpolicy.com/2024/03/08/state-department-us-embassy-ukraine-kyiv-staffing-diplomats-russia-war

11. Patrick Turner, "Macron Sets a Cat Among the NATO Pigeons", CEPA, 28 February 2024, https://cepa.org/article/macron-sets-a-cat-among-the-nato-pigeons/

12. Ivo Daalder, "Macron: The grand master of grandstanding", Politico, 4 March 2024, https://www.politico.eu/article/macron-the-grand-master-of-grandstanding/

13. Iryna Kutielieva and Stanislav Pohorilov, "US Department of State responds to article about "anger at Macron" over statement on troops in Ukraine", *Ukrainska Pravda*, 28 March 2024, https://www.pravda.com.ua/eng/news/2024/03/28/7448496/

14. Olaf Scholz on Twitter, 27 February 2024, https://twitter.com/bundeskanzler/status/1762452584403529830

15. Jennifer McKiernan, "Lord Cameron rules out Western boots on the ground in Ukraine", BBC News, 04 April 2024, https://www.bbc.co.uk/news/uk-politics-68730246

16. Matt Berg And Eric Bazail-Eimil, "Don't rule out troops to Ukraine, Finnish FM says", Politico, 15 March 2024, https://www.politico.com/newsletters/national-security-daily/2024/03/15/dont-rule-out-troops-to-ukraine-finnish-fm-says-00147374

17. Edward Lucas, "Top Job: Running NATO", CEPA, 20 November 2023, https://cepa.org/article/top-job-running-nato/

18. Stuart Lau and Barbara Moens, "In race for top EU, NATO jobs, Eastern Europe asks: 'Are we equals or not?'", Politico, 4 March 2024, https://www.politico.eu/article/nato-eastern-european-union-rutte-secretary-general-commission-russia-ukraine-war-defense/

19. Christoph B. Schiltz, "Scholz verhinderte von der Leyen – nun ist ein Niederländer Favorit als Nato-Chef", Welt, 22 February 2024, https://www.welt.de/politik/ausland/plus250139008/Nato-Scholz-verhinderte-von-der-Leyen-nun-ist-ein-Niederlaender-Favorit-als-Nato-Chef.html

20. Keir Giles, "What deters Russia: Enduring principles for responding to Moscow", Chatham House, 21 September 2021, https://www.chathamhouse.org/2021/09/what-deters-russia

21. Constanze Stelzenmüller, "Germany, France and how not to do deterrence", *Financial Times,* 4 March 2024, https://www.ft.com/content/54b1d958-e111-4f8a-9983-f9f79d997ec6

22. John Deni, "The new NATO Force Model: ready for launch?", NATO Defense College, 27 May 2024, https://www.ndc.nato.int/news/news.php?icode=1937

23. Jacek Tarociński, "Ćwiczenia wojskowe na północno-wschodniej flance NATO. Krok na drodze do intensyfikacji i synchronizacji" (Military exercises on the northeastern flank of NATO. A step towards intensification and synchronisation), OSW, 28 December 2023, https://www.osw.waw.pl/pl/publikacje/komentarze-osw/2023-12-28/cwiczenia-wojskowe-na-polnocno-wschodniej-flance-nato-krok-na

24. Per Appelkvist, "Sweden's NATO accession and its implications for the JEF", Joint Expeditionary Force Newsletter, 25 April 2024.

25. Antti Pihlajamaa, "The Joint Expeditionary Force in Northern Europe: Towards a more integrated security architecture?", FIIA Briefing Paper 389, 28 May 2024, https://www.fiia.fi/wp-content/uploads/2024/05/bp389_joint-expeditionary-force-in-northern-europe.pdf

26. Air Chief Marshal Lord Peach of Grantham GBE KCB DL, Brigadier (Ret'd) Robbie Boyd OBE and Ed Arnold, "Stretching the Joint Expeditionary Force: An Idea for Our Times", RUSI, 8 September 2023, https://www.rusi.org/explore-our-research/publications/commentary/stretching-joint-expeditionary-force-idea-our-times

27. "The Joint Expeditionary Force Newsletter", by email, 7 February 2024.

28. Sean Monaghan, "Joint Expeditionary Force: Toward a Stronger and More Capable European Defense?", CSIS, 21 October 2021, https://www.csis.org/analysis/joint-expeditionary-force-toward-stronger-and-more-capable-european-defense

29. "ENTRETIEN. Stéphane Séjourné: «Ce sera Otan et Europe, on a besoin d'une deuxième assurance-vie»" (Interview with Stéphane Séjourné: It will be NATO and Europe, we need a second life insurance policy), Ouest-France, 10 February 2024, https://www.ouest-france.fr/medias/ouest-france/le-grand-entretien/entretien-stephane-sejourne-otan-et-europe-nous-avons-besoin-dune-deuxieme-assurance-vie-424b1356-c80a-11ee-9a26-b3fe0ec43b85

30. Łukasz Maślanka, "Unijne siły szybkiego reagowania: priorytety polityczne i rzeczywiste potrzeby" (ERRF: political priorities and real needs), OSW, 24 January 2024, https://www.osw.waw.pl/sites/default/files/komentarz_567.pdf

31. Sean Monaghan et al., "Is NATO Ready for War?", CSIS, June 2024, https://www.csis.org/analysis/nato-ready-war

32. Nigel Gould-Davies, "Ukraine: the balance of resources and the balance of resolve", IISS, 26 February 2024, https://www.iiss.org/online-analysis/online-analysis/2024/02/ukraine-the-balance-of-resources-and-the-balance-of-resolve/

33. Anders Åslund, "Germany and France's 'Blind' Russia Policy", Kyiv Post, 26 March 2024, https://www.kyivpost.com/opinion/30044

34. Veronika Melkozerova and Eva Hartog, "Ukraine's army is suffering artillery 'shell hunger'", Politico, 1 February 2024, https://www.politico.eu/article/ukrainian-army-suffers-from-artillery-shell-hunger/

35. Jorge Liboreiro, "Stop exporting weapons and send them to Ukraine instead, Borrell urges EU countries", Euronews, 5 February 2024, https://www.euronews.com/my-europe/2024/02/05/stop-exporting-weapons-and-send-them-to-ukraine-instead-borrell-urges-eu-countries

36. "Miscalculations, divisions marked offensive planning by U.S., Ukraine", The Washington Post, 4 December 2023, https://www.washingtonpost.com/world/2023/12/04/ukraine-counteroffensive-us-planning-russia-war/

37. Andrew Gray, "EU aims to shift European arms industry to 'war economy mode'", Reuters, 5 March 2024, https://www.reuters.com/world/europe/eu-aims-shift-european-arms-industry-war-economy-mode-2024-03-04/

38. Laura Kayali, Jacopo Barigazzi and Joshua Posaner, "More ideas than cash: 5 takeaways from the EU's defense push", Politico, 5 March 2024, https://www.politico.eu/article/more-ideas-than-cash-5-takeaways-eu-europe-defense-push-war-ukraine-ammunition/

39. "First-ever European defence industrial strategy to enhance Europe's readiness and security", European Commission, 5 March 2024, https://commission.europa.eu/news/first-ever-european-defence-industrial-strategy-enhance-europes-readiness-and-security-2024-03-05_en

40. "EU defence reforms won't immediately help Ukraine: Former top NATO official Camille Grand", France 24, 29 March 2024, https://www.france24.com/en/tv-shows/talking-europe/20240329-eu-defence-reforms-won-t-immediately-help-ukraine-former-top-nato-official-camille-grand

41. Luigi Scazzieri, "Can European defence take off?", Centre for European Reform, 19 January 2023, https://www.cer.eu/publications/archive/policy-brief/2023/can-european-defence-take

42. Sylvia Pfeifer and Richard Milne, "TikTok videos vs weapons: defence sector needs priority access to power, says Nordic boss", Financial Times, 19 March 2024, https://www.ft.com/content/dfa3baff-d0c6-4866-a92a-20371c869aa4

43. "EU defence reforms won't immediately help Ukraine: Former top NATO official Camille Grand", France 24, 29 March 2024, https://www.france24.com/en/tv-shows/talking-europe/20240329-eu-defence-reforms-won-t-immediately-help-ukraine-former-top-nato-official-camille-grand

44. Sam Skove, "Europe's still spending too little on defense to suit Estonia", Defense One, 13 June 2024, https://www.defenseone.com/policy/2024/06/europes-still-spending-too-little-defense-suit-estonia/397344/

45. Joshua Posaner & Laura Kayali, "Europe's arms production is in 'deep shit,'

says Belgian ex-general", Politico, February 8 2024, https://www.politico.eu/article/europes-arms-production-is-in-deep-shit-says-belgian-ex-general/

46. Michael Shurkin, "The Abilities of the British, French, and German Armies to Generate and Sustain Armored Brigades in the Baltics", RAND, April 2017, https://www.rand.org/content/dam/rand/pubs/research_reports/RR1600/RR1629/RAND_RR1629.pdf

47. Zico Saerens, "België neemt deel aan Europese operatie tegen Houthi's en stuurt één militair schip naar Rode Zee" (Belgium takes part in European operation against Houthis and sends one military ship to the Red Sea), VRT, 19 January 2024, https://www.vrt.be/vrtnws/nl/2024/01/19/beslissing-belgie-missie-rode-zee/

48. Rudy Ruitenberg, "Belgium postpones Red Sea deployment after frigate mishaps", DefenseNews, 15 April 2024, https://www.defensenews.com/global/europe/2024/04/15/belgium-postpones-red-sea-deployment-after-frigate-mishaps/

49. Alex Luck, "Missile Woes For German Navy Amid Red Sea Operation", *Naval News*, 2 March 2024, https://www.navalnews.com/naval-news/2024/03/missile-woes-for-german-navy/

50. "Report: Danish Frigate's Weapons Malfunctioned During Houthi Drone Attack", The Maritime Executive, 3 April 2024, https://maritime-executive.com/article/report-danish-frigate-s-weapons-malfunctioned-during-houthi-drone-attack

51. Dick Zandee and Davis Ellison, "Germany's Zeitenwende and the consequences for German-Dutch defence cooperation", Clingendael (Netherlands Institute of International Relations), 29 January 2024, https://www.clingendael.org/publication/germanys-zeitenwende-and-consequences-german-dutch-defence-cooperation

52. Rudy Ruitenberg, "Netherlands considers creating tank battalion, but needs funding", *DefenseNews*, 6 February 2024, https://www.defensenews.com/global/europe/2024/02/06/netherlands-considers-creating-tank-battalion-but-needs-funding/

53. Timothy Wright, "Dutch target long-range strike upgrades that expose European shortfalls", IISS, 23 February 2024, https://www.iiss.org/online-analysis/military-balance/2024/02/dutch-target-long-range-strike-upgrades-that-expose-european-shortfalls/

54. Ed Arnold, "NATO Societies Must be Ready for War", RUSI, 26 January 2024, https://rusi.org/explore-our-research/publications/commentary/nato-societies-must-be-ready-war

55. Albin Aronsson et al., "Western Military Capability in Northern Europe

2023", FOI (Swedish Defence Research Agency), March 2024, https://www.foi.se/rest-api/report/FOI-R--5527--SE

56. Claudia Chiappa, "War looms for Europe, warns Poland's Donald Tusk", Politico, 29 March 2024, https://www.politico.eu/article/polish-prime-minister-donald-tusk-warns-europe-pre-war-era/

57. Sean Monaghan et al., "Is NATO Ready for War?", CSIS, June 2024, https://www.csis.org/analysis/nato-ready-war

58. "Would you really die for your country?", The Economist, 17 April 2024, https://www.economist.com/international/2024/04/17/would-you-really-die-for-your-country

59. Matthew Syed, "The storm is gathering, and Europe is still dithering on defending itself", The Times, 14 April 2024, https://www.thetimes.co.uk/article/europe-defending-itself-war-china-west-rqt9pzn3l

60. Lt. Col. Andrew Underwood, Maj. Scott Clark, Capt. Dylan Karnedy, "An Overlooked Ally Observations and Lessons Learned from the First Persistent U.S. Artillery Forces Stationed in Estonia", Army University Press, January-February 2024, https://www.armyupress.army.mil/Journals/Military-Review/English-Edition-Archives/January-February-2024/Ally/

61. Kate Connolly, "Germany's 'Putin-caressers' start coming to terms with their naivety", The Guardian, 28 February 2022, https://www.theguardian.com/world/2022/feb/28/germanys-putin-caressers-start-coming-to-terms-with-their-naivety

62. Steven Erlanger and David E. Sanger, "Germany Braces for Decades of Confrontation With Russia", New York Times, 3 February 2024, https://www.nytimes.com/2024/02/03/world/europe/germany-russia.html

63. Annalena Baerbock, Stéphane Séjourné and Radosław Sikorski, "Germany, France and Poland: This moment may define our children's future", 3 April 2024, Politico, https://www.politico.eu/article/germany-france-poland-this-moment-may-define-our-children-future-annalena-baerbock-stephane-sejourne-radoslaw-sikorski/

64. Alfons Mais, Chief of the German Army, on LinkedIn, undated, https://www.linkedin.com/feed/update/urn:li:activity:6902486582067044353/

65. Sam Jones, "German chancellor Olaf Scholz admits uncertainty over defence spending", Financial Times, 10 November 2023, https://www.ft.com/content/95d47316-b357-4fc3-b25d-34645eef8abc

66. Maria Martinez and Christian Kraemer, "German court deals 60 billion euro budget blow to Scholz government", Reuters, 15 November 2023, https://www.reuters.com/world/europe/german-court-make-key-ruling-budget-manoeuvre-2023-11-15/

67. "Germany's army struggles to recruit new troops, despite official push", Euronews, 2 August 2023, https://www.euronews.com/2023/08/02/germanys-army-struggles-to-recruit-new-troops-despite-official-push

68. Arjun Neil Alim et al., "Russia believed to be behind plot to assassinate Europe's top defence boss", *Financial Times*, 11 July 2024, https://www.ft.com/content/1b685d36-1981-4863-a868-b98d5f17cbe4

69. Didi Kirsten Tatlow, "New Tech Scare Over NATO Ally After Russian Tapping Fiasco", *Newsweek*, 6 March 2024, https://www.newsweek.com/nato-russia-ukraine-china-germany-tapping-espionage-huawei-1876138

70. "Leaked Recording Of German Military Call On Taurus Missiles Is Part Of Putin's 'Information War,' Says Minister", RFE/RL, 3 March 2024, https://www.rferl.org/a/germany-leaked-recoring-military-pistorius-information-war-ukraine-putin/32846128.html

71. Minna Ålander on Twitter, 5 March 2024, https://twitter.com/minna_alander/status/1765095685009916286

72. "Bundeswehr's classified meetings found online", Deutsche Welle, 5 May 2024, https://www.dw.com/en/bundeswehrs-classified-meetings-found-online/a-68999642

73. "Vor dem 700. Kriegstag: Lieferung von 6 Mehrzweckhubschraubern SEA KING", German Federal Ministry of Defence, 24 January 2024, https://www.bmvg.de/de/presse/lieferung-von-6-mehrzweckhubschraubern-sea-king-5730404

74. "Taurus manufacturer criticises German government for slow signing of defence contracts", *Ukrainska Pravda*, 30 March 2024, https://www.yahoo.com/news/taurus-manufacturer-criticises-german-government-100820635.html

75. "German Troops Arrive in Lithuania", AP, 8 April 2024, https://apnews.com/887e3bea39d646e3b147558071d0632c

76. Lisa Haseldine, "How can Germany deploy a tank battalion without any tanks?", *The Spectator*, 27 January 2024, https://www.spectator.co.uk/article/the-dire-state-of-germanys-army/

77. Marina Kormbaki, "Litauen-Brigade kostet elf Milliarden Euro" (The Lithuania Brigade will cost 11 billion euro), *Spiegel*, 24 April 2024, https://www.spiegel.de/politik/deutschland/bundeswehr-litauen-brigade-kostet-elf-milliarden-euro-a-2d633f74-a2db-4827-9598-e2da8ceaeb36

78. Joshua Posaner, "German tanks and troops in Lithuania have one goal: Scare off Russia", Politico, 3 June 2024, https://www.politico.eu/article/germany-bundeswehr-zeitenwende-tanks-troops-lithuania-russia-artillery-nato-steadfast-defender/

79. "France boosts military spending amid war in Ukraine", AP, 4 April 2023, https://apnews.com/article/france-boosts-military-spending-amid-ukraine-war-db213e964b2ff26f3d87e7a4a3ba0cdc

80. Davide Basso, "France not ready for high-intensity war says former Army Chief", Euractiv, 9 November 2022, https://www.euractiv.com/section/politics/news/france-not-ready-for-high-intensity-war-says-former-army-chief/

81. James Nixey and Mathieu Boulègue, 'On Russia, Macron Is Mistaken', Chatham House, 5 September 2019, https://www.chathamhouse.org/2019/09/russia-macron-mistaken

82. Keir Giles, "Myth 02: 'Russia and the West want the same thing'", in "Myths and misconceptions in the debate on Russia", Chatham House, May 2021, https://www.chathamhouse.org/sites/default/files/2021-05/2021-05-13-myths-misconceptions-debate-russia-nixey-et-al_0.pdf

83. Jaroslav Lukiv, "Macron says Russian defeat in Ukraine vital for security in Europe", BBC News, 28 February 2024, https://www.bbc.co.uk/news/world-europe-68410219

84. "How Russia targeted France and radicalised Emmanuel Macron", *The Economist*, 18 April 2024, https://www.economist.com/europe/2024/04/18/how-russia-targeted-france-and-radicalised-emmanuel-macron

85. Martin Fornusek, "WSJ: Macron privately pushed Biden, Scholz to adopt 'strategic ambiguity' toward Russia", *Kyiv Independent*, 3 April 2024, https://kyivindependent.com/wsj-macron-privately-pushed-biden-scholz-to-adopt-strategic-ambiguity-toward-russia/

86. Emmanuel Macron, "Au 20h de TF1 et de France 2 sur le soutien de la France à l'Ukraine", YouTube, 14 March 2024, https://youtu.be/Gdb9L3BBnq0

87. Elsa Vidal, *La Fascination russe - Politique française: trente ans de complaisance vis-à-vis de la Russie*, Robert Laffont, 2024.

88. "French foreign minister says dialogue with Russia no longer in France's 'interest'", *Le Monde*, 8 April 2024, https://www.lemonde.fr/en/russia/article/2024/04/08/french-foreign-minister-says-dialogue-with-russia-no-longer-in-france-s-interest_6667804_140.html

89. "Fact sheet: NORAD modernization project timelines", Government of Canada, 9 May 2024, https://www.canada.ca/en/department-national-defence/services/operations/allies-partners/norad/norad-modernization-project-timelines.html

90. "Minister Blair announces investments in Canadian innovation and launches Artificial Intelligence Strategy at Ottawa Conference on Security and Defence", Government of Canada, 7 March 2024, https://www.canada.ca/en/department-national-defence/news/2024/03/minister-blair-announces-

investments-in-canadian-innovation-and-launches-artificial-intelligence-strategy-at-ottawa-conference-on-security-and-defence.html

91. "Our North, Strong and Free: A Renewed Vision for Canada's Defence", Government of Canada, April 2024, https://www.canada.ca/en/department-national-defence/news/2024/04/our-north-strong-and-free-a-renewed-vision-for-canadas-defence.html

92. "Defence Expenditure of NATO Countries (2014-2024)", NATO, 17 June 2024, https://www.nato.int/cps/en/natohq/news_226465.htm

93. Murray Brewster, "Canada confirms plan to replace submarine fleet at NATO summit", CBC News, 10 July 2024, https://www.cbc.ca/news/politics/submarine-blair-trudeau-nato-1.7259718

94. Patrick Swadden, "What Honda's historic $15B investment means for Alliston, Ont.", CBC News, 27 April 2024, https://www.cbc.ca/news/canada/toronto/alliston-ontario-honda-investment-local-1.7186794

95. Joe Varner, "Canada's selfish disregard of defence is the Achilles heel of NATO's northern security", The Hub, 14 June 2024, https://thehub.ca/2024/06/14/joe-varner-canadas-selfish-disregard-of-defence-is-the-achilles-heel-of-natos-northern-security/

96. I discussed Russian campaigns against Ireland at length in *Russia's War on Everybody*.

97. Conor Gallagher, "Ireland 'scrutinising' Russian diplomats' visa applications amid spying concerns", *The Irish Times*, 17 February 2024, https://www.irishtimes.com/politics/2024/02/17/ireland-scrutinising-every-new-application-from-russian-diplomats-coming-here-amid-concerns-about-espionage/

98. Brian Mahon, "Only Russian 'good will' can keep Irish no-fly zone intact", *The Times*, 28 February 2022, https://www.thetimes.co.uk/article/only-russian-good-will-can-keep-irish-no-fly-zone-intact-0cg6jq23d

99. Tom Sharpe, "Putin's subs have exposed Ireland's shameless hypocrisy", *The Telegraph*, 4 June 2024, https://www.telegraph.co.uk/news/2024/06/04/nato-sea-power-cui-russian-submarines-ireland-eu/

100. Nick Childs, "Gauging the Gap: The Greenland–Iceland–United Kingdom Gap – A Strategic Assessment", IISS, 3 May 2022, https://www.iiss.org/research-paper/2022/05/gauging-the-gap-the-greenland-iceland-united-kingdom-gap-a-strategic-assessment/

101. As for instance "Vinner Putin väntar en större konflikt" (If Putin wins, expect a bigger conflict), *Svenska Dagbladet*, 19 March 2024, https://www.svd.se/a/76XxQ3/debattorer-vinner-putin-vantar-en-storre-konflikt

102. EPP Group on Twitter, 9 November 2023, https://twitter.com/EPPGroup/status/1722562675698438368

103. Sylvia Kauffmann, "Les aveuglés", *Stock*, October 2023.

104. Glenn Hubbard, "NATO Needs More Guns and Less Butter", *The Wall Street Journal*, March 7 2022, https://www.wsj.com/articles/nato-needs-more-guns-and-less-butter-russia-ukriane-defense-spending-security-investments-11646688247

105. Elena Sánchez Nicolás, "Kallas: Russia's defeat crucial to avoid Third World War", *EUObserver*, 21 March 2024, https://euobserver.com/world/158259

106. Alex Vershinin, "The Attritional Art of War: Lessons from the Russian War on Ukraine", RUSI, 18 March 2024, https://rusi.org/explore-our-research/publications/commentary/attritional-art-war-lessons-russian-war-ukraine

6.   READINESS AND RESILIENCE

1.   Helsinki Security Forum, 29 September 2023, https://www.youtube.com/watch?v=wZEk4xJ2r50

2.   John Psaropoulos, "Europe awakens to the threat of sabotage by Russian agents", Al Jazeera, 17 January 2023, https://www.aljazeera.com/news/2023/1/17/europe-awakens-to-the-threat-of-sabotage-by-russian-agents

3.   Souad Mekhennet et al., "Russia recruits sympathizers online for sabotage in Europe, officials say", *The Washington Post*, 10 July 2024, https://www.washingtonpost.com/world/2024/07/10/russia-sabotage-europe-ukraine/

4.   Michael Weiss et al., "Exclusive: Inside Russia's Latvian Sabotage Squad", The Insider, 10 July 2024, https://theins.press/en/politics/272989

5.   Julian Barnes, "Russia Steps Up a Covert Sabotage Campaign Aimed at Europe", *The New York Times*, 26 May 2024, https://www.nytimes.com/2024/05/26/us/politics/russia-sabotage-campaign-ukraine.html

6.   "ISS director: Russian influence activities in Estonia have become harsher", ERR, 12 April 2024, https://news.err.ee/1609311528/iss-director-russian-influence-activities-in-estonia-have-become-harsher

7.   Laura Gozzi, "Russian pilot Maxim Kuzminov who defected to Ukraine 'shot dead' in Spain", BBC News, 20 February 2024, https://www.bbc.co.uk/news/world-europe-68337794

8.   Amy-Clare Martin, "British man accused of orchestrating arson attack in London for Russia's Wagner group", *The Independent*, 26 April 2024, https://www.independent.co.uk/news/uk/crime/dylan-earl-arson-russian-spy-allegations-b2535337.html

9.   "PST har avdekket russisk etterretningsvirksomhet i Vestland" (PST uncovers Russian intelligence activities in Vestland), NRK, https://www.nrk.no/vestland/pst-har-avdekket-russisk-etterretningsvirksomhet-i-vest-1.16868180

10.   Manual Bewarder et al., "Der Ukrainekrieg ist hier längst angekommen"

(Ukraine war arrives here at last), Süddeutsche Zeitung, 21 May 2024, https://www.sueddeutsche.de/politik/sabotage-russland-nato-pipeline-geheimdienst-1.7253897

11. Andrey Sychev and Alexander Ratz, "Germany arrests two for alleged military sabotage plot on behalf of Russia", Reuters, 18 April 2024, https://www.reuters.com/world/europe/germany-arrests-two-alleged-military-sabotage-plot-behalf-russia-2024-04-18/

12. Bojan Pancevski, "Russian Saboteurs Behind Arson Attack at German Factory", The Wall Street Journal, 23 June 2024, https://www.wsj.com/world/europe/russian-saboteurs-behind-arson-attackat-german-factory-c13b4ece

13. "Exclusive: US and Germany foiled Russian plot to assassinate CEO of arms manufacturer sending weapons to Ukraine", CNN, 11 July 2024, https://www.cnn.com/2024/07/11/politics/us-germany-foiled-russian-assassination-plot/index.html

14. Frank Gardner, "We have no Plan B if Ukraine falls, says Estonia", BBC News, 1 June 2024, https://www.bbc.com/news/articles/c722zxj0kyro

15. Zahra Fatima, "Slovakia hit by wave of bomb threats", BBC News, 7 May 2024, https://www.bbc.co.uk/news/articles/c3g523j5elro

16. Isabel van Brugen, "Poland Arrests Nine Operatives Accused of Working for Putin", Newsweek, 21 May 2024, https://www.newsweek.com/poland-arrests-nine-operatives-accused-working-putin-1902883

17. Greg Miller et al., "Russia recruited operatives online to target weapons crossing Poland", The Washington Post, 18 August 2023, https://www.washingtonpost.com/world/2023/08/18/ukraine-weapons-sabotage-gru-poland/

18. Ido Vock, "Man arrested in Poland over alleged Russia plot to kill Zelensky", BBC News, 18 April 2024, https://www.bbc.co.uk/news/world-europe-68848317

19. "Russia 'likely' behind fire that destroyed Warsaw shopping centre, says Tusk", Notes From Poland, 21 May 2024, https://notesfrompoland.com/2024/05/21/russia-likely-behind-fire-that-destroyed-warsaw-shopping-centre-says-tusk/

20. Minna Ålander & Patrik Oksanen (eds), "Tracking The Russian Hybrid Warfare - Cases from Nordic-Baltic countries", Frivärld, 27 May 2024, https://frivarld.se/rapporter/tracking-the-russian-hybrid-warfare-cases-from-nordic-baltic-countries/

21. Steve Scherer, "Canada to invest in technologies to boost 155mm artillery production", Reuters, 7 March 2024, https://www.reuters.com/business/aerospace-defense/canada-invest-technologies-boost-155mm-artillery-production-2024-03-07/

22. "A350 longhaul behind the scenes (in the cockpit with SAS!)", Flightradar24, 5 April 2024, https://www.youtube.com/watch?v=4dG_Whxzdkk

23. "Finnair plane aborts landing at Tartu airport due to GPS interference", ERR, 26 April 2024, https://news.err.ee/1609325847/finnair-plane-aborts-landing-at-tartu-airport-due-to-gps-interference

24. Jerome Starkey and Stephen Moyes, "WAR IN THE AIR Thousands of Brit holiday flights attacked by 'extremely dangerous Russian jamming' in major threat to air safety", *The Sun*, 21 April 2024, https://www.thesun.co.uk/news/27456029/russia-hack-british-flights-air-safety-threat/

25. Patrick Tucker, "Russia's GPS meddling in the Baltic Sea demands NATO action, Sweden's naval chief says", Defense One, 9 April 2024, https://www.defenseone.com/threats/2024/04/russias-gps-meddling-baltic-sea-demands-nato-action-swedens-naval-chief-says/395607/

26. Patrick Tucker, "Russia may be learning dangerous lessons from its space mischief, DIA says", Defense One, 17 July 2024, https://www.defenseone.com/threats/2024/07/russia-may-be-learning-dangerous-lessons-its-space-mischief-dia-says/398130/

27. Andrew Rettmann, "Russia's jamming of EU's TV satellites 'extremely worrisome'", *EUObserver*, 4 July 2024, https://euobserver.com/EU%20&%20the%20World/arf29e45b5

28. Thomas Nilsen, "Russian jamming is now messing up GPS signals for Norwegian aviation practically every day", *The Barents Observer*, 26 February 2024, https://thebarentsobserver.com/en/security/2024/02/russian-jamming-now-messing-gps-signals-norwegian-aviation-practically-every-day

29. Michael Ledeen et al., "Terrorism and the KGB", *The Washington Post*, 16 February 1981, https://www.washingtonpost.com/archive/politics/1981/02/17/terrorism-and-the-kgb/2cfe10f6-c2c9-46f8-a188-177963b9c1da/

30. Keir Giles, "Missiles Are Not the Only Threat", in Michael Jonsson and Robert Dalsjö (eds*), Beyond Bursting Bubbles: Understanding the Full Spectrum of the Russian A2/AD Threat and Identifying Strategies for Counteraction*, FOI, June 2020, https://www.foi.se/rest-api/report/FOI-R--4991--SE

31. Alice Hancock, "Russia is trying to sabotage European railways, warns Prague", *Financial Times*, 5 April 2024, https://www.ft.com/content/f8207823-f5e1-4caf-934d-67c648f807bf

32. Sean Lyngaas, "Russian hackers targeted European military and transport organizations in newly discovered spying campaign", CNN, 15 March 2023, https://edition.cnn.com/2023/03/15/politics/russian-hackers-europe-military-organizations-microsoft/index.html

33. "Urspårningarna på Malmbanan – nu är Säpo inkopplade" (Derailments on the Malmbanan - now Säpo is involved), SVT, 29 April 2024, https://www.

svt.se/nyheter/lokalt/norrbotten/ursparningarna-pa-malmbanan-nu-ar-sapo-inkopplade

34. "Poles and Ukrainians are at loggerheads. That's good news for Vladimir Putin", *The Economist*, 2 April 2024, https://www.economist.com/europe/2024/04/02/poles-and-ukrainians-are-at-loggerheads-thats-good-news-for-vladimir-putin

35. Elisabeth Braw, "Russia's Shadow Fleet Goes Rogue", CEPA, 26 April 2024, https://cepa.org/article/russias-shadow-fleet-goes-rogue/

36. Tuula Malin, "Maakauppoja strategisissa kohteissa" (Land transactions in strategic locations), *Iltalehti*, 12 March 2015, https://www.iltalehti.fi/uutiset/a/2015031119338528

37. "A Dawn Raid in the Archipelago", Corporal Frisk blog, 23 September 2018, https://corporalfrisk.com/2018/09/23/a-dawn-raid-in-the-archipelago/

38. ««Russerhyttene» ved Bardufoss», TV2, 6 April 2024, https://www.tv2.no/spesialer/nyheter/bardufoss-hytte-russere

39. Ian Jack, "Who rules the waves? In my part of Scotland that's far from clear", *The Guardian*, 30 April 2022, https://www.theguardian.com/commentisfree/2022/apr/30/scotland-clyde-estate-globalisation

40. Alexander Martin, "British intelligence moves to protect research universities from espionage", The Record, 26 April 2024, https://therecord.media/MI5-protect-british-universities-from-espionage

41. Josh Glancy, "National service in the happiest country: how Finland faces down Putin", *The Times*, 1 June 2024, https://www.thetimes.com/world/russia-ukraine-war/article/finland-front-line-russia-nato-zwdj28rnq

42. "Comprehensive Security", Finnish Security Committee, undated, https://turvallisuuskomitea.fi/en/comprehensive-security/

43. Olli-Pekka Toivanen, "Evakuointiohje uudistui 20 vuoden jälkeen "Ukrainan oppien" mukaisesti – testaa, tunnetko termit" (The evacuation instructions were renewed after 20 years in accordance with the "lessons from Ukraine" - test if you know the terms), Yle, 29 January 2024, https://yle.fi/a/74-20071816

44. Minna Ålander, "It's the National Security, Stupid", Lawfare, 7 July 2022, https://www.lawfaremedia.org/article/its-national-security-stupid

45. Minna Ålander, "The Nordic-Baltic Region: An Example for NATO", CEPA, 9 February 2024, https://cepa.org/article/the-nordic-baltic-region-an-example-for-nato/

46. Richard Milne, "Finland boosts war readiness in face of Russian aggression", *Financial Times*, 6 May 2024, https://www.ft.com/content/cf28a55d-31d2-433a-a651-e582cca28fa5

47. Kaarle Wikström, "Defence courses keep up with the times", Baltic Rim

Economies, April 2024, https://www.centrumbalticum.org/en/publications/baltic_rim_economies/baltic_rim_economies_2_2024/kaarle_wikstrom_defence_courses_keep_up_with_the_times

48. "Maanpuolustuskurssien toiminta" (Operation of National Defence Courses), Finnish National Defence University, undated, https://maanpuolustuskurssit.fi/maanpuolustuskurssien-toiminta

49. Jacopo Barigazzi, "Von der Leyen asks Finland to prepare the EU for war", Politico, 20 March 2024, https://www.politico.eu/article/von-der-leyen-asks-finland-to-prepare-the-eu-for-war/

50. Press Office, 'Press statement by President von der Leyen with former Finnish President Niinistö', European Commission, 20 March 2024, https://ec.europa.eu/commission/presscorner/detail/en/statement_24_1602

51. Janne Pukkila, speaking in Vilnius, 24 February 2024.

52. Figures in this passage are courtesy of Michael Malm, Department of Total Defence, Swedish Armed Forces Defence Staff.

53. "Poland's capital Warsaw earmarks $30 million for bomb shelters and other security", Reuters, 13 March 2024, https://www.reuters.com/world/europe/polands-capital-warsaw-earmarks-30-mln-bomb-shelters-other-security-2024-03-13

54. Jon Henley, "Sweden's failed integration creates 'parallel societies', says PM after riots", The Guardian, 28 April 2022, https://www.theguardian.com/world/2022/apr/28/swedens-failed-integration-creates-parallel-societies-says-pm-after-riots

55. "It's hard to imagine how the UK could be doing less to prepare for war", Sky News, 3 April 2024, https://news.sky.com/story/its-hard-to-imagine-how-the-uk-could-be-doing-less-to-prepare-for-war-13106724

56. "There Will Still Be No Fighting In the War Book (Part 2)", Thin Pinstriped Line blog, 6 April 2024, https://thinpinstripedline.blogspot.com/2024/04/there-will-still-be-no-fighting-in-war.html

57. Malcolm Prior, "UK disaster response needs 'urgent' £100m upgrade", BBC News, 23 May 2024, https://www.bbc.co.uk/news/articles/c977e91685no

58. Ed Arnold and Si Horne, "How Would the UK's Healthcare System Cope with War?", RUSI, 4 March 2024, https://www.rusi.org/explore-our-research/publications/commentary/how-would-uks-healthcare-system-cope-war

59. Marc Santora et al., "A Children's Hospital in Ukraine Becomes a Scene of Destruction", The New York Times, 9 July 2024, https://www.nytimes.com/2024/07/09/world/europe/ukraine-childrens-hospial-russia.html

60. Poppy Koronka, "British public 'could be called up to fight in war against

Russia'", *The Times*, 24 January 2024, https://www.thetimes.co.uk/article/british-public-could-be-called-to-fight-in-war-against-russia-wh75q6jj5

61. "Britain must train citizen army, military chief warns", BBC News, 24 January 2024, https://www.bbc.co.uk/news/uk-68086188

62. Deborah Haynes, "Deeply cynical' Sunak's 'policy surprise' doesn't change the fact next PM will have no time to play politics with defence", Sky News, 26 May 2024, https://news.sky.com/story/deeply-cynical-sunaks-policy-surprise-doesnt-change-the-fact-next-pm-will-have-no-time-to-play-politics-with-defence-13143319

63. "National Service Numbers - An Objective Analysis of Costs", Thin Pinstriped Line blog, 26 May 2024, https://thinpinstripedline.blogspot.com/2024/05/national-service-numbers-objective.html

64. "How would you prepare for an emergency?", UK Government, undated, https://prepare.campaign.gov.uk/

7. EUROPE'S NEW LEADERS

1. Viljar Lubi, Ivita Burmistre and Lina Zigmantaite, "Our Baltic states are on Europe's new frontline. Nato and Britain must step up", *The Telegraph*, 30 March 2024, https://www.telegraph.co.uk/news/2024/03/30/baltic-states-on-europes-new-frontline-nato-britain

2. Marta Kepe, "From Forward Presence to Forward Defense: NATO's Defense of the Baltics", The Rand Blog, 14 February 2024, https://www.rand.org/pubs/commentary/2024/02/from-forward-presence-to-forward-defense-natos-defense.html

3. Lukas Milevski, "The Baltic Defense Line", Foreign Policy Research Institute, 2 February 2024, https://www.fpri.org/article/2024/02/the-baltic-defense-line/

4. Jan Kallberg, "Code Red: How Russia Conquers the Baltics", CEPA, 30 January 2024, https://cepa.org/article/code-red-how-russia-conquers-the-baltics/

5. Speaking in Vilnius, February 2024.

6. Eliot Wilson, "Why Denmark is sending all its artillery to Ukraine", *The Spectator*, 19 February 2024, https://www.spectator.co.uk/article/why-denmark-sent-all-its-artillery-to-ukraine/

7. Ott Tammik, "Ukraine Allies Have to Outspend Russia to Win War, Estonia Says", Bloomberg, 17 January 2024, https://www.bloomberg.com/news/articles/2024-01-17/ukraine-allies-have-to-outspend-russia-to-win-war-estonia-says

8. Lisa O'Carroll and Dan Sabbagh, "Czech Republic to deliver thousands of extra artillery shells to Ukraine", *The Guardian*, 19 March 2024, https://

www.theguardian.com/world/2024/mar/19/czech-republic-to-deliver-thousands-of-extra-artillery-shells-to-ukraine

9. Jaanus Piirsalu, "Estonia knows where to purchase two billion euros' worth of shells for Ukraine", Postimees, 24 March 2024, https://news.postimees.ee/7986347/postimees-in-ukraine-estonia-knows-where-to-purchase-two-billion-euros-worth-of-shells-for-ukraine

10. Leonīds Kalniņš, "Objectives and reasons for the renewal of compulsory service in Latvia", Baltic Rim Economies, April 2024, https://www.centrumbalticum.org/en/publications/baltic_rim_economies/baltic_rim_economies_2_2024/leonids_kalnins_objectives_and_reasons_for_the_renewal_of_compulsory_service_in_latvia

11. Observations in this section are drawn from comments by Laurynas Kasčiūnas, Chairman of the Lithuanian Seimas Committee on National Security and Defence, in February 2024.

12. "Estonian Defence League", Kaitseliit, undated, https://www.kaitseliit.ee/en/edl

13. Lt. Col. Andrew Underwood, Maj. Scott Clark, Capt. Dylan Karnedy, "An Overlooked Ally: Observations and Lessons Learned from the First Persistent U.S. Artillery Forces Stationed in Estonia", Army University Press, January-February 2024, https://www.armyupress.army.mil/Journals/Military-Review/English-Edition-Archives/January-February-2024/Ally/

14. Valner Väino, "Salm: Europe must play a 'bigger, stronger' role in supporting Ukraine", ERR, 2 March 2024, https://news.err.ee/1609269600/salm-europe-must-play-a-bigger-stronger-role-in-supporting-ukraine

15. "Defense ministry's top official to resign over government inaction", ERR, 12 June 2024, https://news.err.ee/1609369340/defense-ministry-s-top-official-to-resign-over-government-inaction

16. Kärt Anvelt, «Kusti Salm lahkub kaitseministeeriumi kantsleri ametist, sest valitsus ei leia Eesti kaitsmiseks piisavalt raha» (Kusti Salm resigns as Defence Ministry permanent secretary because the government can›t find enough money to defend Estonia), Delfi, 12 June 2024, https://www.delfi.ee/artikkel/120300191/kusti-salm-lahkub-kaitseministeeriumi-kantsleri-ametist-sest-valitsus-ei-leia-eesti-kaitsmiseks-piisavalt-raha

17. Thomas Nilsen, "Norway rearms Finnmark for new security landscape", The Independent Barents Observer, 17 April 2019, https://www.arctictoday.com/norway-rearms-finnmark-for-new-security-landscape/

18. "The Norwegian Defence Pledge: Long-term Defence Plan 2025–2036", Norwegian Ministry of Defence, 5 April 2024, https://www.regjeringen.no/contentassets/27e00e5acc014c5ba741aacfff235d99/no/sved/the-norwegian-defence-pledge.pdf

19. Thomas Theiner, "Gotland – the Danzig of our time", Euromaidan Press, 22 March 2015, http://euromaidanpress.com/2015/03/22/gotland-the-danzig-of-our-time/

20. Minna Ålander, "The Nordic-Baltic Region: An Example for NATO", CEPA, 9 February 2024, https://cepa.org/article/the-nordic-baltic-region-an-example-for-nato/

21. "Would you really die for your country?", *The Economist*, 17 April 2024, https://www.economist.com/international/2024/04/17/would-you-really-die-for-your-country

22. Per Appelkvist, "Sweden's NATO accession and its implications for the JEF", Joint Expeditionary Force Newsletter, 25 April 2024.

23. Robert Dalsjö, "Ukraine's Fate and Europe's Future: A View from Sweden", International Institute for Strategic Studies, Survival Online, 24 January 2024, https://www.iiss.org/online-analysis/survival-online/2024/01/ukraines-fate-and-europes-future-a-view-from-sweden/

24. "Speech by Prime Minister Ulf Kristersson at Folk och Försvars annual national conference 2024", Government of Sweden, 8 January 2024, https://www.government.se/speeches/2024/01/speech-by-prime-minister-ulf-kristersson-at-folk-och-forsvars-annual-national-conference-2024/

25. "Swedish alarm after defence chiefs' war warning", BBC News, 10 January 2024, https://www.bbc.co.uk/news/world-europe-67935464

26. Anca Gardener, "The head of the Army urgently asks for a law to prepare the population: Russia will not stop at Ukraine, if it wins", *Europa Liberă România*, 1 February 2024, https://romania.europalibera.org/a/interviu-one-2-one-generalul-gheorghita-vlad/32799927.html

27. Minna Ålander, "It's the National Security, Stupid", Lawfare, 7 July 2022, https://www.lawfaremedia.org/article/its-national-security-stupid

28. Gareth Jennings, "Finland to acquire JASSM-ER cruise missiles", Janes, 31 May 2024, https://www.janes.com/defence-news/news-detail/finland-to-acquire-jassm-er-cruise-missiles

29. "What is the MPK?", MPK website, https://mpk.fi/en/

30. Paavo Airo, "Maanpuolustuskoulutus MPK teki kaikkien aikojen suurimman koulutustuloksensa vuonna 2023" (MPK achieves highest ever training result in 2023), Reserviläinen, 13 March 2024, https://reservilainen.fi/maanpuolustuskoulutus-mpk-teki-kaikkien-aikojen-suurimman-koulutustuloksensa-vuonna-2023/

31. Elisabeth Gosselin-Malo, "Finland to double ammunition production, build new factories", DefenseNews, 14 December 2023, https://www.defensenews.com/global/europe/2023/12/14/finland-to-double-ammunition-production-build-new-factories/

32. "ASAP Results: Boosting Ammunition Production", European Commission, 2024, https://defence-industry-space.ec.europa.eu/document/download/b694b109-fa2c-493e-bf1e-87768ae6469e_en?filename=ASAP%20fact sheet.pdf

33. Antti Seppälä and Titta Puurunen, "Puolustusministeriö: Oma ruutituotanto tärkeää" (Defence Ministry: Our own gunpowder production is important), Yle, 9 January 2013, https://yle.fi/a/3-6443614

34. Jarmo Huhtanen, "Asevarastot alkavat täyttyä", Helsingin Sanomat, 28 January 2024, https://www.hs.fi/kotimaa/art-2000010110026.html

35. Toni Mikkola, "Finland's Strategic Defense Preparedness", Medium, 10 February 2024, https://medium.com/@virtaava/finlands-strategic-defense-preparedness-3156156582aa

36. Keir Giles and Susanna Eskola, "Waking the Neighbour: Finland, NATO and Russia", UK Defence Academy, January 2009, https://www.researchgate.net/publication/280611718_Waking_the_Neighbour_Finland_NATO_and_Russia

37. Poll, MTV Uutiset, 26 January 2022, https://www.mtvuutiset.fi/artikkeli/mtv-uutisten-kysely-nato-jasenyyden-kannatus-on-noussut-30-prosenttiin-vastustus-laskenut-selvasti-turvallisempaa-olisi-lannen-kanssa/8340650

38. Poll, Yle Uutiset, conducted 23–25 February 2022, https://yle.fi/a/3-12336530

39. Poll, Yle Uutiset, conducted 9–11 March 2022, https://yle.fi/a/3-12354756

40. Yan Xia et al., "The Russian Invasion of Ukraine selectively depolarized the Finnish NATO discussion on Twitter", EPJ Data Science, January 2024, https://epjdatascience.springeropen.com/articles/10.1140/epjds/s13688-023-00441-2
    Laura Halminen, "Näin suomalaisten rivit tiivistyivät ja hajosivat, kun Ukrainaan hyökättiin" (This is how the Finns' ranks were condensed and dispersed when Ukraine was attacked), Verkkouutiset, 16 January 2024, https://www.verkkouutiset.fi/a/tutkimus-osoittaa-nain-suomalaisten-rivit-tiivistyivat-ja-hajosivat-kun-venaja-hyokkasi-ukrainaan/

41. Matti Pesu and Tapio Juntunen, "Finland in a nuclear alliance: Recalibrating the dual-track mindset on deterrence and arms control", FIIA Briefing Paper 375, 16 November 2023, https://www.fiia.fi/julkaisu/finland-in-a-nuclear-alliance

42. Juha Pyykönen and Stefan Forss, "Deterrence in the Nordic-Baltic Region: The Role of the Nordic Countries Together With the U.S. Army", US Army War College, June 2019, https://press.armywarcollege.edu/monographs/374/

43. Terhi Toivonen et al., "DCA-sopimus julki: Nämä 15 aluetta Suomi avaa Yhdysvaltain joukoille – puolustusministeri: 'Kriisitilanteissa voidaan ryhtyä

tositoimiin'" (DCA agreement announced: Finland will open these 15 areas to US troops – Defense Minister: 'In crisis situations, real measures can be taken'), Yle, 14 December 2023, https://yle.fi/a/74-20065054

44. See for example
"PISA 2022: Performance in Finland collapses, but remains above average", Yle News, 5 December 2023, https://yle.fi/a/74-20063678
"Finland to stop paying pension top-ups to recipients abroad", Yle News, 19 April 2024, https://yle.fi/a/74-20084620
"Amnesty report: Parts of Finland's healthcare system have failed", Yle News, 13 June 2023, https://yle.fi/a/74-20036481

45. "Why is Finland the happiest country in the world?", BBC, 28 March 2024, https://www.bbc.co.uk/reel/video/p0hmcc91/why-is-finland-the-happiest-country-in-the-world-

46. Government Communications Department Finnish Ministry of Finance, "General Government Fiscal Plan for 2025–2028 Orpo's Government: Decisions aim to prevent public finances from spinning out of control", Press Release, 17 April 2024, https://valtioneuvosto.fi/en/-/10616/orpo-s-government-decisions-aim-to-prevent-public-finances-from-spinning-out-of-control

47. Anna Grzymała-Busse, "Unity abroad, discord at home: Polish leaders visit Washington", Brookings, 8 March 2024, https://www.brookings.edu/articles/unity-abroad-discord-at-home-polish-leaders-visit-washington/

48. "Stosunek Polaków do obrony Ojczyzny" (Attitudes of Poles Towards Homeland Defence), Akademickie Centrum Komunikacji Strategicznej, 2023, https://www.wojsko-polskie.pl/aszwoj/u/21/7b/217bcefe-a510-4087-b58f-fd1f83c2ecf0/raport_-_stosunek_polakow_do_obrony_ojczyzny.pdf

49. "Jeszcze raz o kwestiach związanych z obronnością" (One more time about defence efforts), CBOS, August 2022, https://www.cbos.pl/SPISKOM.POL/2022/K_103_22.PDF

50. "Beefing up Poland's armed forces", The Economist, 2 November 2023, https://www.economist.com/europe/2023/11/02/beefing-up-polands-armed-forces

51. Jarosław Ciślak, "Liczebność Wojska Polskiego. Mity i fakty" (Numbers in the Polish Army. Myths and Facts), Defence24, 26 October 2023, https://defence24.pl/sily-zbrojne/liczebnosc-wojska-polskiego-mity-i-fakty-komentarz

52. Senior defence official speaking in Vilnius, February 2024.

53. Michał Oleksiejuk, "The key premises of the Polish Homeland Defence Act", Casimir Pulaski Foundation, 18 March 2022, https://pulaski.pl/en/pulaski-commentary-the-key-premises-of-the-polish-homeland-defence-act-michal-oleksiejuk/

54. James Rogers, "How eastern Europe became a fortress", *The Spectator*, 25 April 2024, https://www.spectator.co.uk/article/how-poland-became-the-fortress-of-europe/

55. Ibid.

56. Zuzanna Gwadera, "Poland set to bolster its long-range strike capability", IISS, 23 April 2024, https://www.iiss.org/online-analysis/missile-dialogue-initiative/2024/04/poland-set-to-bolster-its-long-range-strike-capability/

57. Raphael Minder, "'Who will pay the bill?': Poland's defence spending spree raises questions over funding", *Financial Times*, 23 April 2024, https://www.ft.com/content/91590a6d-2739-42c6-bb29-4d2aeac21bf7

58. Zuzanna Gwadera, "Poland set to bolster its long-range strike capability", IISS, 23 April 2024, https://www.iiss.org/online-analysis/missile-dialogue-initiative/2024/04/poland-set-to-bolster-its-long-range-strike-capability/

59. "Poland unveils details of €2.4bn fortification of eastern borders", Notes from Poland, 27 May 2024, https://notesfrompoland.com/2024/05/27/poland-unveils-details-of-e2-4bn-fortification-of-eastern-borders/

60. Raphael Minder, "'Who will pay the bill?'"

61. Zbigniew Lentowicz, "Polskie fabryki idą na wojnę. Produkcja idzie pełną parą" (Polish factories go to war. Full steam ahead for production), Rzeczpospolita, 15 January 2024, https://www.rp.pl/biznes/art39695381-polskie-fabryki-ida-na-wojne-produkcja-idzie-pelna-para

62. Stephen Grey et al., "Years of U.S., NATO miscalculations left Ukraine massively outgunned", Reuters, 19 July 2024, https://www.reuters.com/investigates/special-report/ukraine-crisis-artillery/

63. Maciej Miłosz, "Wiceprezes Hyundai Rotem: Korea jest w stanie przekazać Polsce wszystkie kluczowe technologie" ("Vice President of Hyundai Rotem: Korea is able to transfer all key technologies to Poland), *Dziennik Gazeta Prawna*, 20 February 2024, https://biznes.gazetaprawna.pl/artykuly/9436851,wiceprezes-hyundai-rotem-korea-jest-w-stanie-przekazac-polsce-wszystk.html

64. Zuzanna Gwadera, "Poland set to bolster its long-range strike capability", IISS, 23 April 2024, https://www.iiss.org/online-analysis/missile-dialogue-initiative/2024/04/poland-set-to-bolster-its-long-range-strike-capability/

65. Maciej Miłosz, "Less politics in the army?", Forsal.pl, 20 January 2024, https://forsal.pl/gospodarka/polityka/artykuly/9407125,mniej-polityki-w-wojsku.html

66. Albin Aronsson et al., "Western Military Capability in Northern Europe 2023", FOI (Swedish Defence Research Agency), March 2024, https://www.foi.se/rest-api/report/FOI-R--5527--SE

67. Minder, "'Who will pay the bill?'"

68. "W schronie się nie schronisz" (You won't find shelter in a shelter), NIK. gov.pl, Supreme Audit Office, 13 March 2024, https://www.nik.gov.pl/aktualnosci/budowle-ochronne-miejsca-ukrycia.html

69. Minder, "'Who will pay the bill?'"

70. Paul Taylor, "Could Poland's promotion to Europe's top table be a turning point for Ukraine?", *The Guardian*, 20 March 2024, https://www.theguardian.com/commentisfree/2024/mar/20/poland-europe-top-table-ukraine-weimar-triangle-france-germany

71. Daniel Fried, "Dispatch from Warsaw: Poland's military and economic rise is coming just in time, as the West wobbles", Atlantic Council, 5 July 2024, https://www.atlanticcouncil.org/blogs/new-atlanticist/dispatch-from-warsaw-polands-military-and-economic-rise-is-coming-just-in-time-as-the-west-wobbles/

8. WHAT COMES NEXT?

1. Anatol Lieven, "The war in Ukraine holds two lessons: Russia isn't an imminent threat, and Europe must rearm regardless", *The Guardian*, 23 February 2024, https://www.theguardian.com/commentisfree/2024/feb/23/war-ukraine-russia-threat-europe-rearm-us

2. Keir Giles, "Putin's speech harked back to Russia's empire – the threat doesn't stop at Ukraine", *The Guardian*, 22 February 2022, https://www.theguardian.com/commentisfree/2022/feb/22/putin-speech-russia-empire-threat-ukraine-moscow

3. "*Nemo provocare, nemo audet offendere quem intellegit superiorem esse, si pugnet.*"

4. "Russia – Future Directions", Advanced Research and Assessment Group, Defence Academy of the United Kingdom, 1 October 2008, https://oajonsson.com/wp-content/uploads/2014/03/20081001-russia_future_directions.pdf

INDEX

INDEX

INDEX

INDEX

INDEX

INDEX

INDEX

INDEX

INDEX